God, Kate, and I

by

Ralph Morton

Book cover by Ken Morton
Book cover ideas and pictures by Ken and Ralph Morton
Black and White photograph by Sarah Morton
Photographs prepared and submitted by Ken Morton
Ken Morton Photography Dallas, Texas
ken @ kenmortonphoto.com
(no spaces in email address)

Author can be reach at:
Ralph Morton
5105 G Road
Ingalls, Kansas 67853
spec629 @ yahoo.com
(no spaces in email address)

www.xulonpress.com

Dedicated in Memory of
Mary Katherine (Kate) Morton

Kate

Who in my opinion was taken home way to young, but I
know that God in his wisdom, has his plan and knows best.
I have come to realize that when I get to feeling bad and
cry, it is not for her but for myself, for it is my Hope, my
Wish, my Desire, my Knowledge, my Believe that she is in
a better place. And that her work on earth was completed.
She accomplished so much more, so much faster than some
of the rest of us. I still love and miss you Kate.
Ralph Morton

Table of Contents

❧

Chapter 1:

Beginning of the End

It was August the 28th, 2008, I was in Liberal, Kansas loading 4X4X8 bales of alfalfa on trucks going to Texas, for delivery to dairies. It was in the afternoon and I received a phone call from Kate, my wife, she was at the doctor's office. She had been at work, at the Word of Life Church, in Garden City, Kansas. She had a very sharp pain across her stomach, it had literally doubled her over. This was the first that she had said anything to me about any severe pain in her stomach region. The doctor had started routine blood work and checking of the vital signs. And wanted to do an MRI the next morning. She was worried about her health insurance not taking effect until September 1st, to satisfy the waiting period requirement. This was a no choice, she would have the MRI the next morning. She said that I was not to come home as it would be the better part of 2 hours before I could get there and she would already be home before I could get there. "OK, I will see you as soon as I get in." The full impact of this did not sink in right away. When I was finished, I headed back to the Pierceville, Kansas farm where I am headquartered, for my job. I unloaded and headed on home in rural Grey County, Kansas where we lived. When I got home she was feeling better and had already fixed supper. We discussed the situation and possibilities, nothing looked or sounded good. Our daughter Mary Lynn was off work the next day and wanted to go with Kate, for the doctor and MRI. OK, I would go to work, but if they learned anything they were to call me immediately. No calls and no news. I called Mary Lynn in the afternoon and the MRI was complete and Mom (Kate) had been admitted to the hospital. I got home and went in to see her, she was trying to down play the situation as not to serious and not to worry. I did know that this was for my sake and to help keep me from worrying. It didn't work very well. For my part, I was still worried. I asked her if she had called her Mom and Dad, Mary Francis Teresa Sandoval (December 2, 1930) and George Gilbert Arthur, (March 17, 1926)? "No, I don't have anything to tell them, so I will wait until later". "Well you might start with the fact that you're in the hospital." "No, later." Saturday morning and I'm back at the hospital, nothing new and no news. They were checking her vital signs, it seemed like every 5 minutes, but was every 2 hours, I believe. At lunch, I ask again "Have you called Mom and Dad". She said "No, I don't have anything to tell them yet, I can't talk to them." "You need to call them, now". "No." I very seldom went against her wishes but I told her if she didn't call them, I was going to. She said "I can't, not yet anyway". We waited, then after lunch I said we need to call them, she again said "No". I took out my cell phone and said "I'll dial if you will talk". "No, I can't talk to them". So I dialed, actually I hit a speed dial number. Got Mom and Dad on the phone, they knew if I was calling that something was wrong. I explained everything I knew to them and answered a couple of questions. I then said "That's all that I know for now, but I will call as soon as I learn anything more". Dad responded with "Okay, and we both appreciated your calling and letting us know". I had told them the 'big chicken' wouldn't talk but to hang on a second, and I would see if she would talk now. I told her I had already done the hard part so she might as well talk to them. "Well, okay." I gave her the phone. "Oh no I'm fine and won't know anything till next week." They had a nice visit and she returned my phone. I had asked them to notify Kate's sisters and brother, for me, which they did. Kate was born on September 21, 1950, the first daughter of George and Mary Teresa (Sandoval) Arthur. Next was Mary Margaret Arthur (Reese) Cassero, (April 16, 1952); Susan Grace Arthur Sullivan (April 10, 1956) was the 3rd one; Paul Michael Arthur, (February 26, 1959) was 4th and the only son; Lisa Ann Arthur (August 25, 1961) was daughter number 4 and 5th overall; Julie Felice Arthur Piazza, (February 28, 1967), was daughter number 5 and the last of 6 children. That evening I received the first of many phone calls from Kate's sister Margie Cassero. She wanted to know the whole story, in case Mom and Dad had missed anything. She also wanted to be kept up to date on all new developments. "OK, I can do that, but I will tell you the news, good or bad." She said "That's what I want". She added "If you don't call every night I will call you". My response "I'll be here". Not only did she call every night, if I didn't call her, but sometimes in the mornings before or when she was going to work. These calls were very much appreciated, because after any news was relayed we would just talk. About Kate and anything that pertained to her, past and present. If the day was bad and I needed to cry, whether actually cry or not, she was there with a shoulder and at least one ear. She was and has been a true sister, and I guess I would have made it without her but it was so much better with her there. And I can only continue to thank God for her and her presence through all of the following months. We would talk and we could not go very long before we had to laugh about something, because to me almost everything concerning Kate was good and/or happy. We talked about many things and got to know each other and she learned about her sister and the things we had done for the last 38 plus years. And again she gives meaning to the words, friend and sister, for me. If I look up these words in the dictionary, they have her picture beside the definitions for these words. And I kept telling her and others, when anyone has to go though this kind of thing, that I hoped God would provide their own version of Margie. She told me several times that she couldn't do this for everyone. I kept telling her, I know, and I don't want you to, just that everyone would have their own version or variation of her. And she finally got it, not her, but someone who could be for them what she had been for me. She was having trouble trying to figure out how she was going to be in 73 places or maybe 73,000, all at the same time. In our talks I started telling her of mine and Kate's lives and also mine in a time before Kate. And this is my story.

Chapter 2:

Thoughts of when I was 5

My parents were Orlaff T. Morton, Sr. (August 2, 1915) and Sarah C. Case Morton (April 1, 1917). There were 5 of us kids, eventually, Orlaff T.(Tom), Jr. (October 30, 1938); Patricia (Pat) Ann Smith, (April 5, 1940); Ralph F., (July 5, 1944); William (Bill) G., (February 6, 1946); Kenneth (Ken) D., (Aug 13, 1951).

I will use 5 as a reference age for this because I don't have a sense of time from this period. Some of this could be from others telling me of it and it seems to be my memory and hard to separate now. I had started riding horses at a time before I have memory of it. Dad put me on horses before I could walk, what I am talking about here is most likely when I was 4. I was getting Shetland ponies to ride from a friend of Dad's, Harry Baker, and it seems every time I would get one going good, as in riding and handling, it would sell and he would bring another one. The first that I have memory of was Blacky, a black registered Shetland stallion. I think I could do anything with that horse, so in thinking this, I probably could. I have taken him in the house, when Mom wasn't there, he would follow me and if I set down he would walk up beside me and drop his head and stand there. We played Cowboys and Indians and if I got shot and fell off my horse, he would stand over me with front feet on one side and back feet on the other side of me. I'm not sure he would allow anyone to touch me, he was protecting me. As I remember this horse was sold 3 times while I had him. While this horse belonged to Harry Baker, he was my horse. When he was sold the first time, I don't remember any of the details but Harry bought him back and instead of taking him home, he was returned to me because he was my horse. The same thing when he was sold the second time. He was purchased back and return to me for the same reason. The third time I think I remember and it goes like this, a man, his wife, and his 8 or 9 year old daughter came to look at him and wanted to see what he could do. I showed him, put him through his paces, so to speak. Well they looked him over, I don't remember her riding him but she could have. I knew that this horse was available for sale, knew and understood, so it was with great pride that I showed what he could do. When the man was talking to Dad about buying the horse, Dad was acting as sales representative for Harry, he said he would buy the horse, but had no way to take him home. I have no idea where he was from or lived, but was driving a new 4 door car and was probably as big as you could get at the time. I have often described him as having more dollars than sense. The asking price for this horse was $500.00, a lot of money in 1948. Upon hearing him say he would buy him if he had the way to take him home. Possibly thinking I knew what the sale, for $500.00, meant to Harry, and with the pride that "my horse would bring that kind of money". I butted into the conversation and said "put him in the car". The man smiled, tolerantly, at me and said it was a car not a truck. Having a smart mouth and thinking it was obvious, "He'll go in the car". And he replied that "If you can put him in that car I will buy him". My response, as I remember was "get out of the way". I lead him over to the car and Dad opened the right rear door and I stepped up in the car and he followed me in to the car, between the seats. Dad shut the door behind us, I dropped the lead rope and told him to stay, he lowered his head, a sign that he understood he was to stand there. I opened the left rear door and got out and shut the door. I turned to this man and he was standing there with his mouth somewhat open, as I remember. He took out a wallet and counted out the money to Dad. They got into the car and left. Again this is my memory of this and I do acknowledge that it could be off or different from someone else's.

Doc Blacky
Orlaff Morton Pat (Morton) Smith Ralph Morton

The next one I remember was Peanuts, a brown and white gelding, and he was going good and was gone quickly. The next one I remember was a pony sized mare, she would have been POA (Pony of America) size. I think 48 to 54 inches tall, that was white with a black face. I don't recall her name now but I'm sure she had one. In the days to come I'm positive she was called many things by a number of different people. As I remember we brought her home on a Thursday night. Dad got up at 4:00am to start milking the cows, and I was up and waiting for him. I don't think that this was a real surprise to anyone who knew me. We went to the barn and Dad saddled the mare for me. I'm sure he thought to get anything done he might as well and get me out of his way, so he could get the milking done. I was out of the barn and riding her around. Mom had come out of the house and was at the end of the sidewalk where the gate was. I rode up to her and said "Well, how do I look?" I'm not sure now of her response but do know that it was complimentary, to her 5 year old cowboy, plus 24 days. I rode around some more and the mare decided to go home, I guess. She started down the driveway to the county road and I wasn't having any of that, and it turned into a contest of wills, it was July 29, 1949. In not being quite as knowledgeable as I probably thought I was, I now know that I caused the whole wreck that happened. She wanted to go and I wanted to bring her back, as to the barn or house. We kind of went round and round over this and when I pulled back on her and didn't give her any release, she came over backwards with me. Now I had ridden enough to know to try and get out of the saddle. I tried to throw myself to the left and did get off to the side but not far enough. When we came down a part of the saddle caught me along the right side of my head, the horse came on down. On coming down on me, my left shoulder was driven in to the ground, breaking my left collar bone. The mare rolled to the right, away from me. I do believe this was intentional because she had no desire to hurt me. I would like to input here that I never did blamed this horse for the accident and years later came to realize that I was at fault and caused all of this, with no blame for the horse. I know that others didn't feel this way and I understand. Now the rest will be what I was told, for sure. Mom screamed, she was still watching, and Dad came out of the barn to see what she was screaming about. He then ran, about 100 yards as I remember it being, to me and picked me up and carried me to the house. The horse was standing over me and followed right at Dad's shoulder, clear to the house and would have followed him in if she hadn't been stopped, by the screen door. I was bleeding from my mouth, nose, eyes, and ears, and probably not the best thing my mother every saw. I would guess that they called Dr. Mary (Townsend-Glassen) our doctor, but don't remember, and she did or would have told them to bring me in. Dad and Mom put me in the car, not sure how this was done, as far as the deployment was accomplished. Dad ever being practical and being a horseman told my brother Tom to put the mare away in the barn and not to ride her. And of course being the obedient son that he was, did this, until they were out of sight and then got on and rode the mare at least to the barn. It would be my guess that he rode her around some before putting her up in the barn. They took me to town, three and a half miles away. Upon getting there, I was taken to Doc Mary's Office and examined. It was decided to take me on to Hays, Ks., 60 miles away. If I remember correctly Warner Cunningham drove us to Hays. I don't know if his wife Mary Margaret came with us or not. Warner and Mary Margaret did stand up with Kate and I when we were married in the Catholic Church, in May of 1973. This was after we came home from Ethiopia, when we were married for the second time. Now for this time frame, I have no memory and I don't remember what anyone told me. I was not consciously aware through any of this. The first memory I have was waking up, somewhere, and not knowing where I was at or what was wrong with me, but I couldn't seem to move. I was in a bed, in a strange room with the lights turned down low, actually indirect lighting, and I was staring at a crucifix on the wall. I'm not sure if I had any memory of seeing a crucifix before but didn't know at the time what I was looking at. I'm not sure of how good my vision was either. I have no idea how long I laid there before someone came in and found that I was awake. I asked about the crucifix, and it was explained to me what it was, and then I knew what it was. I asked if I could have it, she said that she would see what she could do. I'm sure this was a nurse, and she did return at some point and gave me a smaller crucifix which I held onto in the days to come. I could close my left hand, and did hang on to it, probably tightly. I don't remember much more about my stay at Hays, don't believe that we were there to long. They had decided that I was going to need brain surgery and wanted me transferred to Children's Hospital in Denver, Colorado. As I remember Lee Mattison, the local Chrysler and Dodge dealer in Phillipsburg, supplied a car, probably a new one, to transport me to Denver. This was accomplished, probably with Mom or Dad holding me in the back seat. I don't remember actually ever asking. We were in Denver for several days and the night before they were to do the brain surgery, to remove the blood clot, it passed or dissolved. I have no idea how they knew this, but they did. So I didn't have to have the surgery, not sure how good this would have worked anyway, the brain would have been very small, but might have worked to their advantage as there wouldn't have been a very big area to have to look in. I was paralyzed on the right side, nothing worked on that side. The eye didn't move and I would have to learn to walk, talk, eat and relearn everything over again. One thing that I didn't know about for awhile was that the nerves controlling the tear glands and saliva glands on the right side of my face were damaged and when they healed, they were crossed. When I cried I had an abundance of saliva in my mouth and when I ate certain foods my eye would water like someone had turned on a faucet and I have moisture in my nose. Was/is somewhat embarrassing when eating, especially when I was younger. I returned home and proceeded to recover and relearn everything. I think I can say that I was very determined to recover and not be restricted or maybe handicapped, would not have used that word then, in any way. I was still going to do whatever I wanted to and try to do it as good as I could or better then anyone else. I'm sure this effected my competitive nature and I don't like to give up on anything. While I do on occasion give up, it is only after giving it careful consideration.

Mom never did like to see me get on a horse again, but knew that I was going to ride and I'm sure had some tongue biting, fingernail or finger biting episodes. She probably worried, maybe more about me, when I was doing or trying to do things over the years. I doubt if I every thought much about her concerns or worrying until I was somewhat older. I was probably inconsiderate but she had nothing to be bothered about, or so I thought. I'm sure she saw that horse go over at least 2 or 3 times in the days after that morning. It has been said, by some, that she liked me better than my siblings. Now I don't think that is true, but I would agree that I did give her cause to worry, sometimes more than the others did. Whether this was warranted or not, I don't know, but I'll bet that she did know. One thing that I don't know about are my eyes, they never cross, they both go straight out, vision wise, in front of me and the doctors say I have no depth perception. I don't know if that has any thing to do with this incident or accident or not. I suppose I could go on about my trials after this but won't as it is a mute point now. Maybe this is an insight into why I am what I am today. Partly I'm here and there has to be a reason why, I guess God has a purpose for me yet and will continue to try and carry out that purpose in the days ahead.

An after thought here, when I was in between 4th and 5th grades I spent part of my summer at Harry Bakers. I'm sure this was a trying time for my mother, as he had over 1000 head of horses on his place at the time. One day while I was there a herd of mares came in for water in one of the pastures. There were ponds for water in the pastures but they could come in for water at the barn/house area and drink from water tanks there. I was drawn to a certain horse, no conscious idea why, and he saw me watching this horse and asked what I was looking at. I told him that mare. And why? I didn't know why. He said "That is the mare that fell on you." "Okay, I want to ride her". He said "No, I'm not ready to die yet and if your mother found out he had let me get on that horse, he figured he would be a dead man, so to forget it and it would be best if I just stayed away from her". He said "She never was rode again, after my ride, as far as he knew". I guess he didn't know, either, about Tom's little ride, that of course didn't happen.

Chapter 3:

School

I started and went to school in a 1 room country school. It was about ¾ of a mile from home. The teacher, Mrs Frank (Beth) Freeman, started having kindergarten 1 day, Friday, a week for me. I'm sure I needed it. I don't think they had a kindergarten class before this. Mrs. Freeman was a good teacher and a really nice lady. I had her for the first and second grades. She was teaching me to play the piano. I'm sure that took a lot of patience on her part. We moved into town and I started school in town for the third grade.

When I started the 4th grade, it was in the same school, same room, and the same teacher, Miss Iva Lake, that my mother had when she started the 4th grade, a few years before. Miss Lake got sick after about a month and we had a number of temporary substitute teachers. A new grade school had been built but was not ready for the start of the school year, but shortly after Miss Lake took sick, we moved to the new grade school. When Mrs. Wava Kaiser came in, she became the permanent substitute, for the rest of the year. She became the permanent 4th grade teacher. Miss Lake came back the next year and was teaching another grade. Mrs Kaiser and I didn't get along very well. Actually I don't think she liked me at all. I could have well given her cause, while not admitting to anything. Anything that happened in that class, was my fault. And I'm not kidding. I spent more time in the hall and in the principle's office than I did in class. There was a desk left in the hall, just for me. Others had to move a desk out into the hall, mine was just left there. It was so bad that Mom was coming to school 3 days a week and spending part or all day in class. I kept telling her, that when I hadn't done something, I wasn't going to admit it. I was still punished at home as well as at school. I don't know how long she had been visiting class, before one day, she was sitting in the back of the room and I was reading with my head down. Someone in the class threw something and Mrs. Kaiser was writing on the blackboard, she never even looked around. "Ralph go to the principle's office, I have had enough of you for the day." It was early, before 10:00 am, and she had forgotten that Mom was still sitting in the classroom. "Mrs. Kaiser, I didn't do anything." Mrs. Kaiser "I don't need your back talk, just get to the office, I'm not putting up with you any more today". So I walked out and went to the office. Mom was in disbelief, and waited for her to correct the situation. No , there were not to be any corrections. She got up and followed me the the office. Mr. Strecker, the principle, wanted to know what I had done this time. I said "Nothing". He thought that he should use the paddle on me. That they had there for these situations. He believed that I was obviously lying and I would be punished accordingly. He was making a big thing of it, banishing the paddle around, and I guess trying to intimidate me. It wasn't my first rodeo, so I wasn't really intimidated. And about that time Mom walked in, "I would suggest that you put that paddle away." And where he had had permission to use the paddle before he no longer had that permission. She told him that she had been in the room and I was telling the truth and had done nothing. She had the name(s) of the people responsible and she had witnessed the whole thing. I was asked to step outside and they closed the office door. After awhile the secretary went and got Mrs. Kaiser and the three of them were in the office with the door closed. Later I was returned to the class. From then on I was only punished if I was caught in the act. Which could happen, but I rarely got caught in the act, and I am saying just that, I didn't usually do anything, to get caught in the act of. Also Mom felt bad because of the times I was punished, not only at school but also at home, when I said I hadn't done anything. If I did it, I admitted to it. In 2 school years, Bill was in this class, with this teacher, and could do no wrong. It was to far for him to walk home, so if he would just wait until she finished up and she would give him a ride home, by the way of the ice cream store and they would have an ice cream cone on the way home. She would drive right by me and never offered me a ride, rain or shine. Just as well, I would have walked anyway, I 'm sure. But I might of taken the ice cream cone, if it had been offered, of course, it never was.

It never got better, because when we came home from Ethiopia, that first winter, I worked part time at Joe Yoxall's Conoco gas station, mostly in the evenings. Her husband, Henry Kaiser did all his fuel business at Conoco, even farm fuel rural delivery. Henry was a nice man and fair, never did understand why she was like this towards me. She was a nice person to other people. I did and do believe that to be true. She would come in for gas, in her car, because they used a charge account at the station. If I wasn't right there she would throw a fit, and sometimes drive off. Joe and Henry have both been there and she didn't know it, and they just couldn't believe it. Then they would hear her version of what happened. Are you sure we're talking about the same time? She would never change her story or opinion. Boy was I glad I had witnesses. Oh well, I guess that goes to show that you can't please everyone or even all the women in the world, no matter how hard you try. And I did try with this lady, when I was working there. I never once said a cross word to her, in all that time. It might have been different in the 4th grade, again not admitting to anything.

I returned to the country school for the last half of the 6th grade and the first half of the 7th grade. And with this teacher I could do no wrong, and it was embarrassingly obvious. I got better grades than I deserved and my classmate, Cheryl Kaiser, worked hard and at times didn't get the grades she earned. We moved from Phillipsburg to Ness City, Kansas in early 1957. We lived there 2 years. I finished the 7th grade, all of the 8th, and started High School there, about 6 weeks. We then moved to Hill City, Kansas in the winter of 1958.

In High School I played football, basketball (until I gave it up as a sophomore and became the team manager, rather than sit on the bench), I participated in track, I ran the quarter mile and then the half mile and threw the javelin. I was the un-official assistant freshman basketball coach my junior year and was listed as the assistant coach my senior year. This got me out of school and I got to travel with the teams. Also do to my 'in' with the coaching staff I got out of study hall, and attended freshmen and sophomore girls phys-ed, as a junior and senior. When I chose to do so, which was on the days when they were not in health class. I did have something constructive to do during this school period, and it always got done, sometime or other. I have been bad a long time. I was also a librarian my senior year, unheard of for a guy in those days in that part of the world. I even found time to help 2 girls pass American History/ Government classes. They set us in alphabetical order which put me between Ruth Morris and Karen Ohman and being reasonably well versed in these classes, I would finish my tests quickly and then watch them. When they got stuck on a question I would, in a gentlemanly way, quietly give them the correct answer. They would continue on, sometimes needing assistance again and tap on a question with their pen/pencil and I would contribute the answer and so it went in the world of school social behavior. I did get decent grades in most of my classes, okay, I passed anyway. I was not very good in English but I liked to read. At one time they were giving us speed reading tests. I did read a lot of books and had developed the ability to skim or speed read. These tests were reading material and on the Go signal you started reading and they would call off "Mark", and you would mark the work that you were at. I believe that we read for 3 minutes, total. You would mark each of the 1 minute intervals. Then during the same hour of class, you were given a comprehension test over what you had read. It seems like now, that my low scores were in the 85 percent range and up to 95 percent or better. It's hard to remember what speed I started out but seems like it was in the 200 words per minute range. My best that I remember was 732 words per minute. I still had about 90 percent comprehension at this speed. The English teacher did not believe I could do it that fast but could not explain my comprehension rate, if I didn't. And these were done over a period of time. I also averaged about 5 books a week that were not school related or assigned books. These books were mostly fictional stories, sports, or history. These things seemed to always get brought up with Mom, when she was at school. I told you I was a trial to my mother. I still survived , although I am not sure how sometimes, as far as my mother went. I went to work after high school. After a year I went into the Army, for 9 years, and met and married Kate after coming back from Viet Nam.

Chapter 4:

After School and finding the Military

Tom had gone into the Air Force (1956) and had served 4 years, he came home and moved to Salina, Kansas. Tom met someone there and eventually got married. Pat had also moved to Salina. Pat met Richard L. Smith (July 16, 1940), of Salina. June 25th of 1961, was when I remember Pat and Rich's wedding as being, white dress, black suits, flowers, and all that stuff. Weddings were for the older folks, and while different and interesting, I could have been doing something better or more constructive, fishing comes to mind. Pat and Rich continued to live in Salina, and in July of 1962, the 14th, up popped Garrett Lee Smith, this seems to happen after weddings, and must be something that only the older people understand. In September of 1962 they moved to Bainbridge Island, off the coast of Seattle, on Puget Sound, in the state of Washington.

After graduating from high school in May of 1962, I went on a Custom Harvesting crew, with brother Tom. Walter B. Hickert, Lenora, Kansas was the owner of the crew. We went from Kansas and started in Oklahoma to Kansas, to Colorado, to Nebraska, to Pines Bluff, Wyoming. While cutting wheat there, we got rained out and we went back into Nebraska to a lake, swimming, and spent the afternoon there. We got back to Pines Bluff and I walked across the grass, barefoot, and my feet were wet from the grass. We had 2 old school buses that we slept in, they had bunk beds built in them. One was pulled by a 1 ton pickup and the other still had a motor and was driven from place to place. I walked up the tongue of the one and stepped across to the other one's back door. I had done this numerous times before. However this time with my feet wet, I slipped and fell head first into the other bus. I tried to catch myself on the door jam and cut my left thumb about 2 ½ inches long and hit a foot locker with my face and broke off my two front teeth and took out the next one on each side. These 2 I spit out on the ground, they were whole and not even chipped. I went over to a water tank, they had horses at the house where we were staying, and tried to wash off some of the blood. I would wash my face with my left hand and leave more blood than had been there before. I claim this to be because I was looking at the reflection in the water tank and couldn't see very well. I finally realized that the hand was cut and I needed to use the other hand. They took me to a dentist. A doctor came there and sewed up my hand and give me a tetanus shot. The dentist arrived and did his examination and said that he didn't think we could save the 2 front teeth, and being mad at myself, I said to pull them out. The shot in the roof of my mouth was the worst pain of the whole situation. The 2 front teeth would not of been able to be saved anyway. They were completely loose and the same as out with just a very small piece of gum holding each tooth. He took them out, mostly by just taking a hold of them and they were out. He put in a few stitches, gave me prescriptions for antibiotics and pain pills and sent me back to the camp. No working and take it easy. I couldn't go to the field because of all the dust. We were taking 2 combines home to Kansas in a couple of days, we had 7 machines there at this time, to cut Milo at home, and so I drove home one of these trucks with a combine.

I made it home and in a few days went to work with my Grandfather, Frank Benjamin Morton (April 1, 1892), helping him with carpenter work and shingling houses, mostly in Norton, Kansas. I worked at this into the fall or early winter, until it slowed down for the season. Then went back to Hill City and worked in a Gas Station through the winter. In April, 1963, I left home for Bainbridge Island, Washington. That was where sister Pat and Rich were living. I lived with them while I was there. Pat has told me that I would get up with Garrett in the mornings change him, feed him and then lay back down with him on my arm and we would both go back to sleep. She would find us that way when she would get up and check on Garrett. I got there and went to work on the Island helping a contractor build 7 houses. He got into financial trouble and we had problems getting out money. I did eventually get all of mine but didn't find any other work right away, so I enlisted in the U.S. Army, in Seattle.

I was sent to Ft. Ord, California for basic training and then to Ft. Devens, Mass. outside of Boston for advanced training. While at Ft. Ord we got to go to the Rodeo at Salinas, California, on pass. We went as a group, the whole company, and were bused by the Army. Probably the thing that I remember the most, from that Rodeo, was a Trick Rider who performed various stunts from the back of her horse, in front of the grand stands. While doing a hand stand, from the back of the galloping horse, she spread her legs apart, like an acrobat or gymnast, in an act of balance, but the seam on her shiny white tight pants split from, more or less, waist to waist. This produced quite a contrast, from the brilliant white satin of her pants, to pink under-wear, to bright red face. She did draw a standing ovation from the stands, which happened to have hundreds of US Army soldiers in them. She was a performer and finished her routine, with something of a red face, still. She had gotten the attention and appreciation of many young men that were away from home and had an unforget-table memory from the Rodeo in Salinas in 1963. I'm pretty sure she survived the embarrassment of the incident and hope that it was, at least, a remembered occurrence, on her part.

While at Ft Devens, John F. Kennedy, President of the United States was killed in Dallas and I marched in a Memorial Parade for him, and attended Military Services in his honor. From Ft. Devens I was sent to Panama.

Chapter 5:

Memories of Panama

I went to Panama in May of 1964, the riots were just over and things were starting to settle down. I'll just start putting some of the things down as they come to me, and see what happens.

I loved fruit and with the roadside fruit stands I was in a little bit of heaven. I would stop and get bananas, oranges, tangerines, coconuts and other fruit. I thought I was getting a lot of bananas for a quarter. Then one day I said "Give me a dollars worth". They brought me a whole stock of bananas. Now in wanting to appear that I knew what I was doing, I took them and I had to try and figure out what I was going to do with a whole stock of bananas. Now I learned that they don't all ripen at the same time, so you can eat from one end to the other, as they ripen. And I kept buying them by the stock. I would take them back to the barracks and hang them from the clothes racks. The clothes racks were pipes that were hung from the ceiling, this was so the clothes were hung up with air space around them so they would not mold, because of the very high humidity. Put them on a rope and you could lower them down as you ate them from the bottom. The guys in the barracks would come by and help themselves to a banana(s). I have never gotten over my love of bananas. And I did eat a lot of them, bought by the whole stock. We went up north into the interior one time and some one drove my car, I had a 55 Buick, yellow, convertible. I rode my motorcycle. We were going up to a car hill climb, ran up a winding mountain road, against the clock. We helped run the event for the car club and then they let a couple of us run our motorcycles for exhibition. We were told, again, why they didn't let us run against the cars, they just weren't fast enough, the cars that is. We stopped at a fruit stand, up north, away from the Canal Zone, and I ordered a dollar's worth of bananas, oranges, and tangerines, they filled the whole trunk, with a number of baskets full, and the bananas went in the back seat, I think it was 2 whole stocks, and we had fruit for a lot of people for a long time.

We had found a back way onto the Post, Fort Clayton, and by going under a bridge on our motorcycles we could get on and off post when the gates were closed. We would go through the jungle and pick up a black top road about 1/4 to 3/8 of a mile from the post perimeter, and then take the road out to the highway and on to Balboa and Panama City. One time in coming back, to the post using this back way, Flip Pallot and I were coming down the black top road and I saw what appeared to be a palm tree leave laying across the road. The problem was that the leaves are not that long, an after thought. It was off the left side of the road and lacked a couple of feet of reaching to the other side. I don't like running over things that I don't have to, so I swerved over to the right edge of the road, on the narrow strip that was not covered, and went by. When I was going by and looked down, it was moving. Whoa, I put on the brakes and turned and went back, I stayed back 30 or 40 feet away. This was a very large Boa. Flip had went around and came back also. The snake was laying there watching us, it was probably about 12 to 14 inches in diameter and the funny thing was his tail. Usually they taper down to a more or less point, he was blunt like a cigar, not sure why this was. This snake was about 24 or 25 feet long. It just laid there and watched us. Flip wanted to see him move so he rode up behind him and bumped the end of his tail with his front wheel. Now I wouldn't have believed how quick a snake that big could move, he came around and grabbed that motorcycle tire and was shaking the whole bike, quite severely. Flip swung his leg over and was getting off and going to give him the bike. Then the snake stopped and slowly opened his jaws and slowly lay back over and started crawling away in the grass. He left a path about 30 inches wide in the grass. We watched as he went down to the stream and went into the water. Wow, that was some snake. We went on and got back to the barracks and was telling some of the guys about this, and they wanted directions to the location. We gave them directions and about 5 or 6 of them went back and looked for this snake. They even went into the water looking and luckily didn't find him. They would have wound up very dead if the snake had got a hold of them in the water.

Another time we were going out to work, about 6 miles out into the jungle, to our operations building. I saw a small snake in the road, he was about 8 to10 inches long. I stopped to look and this snake looked like a Bushmaster, a very poisonous snake that when bitten you have a bout 8 seconds, maybe 10, to get the anti-venom, to be safe. The poison attacks the nervous system and you die when your body functions shut down. I don't know why we were going out there because we were not working on this night. The fangs on a Bushmaster, or Fer-De-Lance, come down and fork so they can inject more venom when they bite. This snake was so small that I could not tell from the markings what it was for sure. I didn't look in its mouth to check the fangs, I don't know if I could've told that way either, as he was so small. I wasn't real anxious to be picking it up anyway. Being overly intelligent, we decided to catch this snake and take him back for the snake hunters to see. When I stopped and looked at him he got very aggressive, a characteristic of the bush-master. I had a t-shirt rag and when he would come at me I would drop it over him, still holding on to the rag, and he would stop and lay still for awhile. There were 4 of us and a couple of the guys went on to our operations building to get something to put him in. They came back with a 1 pound cracker box. By this time the snake was getting tired of the game and would stop when I dropped the rag on him but would almost immediately come out from under the rag and come for me. I would step away and he would come after me. So I used this to lure him into the box. He would come after me, so I stepped over in line with the box. He was very intent on watching me and ran into the box. I dropped the rag on him and closed the box. We had another rag so I wrapped it around the box and tied it. A real secure container for a highly poisonous snake. Anyway, I carried the box in my hand and I did transport him this way back to the barracks and turned him over to the snake hunters. They fooled around with him long enough that he got some what more friendly and they discovered that he was a baby boa instead of a bushmaster. Some bravery, but I didn't know that he was a boa when I was doing the stupid stuff, well anyway not to smart. And I don't like snakes, go figure.

One time I decided to go into the jungle exploring, and 2 other guys went with me. This would have been, I believe late 1964 or early 65. As I remember it, Jim Faircloth and Randy West were the two who went along. Jim was from the east coast, North or South Carolina and Randy was from Falfurrias, Texas. We wanted to see the ruins of a village or town that set on the east side of the Chagres River. This river supplied water to the Miraflores locks on the Pacific side of the Canal and was navigated by the ships in getting between the Miraflores and the Pedro Miguel locks. We had to cross the river to get to this location. Jim had a small canoe that would haul the three of us but not our gear, we were pushing capacity with the 3 of us. So we had to make several trips to get across. Informative thought here, the Panama Canal runs north and south, in case you didn't know. Pacific on the south. This had been a major town or village back in the days before the time of the Canal and the United States. It was the end of the trail, crossing Panama from the Atlantic, Colon side, to the Pacific or Panama City side. I'm not remembering the name of this village, now. Anyway the goods were transported to this location by mule train, as I was told, and am not sure if any other ways were used or not. This was also the end of the trail for smugglers. I don't know what they were smuggling, now, but must have been profitable and/or illegal. Then goods or whatever could be transferred on to the coast by water and to the city or ships waiting there. Anyway I wanted to see this site and view what was left of the history of this location. About all that was left were some foundations and walls or partial walls of houses and buildings. We wondered around and looked over the area trying to imagine the life and times of this historic site. We spent one night at this location and the next morning, at some point, we met up with a local inhabitant of the area. The mosquitoes had been quite bad and we had slept completely covered up. I had put a pair of extra socks over my hands but the mosquitoes bit through the socks and the back of my hands looked like I had the measles or something. That was the only part of me that was like this, because, I assume the mosquitoes couldn't get through the other clothing items that I wore. The man that we met was I believe from Jamaica, originally. He had come to Panama and got a job with the Panama Can Company. They canned, among other things, motor oil for cars and trucks. He had been in some kind of accident and cut off the tip of one of his fingers and even though it had not been his fault, he was fired from his job. As I remember, he had been there for quite awhile. In talking with him, he spoke not only Spanish but very good English. When he learned that we wanted to learn about the region of any and all things. He took us on a fact learning tour and also sight seeing. He showed us lots of things that we would never had seen or learned about otherwise. He showed us plums that looked the same to our untrained eyes. One was yellow on red and the other was red on yellow, in color. Of importance, maybe, if you eat them. One was poisonous to people and the other was good to eat, and I tried one of them but not the other. As I remember, but would not eat them now on this basis, the red on yellow was the one that was good to eat. You also never lay face down to get a drink from a water source, because snakes would wait in the water and grab you by the face or in some cases would lay on a limb of a tree, if available, and drop on you when you were laying down. Why they didn't drop on you when you were standing I don't know and didn't know or ask at the time. Also they had some large cats there and they would also wait on a tree limb and drop on its prey when they went to water, with their head down, but he said they usually wouldn't man if you were standing. They had a tree there that was called an elephant ear tree. I'm sure that was not the scientific name, but the leaves were fairly large, as I remember (could be a little shaky now), they were like 15 to maybe 18 inches across, with a good stem, for a handle. You would fold these into a cup and dip your water and drink from the cup. Something to remember if you happen to go camping where they have these trees. We had expressed a desire to go fishing and he took us to some streams that had a kind of trout in them. If you like catching fish this would have been a good place for you. He showed us these were eager fish or maybe just hungry. He showed us this by flipping something into the water and it was hit immediately by a fish. Of course we had to try our luck as we had brought fish hooks and leaders, fishing line, and other fishing gear. We had to supply native fishing poles, but that was easily done. I did have a fishing reel that had a base that you could use to attach it to the native poles or limbs we used. It seems like I used hose clamps, maybe, to secure it to the pole, don't remember if the others had something similar or not. I do think that Jim did. Also I had figured out a way to put guides on the pole to complete the make shift poles. We baited hooks and cast or flipped them into the water and they were taken instantly by the fish. These fish were like 12 to 16 inches in length and put up something of a fight. They would even hit a bare hook, sometimes, if you tossed that into the water. He told us they were good to eat and while we had been going to catch and release, we decided that maybe these people living in the jungle could put them to good use. So we put them on a stringer and gave them to him or took them to others who could utilize them. We fished for a little while and caught a good number of fish. But in wanting to see everything we could, we ended our fishing bonanza and continued on with our own guided tour. The fish were taken to the area, would not call it a village, where some of the people lived and left with them to be taken care of and distributed to those in need. These people had to pay the government 5 dollars a year to be allowed to live in the jungle. They were suppose to buy a hunting and fishing license for another 5 dollars, for a year, to be able to hunt and fish for food to exist on. Most were able to pay the rent(?) 5 dollars but couldn't afford the other for hunting and fishing. So they poached, by local law, for their food. They did have a few ancient firearms that they shot deer and/or other game with. They did not have the means or knowhow to make snares or just didn't use them, because of leaving something that would catch whatever came along.. They would ambush deer, usually at dusk or dawn when they came for water, as they were careful about where they watered if they wanted to survive their predators. Then the people had to be watchful and careful of the game wardens because they did not have the required license. They did a lot of the hunting from or with dug out canoes. They could hide easily along the water ways and under overhanging vegetation, they were quiet and didn't leave a trail. The also caught illegal fish, no license, by using railroad spikes, pried out of the railroad ties on the tracks of the trans Canal Zone railroad. The spikes were then barbed with a machete, a good machete and this didn't hurt the blade. They were then placed into the split, hollowed out, end of a bamboo pole and wrapped and tied with string, cord, vine or what ever they had to use to secure it with. They would go out on the river at night and light a torch and place it in a holder on the end of the canoe. This torch would be over the water, and the fish would come to the surface, to the light. These were large fish, I believe that they were tarpon or similar type of fish, I think I remember they got up to 6 feet in length. When the fish would come up to the light they would drive the railroad spike into the back of the head as deep and as hard as they could. The fish would then swim off, because they would not die right away, and I am not sure how long it took. I don't know if they did more than one a night or not. They would go and hide out along the shore in a covered spot and watch for the game wardens who sometimes were out on the water at night looking for poachers. They would wait until morning and then go looking for the bamboo sticking up out of the water, sometimes this would be under or in large floating lily pads. These could be up to 50 feet or more across, that I have seen, and were sometimes something of a problem to get them out of. But they would work at it until they managed to do this. If they were considered well off, they would have a rope or cord to tie to the bamboo and then to the end of the canoe and would tire the fish out pulling the canoe and would retrieve it and tow it with them and not have to wait all night to find the fish. Or have to get it out of the lily pads. We went out with him in a large dugout canoe and he showed us watering places for wildlife, places where they fished with and without the bamboo spears. We spotted something splashing in the water and was drifting closer so everyone tried to stay perfectly still. As we got closer we could see that it was turtles trying to eat green apples that were floating on the water. These turtle's shells were like 16 by 24 inches, some might have been a little larger. They were having an awful time trying to bite the apples. When they would try and bite the apple it would spin away from them, just like humans bobbing for apples. This was funny and interesting all at the same time. We drifted clear past them, by turning our heads slowly as we drifted by we were able to get clear past and we were looking over our shoulders before they finally noticed us. They did a double take and were gone under the water. I would guess you have not heard of to many people telling of watching turtles bobbing for apples. Kate always thought that this was a really neat thing and a good story. I did re-tell it to her several times over the years, whenever she asked or mentioned it. We returned to the place where they lived and spent the night. The next morning he helped ferry us across the river, in just one trip, and we were almost back to civilization. Oh before we left we all decided that we were carrying to much weight and lightened our packs somewhat, all the fish hooks and leaders, fishing line, cord, string, and we had some rope along that was to much trouble to carry home so we left it. I am thinking I left the fishing reel too but don't remember for sure, all of that stuff that we were never going to use again, we left. The canned and dried food, this stuff was just weighing us down for the river crossing so we just left it there. Somewhat small change to us but was a small fortune to these people who lived out in the jungle and lived the very primitive life. More friends in strange places, I seem to have made a lot of them over the years, be it Panama, Viet Nam, China, Africa, California, or other far off and exotic places.

I got a motorcycle soon after getting to Panama, cheap and fun transportation. And then I started racing them, the need to go fast, faster than others, the ability to perform better and longer than others, to do the best that you can and to improve your ability. To compete and go to a higher level, to push yourself and your equipment to new levels. To look for a better way and get more out of what you have got to work with. I like motorcycles. I rode and raced them for a lot of years. There was a strip of land between the Miraflores Locks and the dam and spillway on the Chagres River. At some time they had constructed a model of a sea level canal, on this strip of land, it was made of concrete. At one time they floated toy or small boats on it to simulate a sea level canal. They determined that it was not feasible to build a sea level canal, do to the fact that the Pacific

Ocean is 12 or maybe 15 feet higher than the Atlantic. We wanted in and we had to go through the cement canal. A little work with sledge hammers and we had an opening in the cement wall of the model canal. Once behind the canal we went to work and carved out a race track through the tropic growth. We started out with a base course and kept changing and adding to it. Eventually we had a track that we were satisfied with. We used it for a couple of years and held a number of organized races there. Do still have some pictures from this track. On part of the track you came down a small hill and made a sweeping 180 degree turn to the left and back up the hill and a jump. This was on the edge of the spill way from the dam and the water was salt water because of the Pacific Ocean. Interesting race course, having helped built it I probably had somewhat of an advantage, at times. We also had a flat parking lot that we could use for a flat track oval, this was in a different location. I was hooked on flat tracks forever after that and always had a weakness or liking for them. I used to ride in the rodeo arena in Santa Rosa, California, this was a 1/10 of a mile oval , kind of soft but I always liked it, even when I got run over, on the start of a race, in the first turn one night, by 3 different bikes, before I was even on the ground. Then after the races we drove, during the night, down to Edwards AFB to ride in the desert. I was somewhat sore by the time I got there. This was before I met Kate, and took place in 1969.

We worked closely with the sports car club and helped with their races and events, and once in awhile we ran in their events, and they would help us with ours. There was an International Grand Prix held in Panama each year and the car club helped put this on and the motorcycle people worked security and crowd control. The first one I don't remember much about except I met a girl from Columbia and we became friends. She was bound and determined to help me learn more Spanish, and sometimes we worked at it real hard, learning Spanish that is, maybe. She had the most beautiful eyes and the rest of her wasn't bad, either. It is still not to hard to remember how she looked, ah but the eyes. At the second one, it was held on the Atlantic or Colon end of the Canal Zone. I worked crowd control where the cars came down a long straight away and did a high speed turn onto another straightaway without slowing down. On Saturday I took my shirt of for about an hour, it was kind of cloudy, and then I put it back on. By sundown I had 2 and 2 ½ inch blisters and was sick. I felt terrible, but knew I wasn't going to die, I would have to get better to die. I missed the big party but the girls kept coming upstairs in the hotel to check on me and put lotion on my back, it was still miserable. But I was ready to go the next morning, and was at least able to function. I was a little tender, but was ready and willing. This turn was a favorite spot for the crowd. We had hay bales set up and a rope to keep the crowd back but they were constantly ducking under the rope and getting out close to the track. One Panamanian couple kept ducking under the rope and going up to the edge of the track to watch the cars come through this corner at over 100 MPH. Now this couple had a baby that was less than 6 months old, and it was wrapped up in a blanket and the man was carrying it. I had gone down the edge of the track/crowd area and moved some people back behind the rope, had turned around and was headed back. This couple had again moved out to the edge of the track. I was headed back to move them back, again, with cars coming in to the turn. One was an Austin Healy, that had a 327 Chevy engine. I knew the driver/owner. He blew his engine coming into the turn, a rod (or part of) and a piston or what was left of one, went through the pan and blew out from under the car and into the air. He straightened out and was trying to stop while going off the track, right at this couple. One ran to the right and the other to the left, and the man threw the baby up into the air. The car went through the spot where they had been standing and when it had passed the baby dropped to the ground behind it. I was the first one to the baby, he was crying but was apparently not hurt. I did take him to the doctor that was standing by, in the pits, and he was checked out and then returned to his mother/parents. Did not have anymore trouble with people wanting to cross under the ropes or go past the hay bales to stand on the edge of the track, for the rest of the day. I really couldn't believe what I saw when he threw the baby into the air, but thankfully it turned out okay. Just another in the long list of things I saw and did. Amazing what the human body sometimes endures and keeps on ticking. When you think about it, I guess it was really not that bad for the baby, other than the landing, and he was wrapped in a blanket and it was the ground rather than the hard surface of the air base runway.

In joining and working with the Sports Car Club, the motor-cycles were a part of the car club. We eventually split off and started a separate Motorcycle Club. We still worked and ran in some of their events. In the socializing with these people, you would always seem to have arguments about the speed of individual's motorized vehicles. Whose was faster or faster over a certain type of terrain or course. Having heard all the arguments, I was thinking how sense-less some of these arguments were. Ah ha, I see a practical joke in this somewhere. I would get tired of listening to these endless and unsolvable arguments. I decided to add to or join in the utter nonsense of them. I would enter into the conversation and say that if all things were equal then the one that was painted Red would win. It was scientific, proven in the laboratories, it had something to do with the molecular make up of the paint. Red was the fastest of all the colors. Now this was by its self assured of starting an argument. But you can't argue with the proven facts of science. I even had a list of schools where the experiments were conducted and results were available upon request. This could go on for hours and when things start to lag or get out of hand, you just inject some new information or changed the direction of the conversation. By the way do you happen to know what color is the slowest? New discussions and or new arguments soon started. And what you ask is the slowest color? Blue, of course. More new discussion and or arguments. This was and is never ending, unless you put a stop to it, and of course I never let it go on for more than 6 or 7 hours, without taking a break. Over a period of time I even produced a Color Speed Chart, to serve as a training aid in teaching the uneducated about the truth of the speed of the individual colors. Also reference materials were faked, I mean, produced to substantiate all of my scientific claims and facts. I think I probably hold a world record for starting arguments and prolonging them, whether there is any real basis for them or not. You might jump to the conclusion that I like to argue, and you would be right. I also like to have fun and if it's at others expense, preferably with no open or bleeding wounds, I can live with that.

Color Speed Chart

Now this is a reproduction and is used for reference, colors may not be actual due to the printer/monitor being used. Also is not done in complete detail as far as color dilutes and variations are concerned. But you should be able to get the general idea. It is very hard to duplicate all of the different color variations here. But please understand that under Laboratory conditions this of course would be more complete. Please feel free to ask any questions you may have and will try to answer them. Also paint from different companies may vary the speed index, and methods of application may also vary the speed index of the various colors. But be assured that the scientific data is available and will back up the information contained on this chart. And should be interpreted in the spirit that it is offered. Thank you for your consideration

Color Speed Chart
From fastest to slowest, shows the ranking of
individual colors relative speed to the other colors!

Fastest: RED

ORANGE

PURPLE

BLACK

GOLD

PINK

SILVER

GREEN

WHITE

GREY

YELLOW

BROWN

TAN

Slowest: BLUE

I seem to remember one time we had some kind of a gathering of these individuals at a hotel or restaurant in downtown Panama City. It lasted until about 2 or 3 in the morning and I, in being in good humor and challenged, to race back to the Canal Zone and on to Ft. Clayton. I was on a motorcycle, as were the others, and we all started in the parking lot. As I remember there were about 18 to 20 of us who were going to make this run. Some were more into the taking of chances than others. We all started out of the parking lot at the same time and I was a little quicker in getting away, so I was in the lead. In knowing the city and the different routes I chose the one with few or no stop signs and/or stop lights. I had soon opened up a sizable lead and was going around on a causeway, with no traffic and no traffic signals, and was almost obeying the 40 mph speed limit. Really I wasn't going over 75, or so. I came flying around the causeway, there was a blind spot where you couldn't see ahead, I rounded this point and there was a road block set up by the Panamanian La Guardia National, the National Guard or what serves as a Police Force. I was going so fast that by the time they even saw me, I was by them. They didn't even look at my tag number, even if they could have read it. They had no idea who it was, while I was home free, the rest of the group would not be. So I slowed and went back and as luck would have it they all had their attention on me when the rest of the group started through the area. They were able to slow down and proceed at a more reasonable speed and were waved on through. I think these men were more interested in my bike, than in me for speeding. We had a nice and lively conversation for about 10 minutes and they told me to go on, maybe I should slow down a little and try to be careful. I definitely would, at least until I got out of sight. Some of this I knew from my conversation with the local Policemen. About a half mile down the road the rest of the group was waiting for me. They were waiting because they figured they would have to come bail me out of jail and if you had enough money you could get out of most things in Panama. I stopped and assured them that everything was alright and no ticket (s) were issued and I was slowed down and being careful but was still going to be first to the Canal Zone and then would obey speed limits on to Ft. Clayton. And with that I started my bike and beat them all to the Canal Zone. Of course I was careful. I was watching out for road blocks. I even had a helmet on and never did go faster than the bike would run. I'm sure of that, unless it was downhill.

Some time in 1966, I remember, we had a company of Marines come in, TDY, temporary duty, for us to train in the work that we did. While we had at least 50 men working on shift, they had a skeleton crew of about 8 who worked with us and that we trained. Now being the good conscientious, patriotic, American Soldiers that we were, and being assigned to teach these marines in all aspects of our work, we were duty bound to also take them down town and show and teach(?) them of the public relation responsibilities of the American Soldier. It seems that after several forays in this direction, we had finished the evening set of 6 work days and had 2 days off. So at midnight on the 6th evening shift we proceeded, with a lot of our men and all of the marines assigned to our shift, to go down town and work on public relations with the local populace. I am not sure now where we started at but we got to the Pan American Bar. We were doing quite well in the spreading of good will with the locals. Now it just so happened that a certain young lady got off about 3 in the morning at the Pan Am Bar. She and I thought we should go else where, somewhere of a more private nature. Which we did and I didn't see any of these guys for a couple of days, but will relate to you, what was told to me about the happenings after I left. I'm not remembering the names of the Marines, now, but will try and tell of the happenings as best I can. The Sargent, E-5, and ranking member of this group was from Texas and while I still remember his face, I can't speak his name. He and 2 of his men wound up with my 2 roommates, from my military barracks, Randy West and Ron Hoffman. They were getting ready to go somewhere and get breakfast and head back to the post and go to bed. When leaving the area of J and K streets, mostly bars and entertainment establishments, for 2 solid blocks. Our friendly Texas Marine decided that he needed to go to the bathroom, and proceeded to do so at curb side. Three La Guardia policemen were where they could observe this and took exception to this public display. Approached and arrested him for this offense. Since the others were just present they were let go. Our Texas friend, spoke Spanish, and told the policemen that he needed to finish what he had started, so they let him go into a blind alley between 2 of the buildings close by. He went into the alley with a policeman standing, back turned to him, on each side of the alley entrance. After waiting a seemingly respectable time, one of them did turn and look down the alley, didn't see anything and turn back around and thought for a second then turned and looked again and appeared to get excited and rushed into the alley, followed by his fellow policeman. After a short time lapse they both rushed back out on the street and looked up and down the street and one of them approached the 4 remaining servicemen, who were still standing on the street and watching. "Where's your friend?" he wanted to know. They didn't know either and told him so. The third policeman had moved on down the street and he returned to the scene (?) of the crime. The 3 had a animated conference, and then 2 of them ran into the alley again, for another look, and came back out and all ran up and down the street and checked in all the open establishments. No luck. I seem to remember that other policemen showed up and helped in the search, but none had any luck in finding said Texan. My 4 friends discussed this situation and decided they should leave the area, to avoid the possibility of guilt through association, out of sight out of mind thinking. They did go a couple of blocks to a restaurant, where they had been headed anyway, and waited and had breakfast. After waiting for maybe an hour they were joined by our Texas friend of was laughing and trying to contain himself. They decided it best if the just caught a bus, at the near by bus stop and make themselves unavailable to the local police, should they show up. It so happened that our Texas friend had up on entering the alley had proceeded to climb the brick wall until he got high enough to get a hold of pipes that would have been on the second floor level and proceeded to climb on up to the roof of the buildings. Which I remember as being 3 stories high at this location. He had then walked across the roofs and went several buildings down and lay down peeking over the front of the building and laying there and watched the action taking place down below. He said he had a good view of everything taking place. Eventually some one did climb a fire escape and look on the roofs but was very tentative and didn't expect to find anything and didn't. After awhile he traveled about 2 blocks, solid buildings, and went across the alley, on pipes, and got to the next street over, the opposite side of the block and climbed down a fire escape ladder and joined the others at the restaurant. As far a we know they may still be looking for him, in Panama City. Extra training provided, free of charge, to our comrades in the Marines Corp. And did make for some lively conversations in the days that the Marines were still with us And gee I actually missed this one, but am still pretty sure that I still had more fun, at the time, and could still get in on the conversations, at a later date. And could up on questioning about it. honestly say, "I wasn't there, and I did not witness anything". With the story making the rounds, some of the higher ups wanted to know about it and if there was any truth to it. And for some reason I was always included in the questioning for things like this. If anything actually happened. I'm not sure why I was always asked about these type things. I believed I must have been home in bed, well I was at least somewhere else, and maybe I was just otherwise occupied. That must have been the way it was, at least this time. And yes I do know where I was at, but with no witnesses, I'm not telling.

I liked to play basketball, probably picked it up in girls phys-ed. I was not good enough to make the company level team, so I started a league of my own. There was a team from each of the 4 shifts from work, 1 from the headquarters personnel, and to make 6 we had enough players from my platoon for an extra team. I did the scheduling, stats, and all administrative work, and got the officials for the games. Starting out I coached the first team and played on and coached the second team. Our 5 best players were on the first team and we did wind up winning the league. As time went on and we were short of players, for whatever the reason Brian Younger and I played on both teams, usually as subs on the first team and we both started on the second team. And for those that think I might be prejudiced against the color blue, the first team's shirts were blue, my choice. We could play at the YMCA gym in Balboa or in the post gym, Ft. Clayton, when it was available. So we had a good time and played a lot of basketball.

We also had a tag football inter mural league, played rain or shine and it was mostly in the rain. Had a lot of fun with this also.

My third year there I decided to play in the regimental level flag football league. We were combined with other outfits to bring our man power count to a high enough count to qualify for this level of competition. There were 11 teams in the league, I'll see how many I can remember now: 4th Mech 10th Infantry, Ft. Amador, U.S. Navy, Special Forces, 2 Air Force teams, 1 was Howard AFB, Rodman Naval Air Station, 10th Air Borne Red Devils, another fort from the Atlantic side, 4 Mech 20th infantry (?), and us (can't remember our name, now, something to do with Ft. Clayton). Most of these teams, if you made the team, that was all you did, all other duties were relieved and you just played football. Not so for us, we had to work, except for practice and for the games. I went out for the team as an offensive guard, and I made the team at this position, right guard. We had a coach that had played football at West Point but before the first game received orders to go to Viet Nam and quit. They asked Bob Irwin to coach, he was the starting center linebacker, but he said no. He would only until games started or they found a permanent coach, he was going to play not coach and play. One day in practice, the starting center was just going through the motions of playing. There was a kid playing center line backer, while Bob was coaching, and he wasn't a football player. He was also just going through the motions. Bob got mad and went into the defense, told the kid to get out and watch how it was done. Bob told the center, "you better hit me". Bob lined up about 2 yards off the ball and when the quarterback called signals and the center started to snap the ball, Bob would hit him before he could get the ball to the quarterback. Knocked him and the quarterback into the backfield on their backs. This was starting to hurt to just watch. The center never got the ball to the quarterback again, and the quarterback was up under center, for the football knowledgeable. After a while Bob said "Ralph get in here at center". "No, I'm a guard". I did play center in passing drills and as a back up at times. You are now playing center. Oh boy, if he's going to hit me like that then I'm going to do what I can to him first. When I snap the ball I also take a stride with my right leg, so I am in motion with the motion of the ball. I would meet Bob coming in and it felt like hitting a wall. But he didn't move me back either. We ran plays for awhile and he had the other center come back in to play center, same results, he couldn't get the ball to the quarterback. "Ralph you are now the permanent center." "No, I'm a guard." "Not anymore you are the center." So I was now the center. We were running plays and it was a sweep around left end. Bob faked coming in and stepped back and went into coaching mode, and was watching the play develop. I nailed him good, drove him into the ground, and thought 'Oh no, I didn't do that, he was over being mad', I helped him up and said I was sorry. He just smiled and said "No you're not". He was right and he didn't get mad, but he never stopped and watched any more plays develop, either. Keep in mind that for these teams, I, at 5' 10", 180 pounds was a little guy, most players being full grown. They were 6' 3" to 6' 7" and would weigh 220 to 280 pounds. I looked little league playing with the big boys. Gates Winters and Pedro "Pete" Macias , starting left guard and defensive tackle were in the same boat, Gates was 5' 9" and 180 and Pete at 5' 10-11" and 175 felt undersized also. The other center was 6' 4" and weighed 240 to 245 (at weigh in when starting the season). But we played with a lot of heart and made our presence known during the season. I would state that pound for pound I think that Bob Irwin was the best football player I ever knew. We would stand flat footed facing each other and he could grip my shoulders from the top with his hands and staying flatfooted with his arm strength lift me off the floor, of course that's not so much he couldn't hold me there. Give that a try with some one your own size some time and see if you can get their feet off the floor. He was 5' 10" and weighted 170-175. After practicing against him 5 days a week, games were a blast. He averaged tearing a shirt off me, 4 days out of 5, we had light practices on Fridays. Pete and I were the only players that made it from our platoon or work shift, there were some others from our company but were on different work shifts. The original center wound up making the team as an offensive lineman and played quite a bit at right guard. He didn't have to practice heads up with Bob. I was also the punter for the team, you should of seen me snap the ball and catch it and make the kick, not really, we had another guy that snapped the ball for punts. Our first game was with the Ft. Amador team, the guy who was the coach was also the center line backer and was better at talking than playing line backer. He started out the game saying "come on bring it up the middle, right here, bring it on", so our quarterback after the first play, says, quarterback sneak, right up the middle and right over the top of the center line backer. He was a Captain in the Army. We made a first down. "Just try that again, come on guys". Okay, quarterback sneak, another first down, and so it went, every play was a quarterback sneak until we scored a touchdown. And this guy never learned and we went back to this system off and on for the whole game. The only way they could stop it was to bring in the halfbacks or outside linebackers and this left it wide open for a fake and quick pass to the outside, for big yardage plays. In the second half he was going backwards at the snap of the ball, so I told the quarterback to step back, fake a hand off to a back, and then hit me up the middle with a pass, everyone was pass eligible, this worked very well. Like I said, games were a blast, except for 1 that I will get to later. The score wound up like 60 to10, ours was the big end. Our next game was with the Airborne unit Red Devils and it was a lot tougher but we won 10-0. We continued to roll and were doing good and when we got to the 4th Mech 10th Infantry. We were still undefeated. When we played them they moved a defensive tackle in to play heads up on me. He was 6 ft 7 inches and weighed about 250, they called him 'Big Red', he was a African American with red hair and red skin, I never saw another man with his hair and skin color. I couldn't move him out but he couldn't go through me either, we had a very long day of football. The only thing I can say was he didn't pick me up and throw me around as much as Bob did in practice. We actually became friends after this game and I would occasionally see him, when we went somewhere, he was better for a friend than as an opposing football player. Our knees were the same height off the ground and our right knees banged together all day long, in that game. On Monday after this game, I played in a inter mural game. I had to play out of position because I was on the other team. Billy LaMonte hit me on my knee and it puffed up like a balloon. Billy was so sorry that he hurt my knee, he was 5 ft 5 and weighed about 130, after a meal. He never did understand how "Big Red" had done the damage on Saturday and he hit me on Monday and made it swell up. I didn't get to play the game that week. I wanted to but they made me set out, and we lost our first game. I was back the next week and we won again, maybe I was just a good luck charm. We ended up the season with 2 or 3 losses, I know we lost 2 but not sure if we lost 3. The team that won the league was the team we beat 10-0 the second game of the season. They only lost one game, us. I think we wound up in 3rd place, not to bad when you remember we were playing with some little league players on our team.

Now something happened while I was playing football, on this team. Pete and I had been friends before this but got to be good friends while playing football. When we were working the evening shift, we would go to practice and then we were suppose to go to work after practice. Being the assistant trick chief, I would call in and check how they were doing and almost always they were okay, and SSG Frost, the trick chief, would tell me to go ahead and take the night off. I had told him about how hard the practice was and we were really tired, he said he understood and to take off and get rested up, big game on Saturday. OK, we would. We would then take our showers and put on civilian clothes and head down town Panama City. I guess you could call that restful, but that might be stretching it a little bit. We would always find something to do. Pete was Mexican, from Texas, and we both had very active senses of humor. I'm not sure how this came about but we decided we would convince people that I was a Mexican. Now this, like the Speed Color Chart, sounds pretty far fetched and maybe even ridicules. However with persistence and determination, you can do a lot of things and we were and did have. We would go in a bar, restaurant, or club and start talking with people, we didn't know, locals mostly. And they would usually ask if you speak Spanish, they didn't bother to ask Pete, he obviously did, but would ask me and I would say, no. Pete would direct the conversation, in Spanish, to something he knew I would understand. I did speak and understand some. I would comment about the conversation and they would say "I thought you didn't speak Spanish". Well "Poquito", just a little. They would then kind of keep an eye on me, something going on here. Pete would then steer the conversation else where, again where he knew I would understand and I would again comment on what they were talking about. Wait a minute, you speak Spanish. "Well, yes a little". Not fluent like all of them, of course they never believed this, again. Why and how come I spoke such good Spanish. I really don't. Yes you do. Well, very hesitant, the truth is I'm Mexican. Oh no, no, no, you can't be, you don't even look like you might be. Well I didn't want to tell you in the first place, and I would clam up and not talk to anyone. Pete would explain that I was very sensitive about my heritage and would they please be considerate and not ask me any more questions. Talk about setting the hook, of course this just made them more curious, which it was intended to do. I would stay quiet, with my hurt feelings, for a while, and then get over it and be willing to talk again. Pete would ask "You okay?" "Yeah I'm okay, just a little sensitive about it." They would start asking questions again "You're really Mexican?" "Yes but I'm from the Northern United States and we don't get much sun light up there, not like Texas where Pete is from, so my skin never got brown like his." Sometimes they would show disbelief again and I would even get up and walk away, with my hurt feelings. They didn't believe me. I would walk to the bar or across the room and stand by myself to hide my hurt feelings. Lots of times there would be women and men both in these groups, one of the women would usually come over to console me and try and get me to come back to the table or group. They didn't mean to hurt my feelings, it was just kind of hard to believe this story. Well I didn't want to bring it up anyway, because this always happens, no one ever believes me, so just forget it and we'll talk about something else. And I would be convinced to go back and we would not talk about it any more. So if no one else brought it up, Pete would. And we would be off again, I lived way up north, had they ever heard of Kansas, I don't think anyone ever had. Well that was way up north and there weren't any other Mexican families up there. We didn't get enough sunshine to turn our skin brown like Pete's. My parents could speak Spanish but they didn't want us kids to because that branded us as different and they wanted us to be like everyone else. And we weren't to be speaking Spanish, we had to speak English in school so we would speak English all the time. Of course they still spoke Spanish to each other, but that was okay, but not for us. This sometimes took place over several visits and we painted a very convincing story. If we met with disbelief than I would just stop talking or walk away, but I always came back. This whole thing went on for several months and with a number of different groups of people. But always the same theme and story, it was easier to keep it straight if you told the same story, and of course this was all true, if you don't believe me than ask Pete. Now I suppose you don't think I'm Mexican either. Well we will get to you, don't go away. After football season we would be downtown in some of these same establishments and some of these people would tell someone that "See that guy over there, he's Mexican". No way and the argument would be on. Sometimes we even got drug into these arguments but if possible, and if I was watching, I would try to slip away before it got to me. I must have something against arguing or starting arguments. You do believe that don't you? I have been bad a long time.

My sister, Pat, ask if I thought my Mother had any idea what she was turning loose on the people of the world, and I think the answer would have to be no, or I would not ever have survived my childhood. Almost didn't anyway.

Another guy I worked with, in Panama, was David Gajewski, from Wausau, Wisconsin. He was a lot of fun and we played a lot of cards, mostly pinochle. He also was a pool player, and a hustler, if he wanted to be. He was good when it came to shooting pool, billiards. He lost his father when he was 5 and his mother had to work full time or more. He had 3 older sisters and so was kind of on his own after school. In walking home from school he went by a pool hall, maybe several, and started stopping in at this one and would quietly watch and stay out of the way, so they let him stay. After awhile they had him start racking the balls for games and he would make a little money. When he wanted to start playing they would let him practice on a back table when they weren't busy. And then some of the guys started helping him with his game and techniques and he got really good. And was sometimes used in their games and as a ringer in some of the betting that took place in this establishment. He got a lot of experience and I'm not sure how he sometimes used it before I knew him. When I knew him, he never drew someone into a game or a bet, but as always seems to happen, others would start wanting to bet him or us, because we played a lot as partners. Mostly he would decline or walk away, but sometimes if they were really pushy or he didn't like them for whatever the reason, he would play. I never heard him or remember him naming stakes, but he would play for whatever they wanted to and when he was serious, he never lost. When it was just a game, no big deal but when you made him mad or he got serious, don't bet against him, you were going to lose. Sometimes he would be setting around and nothing going on, he would seem to start sniffling and almost ready to start crying, he would reach up over his shoulder and pat himself on the back "You'll be alright, Davy, you'll be alright". He might do this several times, and if somebody didn't know him, they would be concerned and ask him "Are you alright?" "No not really". Then he would laugh and laugh. Maybe that's why we got along so good, his sense of humor must have fit in with mine, that and we were both big Johnny Cash fans. I had a number of Johnny Cash albums and we would listen to the music and talk for hours about whatever came up for conversation. We would also play cards. We would play partners and won more than our share of the time, we thought and played alike and this made for good team play. Completely lost track of him when we left Panama. Seems like he was on track to get married when he got out of the Army shortly after leaving Panama.

The place named "Calvin's", and called "The Fort", was a bar, dance hall, and meeting place for lots of people, for lots of different things. This place was located in Rio Bajo, the poor, less fashionable part of Panama City. The bar was utilized, primarily, by persons other than Caucasians. Very few patrons were white, as in skin color. Reportedly about 75 percent of the drug trade, for Panama City, went through this establishment. On busy nights there were girls selling candy, gum, peanuts, and other things from trays supported by a strap around their necks. They did sell some high priced things off these trays. I have witnessed a small bag of peanuts sell for amounts of more than one $20 bill, this in the mid sixties. Now you ask what was I doing there? Maybe that's a good question, and then again maybe not. I started going to this establishment when there was a party for one of the guys I worked with. I had friends from all races and all kinds of backgrounds. If you wanted to feel in the minority this was a good place to start, if you had light colored skin. At that first party there were probably less than 6 people there who were white skinned, and there were several hundred people there.

When you came in the front door, there were several doors, on your right front was a small bar, with 10 to 15 stools. Seems like there were maybe a half dozen small tables to your left and along the wall. Down the front wall, on your left was a door that went into a room with a number of booths with tables, they were very nice and comfortable. The benches were very well padded and had leather covers, red if I remember right, the lighting was soft and red also. Very plush, nice, and kind of private. Seems like I remember about 15 booths in this room. There was a door at the end of the room away from the front of the building. This door went into another room with more booths with tables, and I don't remember this room as being quite as plush and nice as the first one was, but were still nice and also fairly private. Seems like there were about a dozen booths in this room. There was a door from the bar, in between the bar and the tables into this room and offset on the opposite wall there was a door that lead into the back bar and dance floor. Also there was another door that was to the right of the door that came in from the front bar. This was a big dance floor, I'm guessing from memory, that this room was something like 250 feet by 200 feet. There were a lot of small square tables and chairs in this room, taking up about half of the space , there was a small bar in the front right corner of the room and the bandstand was in the back left corner. There were a number of doors out of this room. The main exit was midway on the right side of the building, opening on to the parking lot. The building had to be 200 by 500 feet, I'm guessing from memory. Behind the front bar to the right was more space but was never in there, office (?), storage, and I think there was a kitchen back there somewhere, because there was some food served at times, I don't really remember much about the food. On the busy nights in the back, not sure where all the drinks came from but don't think that they all came from the small bar but could have. There were a number of waitresses in this place and I'm sure they each had individual areas that they took care of, but don't claim to know the areas or patterns. After coming to the original party I came out here a number of times and was accepted, so I never had any trouble. There were a number of people who looked out for me and saw to the fact that I didn't have any problems from anyone.

We came to a big party, one night, now the reason escapes me but I'm sure that it was for a very good reason. There had to be 500 people in the room. We had a number of tables pushed together and we had 2 of the light skinned persuasion at our tables. We had 30 to 35 people at our tables, as I remember. There were only 3 whites in the whole place, as I remember. In another section of the room the 4th Mechanized 10th Infantry were having a going home party for some of their people who were leaving, probably going to Viet Nam. Sometime during the evening, after a lot of the people had to much or maybe enough to drink, an argument broke out among the 4th Mech people with a guy that had been in the Marine Corp. and stayed in Panama. They were both dark skinned and were told to take it outside, which they did, with the ex-Marine whipping up on the current soldier quite severely, but just with his hands and maybe feet. The third white guy decided he had to take up for his worked over buddy, and did his best to pick a fight with the ex-Marine. This guy was on the small side, about 5 ft. 8 inches , and 145 pounds of pure D dumb. Not only did he pick the fight but when they went outside, I was setting where I could see out the open doors and watch. He pulled a switch blade knife and made some very dumb comments, the ex-Marine tried to talk him into putting away his knife but like I said he was very dumb. He wanted to know if the ex-Marine "Was afraid of a little knife". Ex-Marine "No, but you better put the knife away". Dumb GI "Afraid of a little steel huh". Ex-Marine "No man, put the knife away". Dumb GI "Come on man lets get it on". Ex-Marine "Okay but this is not my idea". He took out his straight razor and proceeded to slice up one dumb GI, he cut him wide and deep several times in the stomach area, dumb GI dropped his knife and tried to hold his insides, inside, with blood running somewhat freely through his fingers. When this was starting, a number of the local regulars came to our table and said "Hey Man, let us buy you a drink", sure buy me all drinks you want, "You don't want to go out there, do you?". My reply "No way, I don't even want to go to the bathroom, for at least an hour after its over". They bought me a half dozen drinks and stayed there until everything had settled down. Someone called and an ambulance came and took the dumb GI away, I don't think I ever heard if he lived or not. The Police and Military Police came but nobody knew anything about what happened, so after looking around they left. These people were okay, as far as I'm concerned, they always took care that I was not bothered and I sure never gave them reason to do anything else.

Several times at the end of the month, when everyone was broke, I went out there and got a set up, a couple of bottles, usually Rum, with about 6 Cokes per bottle and then a bucket of ice with glasses, set these on a table and invited who ever was there to have a drink, they would accept and make a small drink and make it last a long time. So I was known whenever I showed up. Now I didn't like Rum and Coke, and usually drank beer, but at this time of the month, so as not to offend anybody, I would get a Seven-Up and drink a light Rum and Seven-Up. I know, you knew I was different but you didn't know how much. If I ever needed something or had to find something or somebody, I had but to ask and they would usually be able to find or supply whatever I was looking for. Nice to have friends, in high (?) places.

I had some things stolen once, and went out and told the people who ran this place about it. By the afternoon they had found the person and my property, less the small amount of money that she had taken. They brought her to me and let her return the property and said she had 24 hours to come up with the money, I believe it was 5 to 8 dollars. I told them to forget the money I was just glad to get the property back. They said okay and let her go with the advise to not come back and to not bother any of their friends again, she took them very seriously.

I could go on about some more of my happenings in this scenic place in the tropical paradise known as Rio Bajo but will spare you of that, at least for now.

Another one of my escapades in to the field of group humor happened during my stay in Panama, in probably late 65 or early 66. It seems we had a guy transfer in from Japan, where he had served and then been rotated to Panama. His name was Phil Read, and he had a Yamaha Motorcycle, that he had purchased in Japan and had shipped to Panama. Now it just so happens that a Phil Read, same spelling of names, rode for the Yamaha International Motorcycle Team on the International Grand Prix Circuit. We were going to have a big Drag Racing Meet at La Hoya Air Strip in the near future, so, I decided some additional advertising was in order, and just happened to mention at the local Honda dealer that Phil Read, who was from Japan, was going to be here for the drags, and if his Yamaha bike, which had been shipped, got here in time he would bring it out to the drags. "You mean Phil Read is going to be here, for the drags at La Hoya"? "Yep, that's what I heard". Now a few comments like this and things were off and running. And it spread like wild fire, maybe to fast. In starting this off there were 5 or 6 guys in on this and that seemed to be plenty. Bobby was from Columbia, South Caroline, and was I thought one of these. He was really into this and was doing a bang up job of spreading the word, with very much enthusiasm. In watching him, it dawned on me that he was not that good an actor, he really believes this is going to happen, with the 'other' Phil Read really showing up. Now, how to you tell 6' 1", 200 pounds of unbridled enthusiasm that he needs to back off. Bobby was really promoting this and the whole thing had spread to hundreds of people, maybe several thousand. After this had been going on for a week to 2 weeks, Bobby found out, from someone, that this was not for real, that he was upset, would be putting it mildly. We were working the evening shift and I was in the mess hall eating at midnight when he came in. The mess hall had double glass swinging doors, and when he came in both doors hit the stops, very hard. No doubt, he was hot. He spotted me setting at a table in the center of the room and came stomping over, he placed his hands on the table and leaned across toward me and said "I'm going to kick your ass". Well I was surprised, maybe, and looked around and over my shoulder, "Who me?" Bobby "Yes you". "What did I do?" Bobby "You know, does the name Phil Read ring any bells?" "Well yeah, but what are you talking about?" Bobby "You know, about 'the' Phil Read being at the drag races". "Oh that, I thought you knew about it and was just playing up the situation". Bobby "No, I didn't and boy was I looking stupid". This went on for awhile, 5 to 10 minutes, and then Bobby said again "Boy was I looking stupid". "Welllllll, yes, but it looked good on you". He laughed and said "I'll bet it did".

We were friends again, and I didn't have to worry, for a little while anyway, that someone was looking for me to kick my .... ah... butt. I do have a way of getting into things, at least at times. The situation went on and gained a lot of momentum and/or followers. When the weekend of the drags got there we decided that, 'some' Phil Read might be better served by not showing up. If 'the' Phil Read didn't, so none did. I and my cohorts had to show as we were entered in the drag races. Someone passed a note to the organizers that do to other commitments Phil Read was unable to attend and offered his apologies for any inconvenience that announcements of his possible attendance may have caused. There was some disappointment but the fact that he had sent a note of apology made everyone, seemingly, feel better. And it was with relief that the drags proceeded without any interruptions. I got blown away in the first round by an 883cc Norton, my 350cc Honda beat him off the line and lasted until I shifted to 2nd gear and then he just disappeared by me. Oh well, I shouldn't have been in his class anyway, but that's where they put me because of the work I had done on my 250cc motor. It was fun for about .025 seconds and then I was finished and went to the pits, done for the day. Another month of work, appreciated by some, and by others, who didn't really know, I was still a nice guy. Yes Mom, I heard you, I'll try to do better next time. But I don't think I did any better, maybe the story just wasn't as good, but I'm sure I was trying, at something.

Talk about a small world, Rollie was here a few days ago and while we were talking, I mentioned this story about Phil Read. He said I know a Phil Read, from back east, somewhere, really that's where Phil was from. In comparing notes this man had been in the Army in the 60's, been in Panama at that time, and worked in the communications field. He still rode motorcycles after all these years. This was the same Phil Read that I had known in Panama in the mid 60's, and who had decided not to go to the drag races on a day so many years ago. He is gone now, cancer, but I would have liked to have talked to him, why didn't it ever come up before, I don't know. It really is a small world.

I doubt if very many people knew that I was also a Ham Radio Operator, not much work involved in getting my license, considering my line of work. And did enjoy operating on the radio. We had a Ham Station right in the building, on the ground floor of our Headquarters. This was set up and maintained by the Ham Operators in the unit. Then Fort Clayton had a station set up, in it's own building with top of the line equipment and there were at least 3 individual complete stations for the individuals to work on at the same time. The post station was KZ5AA, and the company station was KZ5FC, my own call sign was KZ5MO. At Christmas in 1966, 3 of us were taken off duty status and for a week or more and ran the KZ5AA station, for the purpose of getting phone patches through to the states for anyone who wanted to contact people at home with holiday phone traffic or written messages when phone calls were not possible. We also sent some messages that were delivered by Ham Operators in the states. This got to be work but we had a blast doing it and did make a number of people happy over the holidays. We worked harder than if we had been going to work, we spent 12 to 15 hours a day on the radios and talked with people all over the world in the process. Kilowatt, Zanzibar, the number 5, America, America calling CQ and standing by. After saying that phrase a few thousand times it is still remembered after all this time. Due to 3 of us being on the air at the same time, or more, we were joined by other Ham Operators at times, we used not only KZ5AA, but other calls signs as well when we were on the air at the same time, each one had to use a different call sign. The first one used was the AA, and then the next operator used his own call sign. I was normally AA. Multi talented, that's me, I did not find something I excelled at, so just kept looking.

The Special Forces ran a Jungle Survival School in the Canal Zone, with the base school being on the Atlantic Side of the Canal Zone. They had open air class rooms as well as conventional class rooms. The open air class rooms had walls around them, with trees growing inside of them. They also, at times, had snakes loose in them, roaming around where ever they wanted to go. I only remember them being Boas and they were suppose to be kept well feed, but 20 feet long any kind of snake bothers me. Luckily I didn't get to or have to go through this school, although I did ask to go, but never got to. The guys said that you would be listening to a lecture in these class rooms and a large reptile would go sliding under your bench and across your feet, I would think this would be distracting, from the speaker, but having not tried it could not say for sure. Was thinking that they also introduced you to other wildlife and animals in some of this schooling. This was to help prepare you for service, primarily, in Viet Nam. One of the guys I knew that went to this school, and was on assignment to Viet Nam, said that during the second week they were taken up country, toward the US of A, and at night were dropped out of Helicopters into unfamiliar territory and had to find your way back to the Canal Zone. You had only your basic gear with you, a canteen of water and no food. As I remember you were about 20 miles from the Canal Zone and there were lots of natural obstacles in your way. One guy was dropped, literally, and missed the ground and went into a body of water. When he came up he put his arm over a handy log, which moved out from under his arm, what a wonderful feeling that was, something as big as a log in the water with you. I'll bet he still wonders what it was and is glad it wasn't hungry or hostile. He did make it out of the water and if I remember right made it back to the Canal Zone without being captured by the enemy forces. Oh yeah, I forgot to mention that there was a line of enemy forces across between you and the Canal Zone, that you had to make it through or if you were captured you went to a POW Camp, Prisoner Of War, and were treated accordingly. If captured you are not to talk, give name, rank, and serial number, only. Just like the real thing. When captured you were taken to a compound to be held for interrogation or just held. Nice place to visit, you entered by crawling into a pipe or tunnel and it wound around until it was dark and you couldn't see and it ended and you were dropped into a hole with water in the bottom, at least you hoped it was water. When you would crawl to the top of the slope an interrogator would be there and ask questions, where were you stationed, what was you unit, who was your commanding officer, and stuff like this. When you didn't answer these questions you were pushed, with a foot, back down the slope, into the water and/or slime and had to crawl back up again. This continued until you answered or they got tired and you were allowed out of the hole. Another thing that they did was put you into a wire cage, that was not to large, and you couldn't stand up but were bent over and some what compacted, oh and in this container was a large snake, probably a boa constrictor. Not sure how long they left people in with the snake but I'm thinking that it was successful in making some talk. In 66 they did this to a class and a guy that was captured was going to be put in with the snake, he told them and begged them not to put him in with the snake as he had a phobia about snakes. They treated him like an enemy would and put him in any way, he had, I believe, a heart attach, he was in his 20's, he did die. There was a big investigation over this and this practice was suspended. It was not reinstated while I was still there. Now I guess I have mixed emotions on this, I would not like to be put in with the snake, either, but if I were captured by an enemy, i.e. Vietnamese, they wouldn't give a damn whether I was afraid of snakes or not, in fact if I showed I was they would put me in there that much faster. So if you are going to train people in the art of war, I guess this should be included, if the enemy is going to employ these tactics, you should be aware of what you are facing, if captured. Maybe this individual should of been taken out of this, or this position, but that wasn't my call, thankfully, and somebody had to make it. This did expose you to the real world of war, if you were captured, you had a idea of what you might be in for. Nobody ever said that war is fun or fair. Ah the life of a sailor, oh right, I was in the Army.

Back in 1964 when the riots started in Panama, at a school in the Canal Zone, as I remember, supposedly they started when Panamanian students brought out a Panamanian flag, and were going to take down the US Flag and replace it with their flag or fly it over the US flag. The American students said that the Panamanian students were not going to be allowed to take down the US flag, but could fly the Panamanian flag beside it. In the altercation that took place at this time the Panamanian students said the US students tore their flag and that was when the riots started. I have a series of pictures that show the Panamanian students coming from the school building with their flag, it is already torn, and the same tear was in it after the riots actually started. This was a very destructive and costly occurrence. I was at Ft. Devens and was put on standby status, 60 minutes notice, and I had to have civilian clothes, Class B uniform, and Class A uniform ready. The orders came, civilian clothes and we were on our way on commercial aircraft and landed in Panama City, Panama, at the Commercial Air Port. We were transported in unmarked vehicles to Fort Clayton in the Canal Zone. Through the burnt out and shot up, yes real bullet holes, Mom, part of town, maybe all parts along the Canal Zone were that way, I didn't see much of it till later and I was there for awhile. This was known as 4th of July Avenue, then it was changed to John F. Kennedy Avenue while I was there.

There were riots again in 1966, and as luck would have it I was down town Panama City when they started. I'm not sure what I was actually doing, but am sure that I had a date with my girl friend at the time. When these festivities started I was sure I wasn't going to try and get back to the Canal Zone. The major problem areas were between me and the Canal Zone. This girl, Teodosia Cruz and I decided that the best thing to do was to go to her home, at her invitation, and wait it out. I can assure you that I was very much in favor of this, especially the waiting it out part and at her home. Seemed to be the best idea anyone had, even if the riots hadn't been going on. Now she lived out in the suburbs and it would have been like an apartment building, all apartments adjoining on the ground level, no upper level. We took a bus, got off on the main road or highway, and walked the block and a half to her apartment. I hadn't been there before and didn't know that she had her mother living with her, at least part of the time. You know how Mothers are, they can put a damper on things, at times. But under the circumstances it was still the best idea in town. I stayed there for 3 or 4 days. I was able to get to a phone and call in and let the company know where I was at and that I was okay. I was told to stay right there until it was safe to come back. Talk about leaving the door open and the cookie jar out. Sounds good, don't it. But as luck would have it there was only a small apartment, 1 room, combined kitchen/dining room/bedroom with a separate bathroom. Only 1 bed, 3 people, no sofa, so I was wondering how do we do this, well she explained it to me. Mother will sleep on the backside of the bed next to the wall, she would sleep in the middle and I would be on the outside. Now this might seem to be a nice situation, you make it to your girl friends home and bed. But her mother is there too. Oh well, you could at least sleep close together. Some of you maybe thinking, maybe ahead, you get to sleep with your girl friend and sleep with her mother at the same time, I do know people who would like that idea. However this was sleeping with your girl friend and her mother at the same time, but in as sleeping in the same place, not as sleeping with anybody. I said I was always getting into these situations, remember. But it still beat being out in the rioting city. We did have a good time and some fun, and I think her mother even liked me, a little anyway. Well anyway, she didn't do me any bodily harm, when I was sleeping or otherwise.

I even went to church with her, the daughter not the mother, a couple of times, I ran across a picture of this church a while back when I was looking for other things. It was a beautiful old church, with a lot of cut glass windows. I want to say it dated back to the 1700's, or before, but am not sure any more. But what a feeling when entering, a feeling of entering history, and to know that people had been worshiping God here for more than a couple of hundred years. I think, it was a different feeling, that I have never had in any other church. Another I can't explain it.

Let me see here, how many people do you know who have watched turtles bobbing for apples in a river; survived riots with the help of a friend, to have time to promote drag racing in a foreign land, with special advertising, not to mention the Color Speed Chart educational material. Such is life, in the fast lane, in a foreign city, in a foreign country, on a rainy day.

Chapter 6:

Still in the Hospital

We were still in the hospital on Sunday, waiting, with nothing happening over the weekend but checking vitals and drawing more blood. I wanted to take her somewhere else, for a second opinion and maybe more experience in dealing with this type situation. But no, she would not agree to go, she wanted to stay in Garden City, for reasons of her own. I couldn't go against her wishes. Monday was a holiday, so more of the same. Tuesday was more of the same. With Wednesday, the Doctor stopped by and said they suspected cancer in the stomach, right lung, ovaries, and liver. Kate called me, as I had gone to work, and told me. I left work and headed to the hospital to be with her. On Thursday they did a C-T Scan and eliminated cancer in the right lung. On Friday they scoped her stomach and eventually told us her stomach was cancer free on the inside. On Friday afternoon I had an appointment at Dr. Walker's office and was not there when Pastor Lenoir Randle stopped by to visit. After praying and talking, Lenoir told her that she should go somewhere else for a second opinion. When I returned she told me of Lenoir's visit I'm not very good with titles, so Pastor Lenoir is just Lenoir to me, no disrespect intended. So now she thought we should go some place else, so I said a quiet "good idea", my conscious thought was "ALRIGHT, AMEN, FINALLY", after asking her every day and getting a "No", she was finally ready. My thought was also "I could kiss that woman, and I may still". Dr. Watkins, from Kansas

University Medical Center in Kansas City, arrived late on Friday to fill in for another doctor that had to be gone on some kind of an emergency. On Saturday morning Dr. Watkins came in and visited with us and told us more in 5 minutes that we had learned in 8 days. When he was finished updating us, I asked him about going somewhere else and getting a second opinion. He said yes and recommended it. I asked if he had a recommendation as for where. Yes, he could recommend the KU Med Center, as he was on staff there and had first hand knowledge of it. I said "YES" and Kate agreed. Thirty-Five years ago, almost to the day, I brought my father home from KU Med Center, with terminal lung cancer. Dr. Watkins said he would get to work on it and make it happen as soon as possible. Mary Lynn, Lance, Katy, Logan, and friend Rollie Leighton were all there and we could and did wait some more. On Sunday morning Dr. Watkins and Dr. Booker were both suppose to meet with us at 10:00 am, although all our paths did not cross until later, Dr. Booker came in and left, Dr. Watkins came in and everything was a go, to go to Kansas City, by 11:00am. We needed a bed assignment in Kansas City, before they would let us leave. Rollie's sons came from Quinter with a large stock trailer and loaded all the horses, except Dolly, and took them home. Mary Lynn went home and packed me a bag and if needed would meet us at the airport, which is only 6 ½ miles from our house, with the hospital being about 20 miles. It was a long wait until 3:30pm when the call finally came. We loaded in the ambulance for the ride to the airport and had to wait a little while for a plane, as the one that had been waiting for us had to leave for another emergency and they flew another one in. And then on to Kansas City.

Chapter 7:

Viet Nam Revisited.

When I left Panama I had volunteered for Viet Nam, but was turned down. I was sent to Ft. Carson, Colorado instead. I didn't like this very much, I preferred a little more action. When they came down and asked for 5 volunteers for special assignment in Viet Nam, I was first to go. Ronnie Rooker and Jimmy Smith were right behind me, Tom Cole was the fourth man, and the fifth, Hank, unable to remember his last name, came from Vint Hill Farms, Va. Ronnie was from Missouri, Jimmy from Oklahoma City, and Tom was from Baltimore. We had to go to Vint Hill Farms, Va., for 2 weeks training and then to Travis AFB, California. We departed Travis on the 4th of July, 1967, we crossed the International Date Line after 10:30 pm. So my birthday was only about an hour and a half long. To make a special day really special, I was developing a boil, a big boil, on the back of my neck at the top of my spine, centered of course. Up on arrival in Saigon, Viet Nam, I had to go on sick call and have my boil lanced and drained. It was located right over the spine so they couldn't deaden it, so I had to just bite the bullet and let them cut away, oh what fun.

They held us up on our assignments, our positions had already been filled. I wanted to go ARDF and would be flying and getting flight pay, but no we were on special assignment and I couldn't get approval, another catch 22, the military has lots of these. They held us up about 5 extra days and then sent us on to the 330th Radio

Research Company, in Pleiku by way of Nha Thrang, 313th Radio Research Battalion, part of the 509th Radio Research Group, Saigon. Since our positions had already been filled, because they went operational early, before we got there, we were assigned to our regular MOS jobs.

In the company we had some more of the people who liked snakes, just like in Panama. Now I personally could do without them, but like everything else, the snake has its place, in God's order of things. There was an 8 foot python that one, or some, of the men kept in the company area. It seems like now they had some kind of a cage or container that they kept him or her in. It would only eat live animals. It seems like I remember that a full grown chicken would last it about 3 weeks or so. I still have pictures, somewhere, of the python taking and eating a chicken. It was another interesting incident, that I have been witness to. And they didn't have rats around where that snake was, and maybe they let it loose at times to help with the rat problem. I seem to remember that, but couldn't swear to it now and it wasn't, as far as I know, around me loose or it would not have been. Interesting people, places, things, animals or reptiles everywhere I go, some more so than others.

In September I was asked to volunteer to work at putting up 17, 100 feet long by 20 feet wide, buildings to house the company. I agreed, along with 4 others, to do this and we were assured that this would not effect us for promotion or anything else and we were relieved of all other duties. SFC Rodgers was over us, but we didn't see much of him. I was in charge of the 5 who did the work. At Thanksgiving I was sent to Nha Trang for my E-6 promotion board, I even missed Thanksgiving Dinner because of traveling, such is life in the military. SFC Bradley was on that board and had been on my E-5 promotion board in Panama. He was also with General Goding, 3 star general, Commander Pacific Forces, who was to inspect the 330th, prior to this promotion board. We were to be standing by for inspection, at 0800 hours, at the company construct site. When the General was late, Mark Harbin and I decided that we would go ahead and get to work. We were trying to complete a building, less the concrete work, in 24 working hours. We worked 7am to 9pm at first, then 7 to 7. I was hanging a screen door on the back side of the building. I was using nails for the hinges as we didn't have screws, and was bent over nailing the bottom hinge. I looked down and right behind me, a little to my right, were a pair of very highly polished combat boots. Someone cleared their throat, somewhat loudly, and I said "just a minute, I'll be right with you". I finished driving the nails and turned, putting my hammer in the leather strip that I wore on my fatigue pants for that purpose. I turned and saluted General Goding. He wanted to know if I was aware that he was coming to inspect us and we were suppose to be standing by for his inspection. "Yes Sir, but you were late and we are trying to get these buildings done and the men in them, before the rains started, and figured that was more important, and the General might have changed his plans or something and no one remembered to tell us, so I figured that this was more important than waiting". "More important than a 3 star General?" "Yes Sir, getting the men out of the tents and into the buildings before the rains start". "Good answer". My Commanding Officer, Major John Tunnell, and the 1st Sargent were about to have heart attacks, but oh well. We talked for a while and he said "You must be a farm boy?" "Yes Sir, Kansas". "I though so." He asked how long it took us to build one of these buildings. Well, we're trying to get this one done in 24 working hours. He turned to the Post Commander, who was a combat engineer, and said "I thought you said your boys could put one up in 72 hours". "Yes Sir" the Colonel replied. He than ask me how we could do it in 24 hours. I reminded him that was 24 working hours and that everything just went right. This was one building, the combat engineers put one up every 72 hours. I was aware that I was going to be there and the Post Commander was going to be still there also. The nice thing about 3 Star Generals is they know who they are and where they're going and don't have to prove anything to anyone. We talked a little more and he said that he was running late and needed to move along, and he was holding up important work here. He said it with a smile, I saluted and he returned it, and they moved along. My CO gave me a look when he went by and the 1st SGT was shaking his head when he went by. Later told me, that I must like to push my luck, and I asked him what he was talking about and what could he possibly mean by that, he just said 'never mind'.

So when SFC Bradley got his turn to question me on that promotion board. His first question was "Where are you working and what are you doing, right now?" I told him that I was working at building the buildings for the company's semi-permanent quarters. He knew anyway. "Was I aware that my recommendation for promotion stated that I was still working in operations?" "No Sir, no knowledge of what was in the recommendation." He went on to other things and I passed the board. I didn't get my promotion until about the first of June 1968. Nice to be appreciated.

Sent to Mom, Dad, and others in October 2008.

In going through some things, I came across the in and out letters from when I was in Viet Nam. Mom had gotten them from me when I came home and kept them, and then gave them to Kate. In looking through some of them I ran across one in which my Mother was referring to packages she was sending me for an orphanage. This brought back some memories.

Sometime in the fall of 1967 I had run across an orphanage, it was out in the 'thickets' and was run by, I believe they were French, Catholic Nuns. They took in any kids that needed to be taken in and were having a tough time of it. Taking any kids that needed to be, means that children of mixed races, who were social outcasts, and were not accepted by some of the people, were taken in or accepted also. Babies of mixed races were often times killed, if they were abandoned, orphaned, or put up for adoption. These ladies or Nuns took any children in and were not concerned with race, just the needs of the children. It is hard to believe that this was the case, but it was. In some places of the world race is still a major issue, babies and children not excepted. As not too much was available to me. I was able to get hand soap, laundry soap, and things like this, that they needed, but so much that they needed was not available to me. I talked with them some and asked of the things that they needed and said that maybe I could help, and would try to do so, if I could. I then wrote Mom and told her of this situation and ask her to gather up anything that she could and I'm sure she used money from my account and purchased some of the items that I wanted and they needed. The things that were not available to me. This material had to be sent in packages that were limited to a certain size, so she would have to send several 'smaller' packages to get things to me and keep within the limitations of package size requirements. She also contacted the Red Cross, Salvation Army, American Legion, VFW, VFW Auxiliary, local church groups and also local individuals for any and all assistance in gathering used clothing. I do know that new items were purchased by some and sent in the sizes, for the kids, that we requested. While Mom sent at lot of this, some of it was sent to me by others, groups or individuals. All packages were supposed to be marked in some way that we had come up with. This was so that I would know without opening them that they were for the orphanage. I don't think I ever opened one of these by mistake, so the marking system that we had come up with must have worked. I was thinking about this the other day and wondered if something intended for me was taken to them by mistake and I do hope that if this happened that it was candy, cookies or whatever 'goodies' Mom had sent for me. They would have been better utilized by them, than me. I'm sure that some of the mail personnel wondered why I was getting all these packages and what in the world could be in them, and I never told. I was what was known in the 'Military world' as a "scrounger". So I was able to get a vehicle, usually, to look for "things". Which the unit needed, but maybe didn't want to know where I got them, but did want whatever it was that I was getting. So when I wanted to use a military vehicle I was never questioned or not questioned very closely about what I was going to do. So I would get a Jeep or whatever was available at the time and I would go by the orphanage. They had a drop arranged where you would put an item in a door on the outside and they would be able to get it on the inside. The idea was that the donor would remain unseen/unknown. I would put the packages in the door, and

I am not sure that door would be the correct term, and then leave. Sometimes I would have more than the opening would hold and had to, happily, pile them on the ground around it. I don't remember if you knocked or not, and then left. I do know that they knew who was leaving these things. Most of them had my name and address on them, this just occurred to me. I took real pleasure in doing this, as you 'might' remember, my affection for children was of long standing. This continued after I was injured in the truck incident and until the Tet Offensive started in late January of 1968. After the Tet Offensive I went back as soon as I could to check on the orphanage and it was no longer there. I never did try to check on it as I didn't want to know what had happened to it, although it was my hope that they, or someone had, moved it to a better place and out of harms way. I have often wondered but don t think that I still want to know what happened to it. Kate and I spoke of it once in a while and I take kind of a sad pride in the remembrance of this.

In writing of this, I guess, I just wanted to tell you of this, to share with you what I had shared with Kate, of a side of me that was very seldom shown or shared with anyone. I think that now I would like Mom (Teresa) and Dad (George) and others to know this and understand that Kate and I were alike in ways that they might not have known about before. I don't think that I do this for any recognition but rather to share with you something that at that time and place was important to me.

Ralph

Back in August, I, along with several other guys, made arrangements and got a dog from a guy in the Air Force. He had brought it's mother over on a plane and then she had pups and this was one of the pups. We named him Big Dog or BD for short. He kind of evolved into my dog, he slept under my bed and pretty much went where I went. I have said that I get along with kids, dogs, and horses, you might remember. BD didn't like Vietnamese, and at first wouldn't let our house girl into our tent to clean up and get our laundry. I made him aware that it was okay for her to come in but he wouldn't let any other Vietnamese in that tent. He never took his eyes from her while he or she were in the tent. We didn't have anymore breaks taken in our tent, by the house girls. They were taken somewhere else. I will have to look for his pictures, I still have several. If he was asleep under my bed when a Vietnamese entered the tent he would stand up and then come out from under the bed. He turned my bed over a number of times, several with me in it. I finally got him to come out and then stand up. He had a collar on and I have grabbed him in mid leap several times, to save some little house girl that didn't know to not come into our tent, especially unannounced. I pulled guard duty on the perimeter once after I got him and he stayed on the line with me all night. After I went to the building crew I didn't pull guard duty anymore. Later when we had all moved into the buildings, anytime there was an alert we had to clear the company area, and I was in charge of that detail. When we were clearing an area he would be up and down the line like a bird dog. When we cleared the barracks, we would go in the door at one end, leave a guard at the door, check everything inside and he was there, in every corner, under every cot and then out and leave a guard at that door and on to the next building until they were all cleared and the area was cleared. Guards were posted until we knew that there were no unwanted visitors or guests present. He was very helpful and I believe everyone felt better with him around, because you knew that there were no unwelcome ones around when he was there. Not to long before I was due to leave the country, the Army came down and said that the dogs all had to go, and I said no, BD was staying, We had an SSG who had a small black and white dog, he went out and shot his dog, then made a point of telling me that I had to get rid of BD. I told him no, and to stay away from BD, because if anything happened to BD then he wouldn't have to worry about packing to go home. Shortly the Army changed its mind and said the dogs could stay, because they were worth the extra problems. He got a chance one night and shot BD, said that BD had attacked him. This was after the Army's decision to allow us to keep our dogs. The CO had him removed and he was taken else where, before I found him or some of the others did. Because the CO figured that he might have an accident, or I or someone might, I guess, shoot him, and the CO was a smart man. This was Major Keener who replaced Major Tunnell. If the man in question had stayed there he would not have survived. I'm sure a sniper or something else would have gotten him. It was a dangerous place to be and all kinds of dangers lurked in this place. Some were closer than others, it would seem. I don't carry a grudge but I also never forget.

On December 15, 1967, Mark Harbin and I went with a convoy, destination, Qui Nhon. We were going to pick up, I believe, beer. We had other trucks going too, so maybe were picking up something else, as we never got to the end of the line, I guess it is a mute point now. We were at the back of the convoy until we got to Anke. There we stopped for lunch and the convoy split up with some going in a different direction and we were to continue on to Qui Nhon. We were moved to the head of the convoy, as I remember only a 3/4 ton was in front of us, as far as convoy vehicles were concerned. Guard vehicles were in front, but they moved around at times, so not sure what else was in front of us. When we came over Anke Pass and started down we met a convoy of tankers coming up and they were carrying aviation fuel. They were the target, not us empty trucks. We were told to never go off the blacktop or asphalt of the road, but on this hair pin curve, it was more than a 180 degree turn, like 190 or 195 degrees, doubling back under its self a little bit as you were coming down. The 3/4 ton went off the blacktop in front of us, so Mark, he was driving, followed in his tracks, thinking we would be safe. Have you ever heard the term "wrong again"? Well, we fit into that category. There was a loud explosion, that I don't remember hearing, and we couldn't see the windshield. Dirt and smoke were blocking our vision. I remember having the sensation of falling for a long time, the angle of the truck seemed to be down, at about a 10 degree angle, maybe, and eventually I realized we had stopped falling. I remember looking out my window and all I could see was down. About 150 feet below I could see tree tops. Well, I'm not getting out on this side. I was going to roll across the seat and get out on the left side but I couldn't pick up my left foot. At this point it never occurred to me that I was hurt. I had a tremendously loud ringing in my ears and any sound seemed to be way off in the distance. I took a hold of my left pants leg, on both sides of the knee, and pulled my knee to my chest and rolled across the seat, and got out the door. Mark says he helped me out and to the ground, but I don't remember that. I remember walking along the side of the truck, to the rear. I had to be hanging on to the side of the truck but I don't remember doing it and would have said that I hadn't if I had been asked. When I walked past the back of the truck, I remember falling forward. I was able to reach out and grab the bumper of the truck stopped behind us to keep from landing on my face. I pulled myself up and was wondering what I had tripped over. There was nothing there, my left leg had just not held me, but I still didn't realize it. Using my M-14 as a crutch or cane, I moved back to our truck and went part way up along the side of it. I was leaning against the truck when they set the helicopter down in the road. A Warrant Officer, who was the pilot, got out and was checking for injuries. He came over to me and asked "Are you okay?" "Yeah I'm OK". "What's the matter with your head?" I had a knot on my forehead that stuck out over 2 inches and the skin was split from the right of center, up in my hair, into my left eyebrow. The split was 3 ½ to 4 inches long, and was bleeding lightly. I put my hand up to it and it stopped over 2 inches from where it was suppose to, and I said "I'll be damned". Then "I'll be okay". He said "You're sure?" I replied with "Yes". He went on, looking for Mark and spoke to him, as I remember, and then came back to me. "You sure you're okay?". My response was "Yeah, I'm okay". He looked down at my left leg and asked "What about your leg?" I looked down and said "oh", very scientific and medical. My pants leg was soaked in blood from the knee down. "Get in the chopper". "I'll be okay". "It wasn't a request". So I hobbled to the chopper and climbed in, and we were soon airborne over the pass. They took me to the Heli Pad in Anke and was met by an ambulance which took me to the field hospital. That place was a mess, stretchers everywhere with casualties. This is not meant to be a judgment, just an observation. Some stretchers were stacked 3 deep in the halls, most were coming in from up north, the DMZ, Hue, and Da Nang. I was processed in and taken to a small examination room and told to wait for a doctor. After a while a doctor came in, looked around and went out. In a few minutes he was back, looked around and asked "Is there anyone else here?" "No, just me". "Oh,OK", and he went out again. Came back with the medic, who told him "This is him". "No, I wanted the guy that hit the land mine". "This is him." He looked at me, up and down, and said "Are you hurt?". I came back with "I thought you were going to tell me". He looked at my head and said "it'll heal". He looked at my knee and told the medic to x-ray it, clean it up and we'd look at it again. They x-rayed it and cleaned some of the blood away, the doctor came back, looked at it, and said "It would be okay, some day" and left. The left knee had, I believe, 7 pieces of shrapnel in it or through it. The medic took out what shrapnel he found, but there were more holes than pieces. We thought that some had gone on through. He did give me the pieces that he took out and I gave them to Mom, eventually, and she gave them to Kate. They are here, laying on the desk, in an envelope. I didn't remember even saving them until I was looking for something and then found them after Kate died. Both knees had been put up into the metal dash of the truck, about 10 inches. There were 2 nicely shaped "U's" in the dash and both knees were badly bruised with possible ligament and tendon strains, tears, and/or damage. And the knees have never been normal again and I never did return to my running form because of the damage. When I went over there I could run 20 miles or more with full field gear, when I came home I was lucky to be able to walk 5 miles and some days couldn't have done even that. The medic said "He's a little stressed out, do to all the casualties coming in from the north, and usually land mine victims are more shredded, with more damage, just be glad you're not". "Did I have some place I could go?" As they didn't have any room at the hospital. "Yeah I do." And they let me walk out. I went to the airport. I wanted to go on to Qui Nhon and hook back up with Mark and the rest of our guys. On this day there were 5 flights out to Que Nhon, but 2 were already canceled, to go north after casualties. The next one, I went out to get on the plane, we were boarding, with some were already on and they announced that everyone was to get off. The flight was canceled and was going north. The second one, I was already on and it was canceled and I had to unload, it was going north, The third one was called for boarding and as we were going out of the terminal, it to was canceled and was going north also. This was the last one for the day and I would just spend the night in the airport. I got a couple of sandwiches from a vendor and something to drink and was set for the night. I slept on a bench, the little I was able to sleep, and hurt in places I didn't even have. It was just in one spot, all over. We were under attack most of the night and it was pretty much sleepless in the airport. The next morning I booked on a flight back to Pleiku and got out of there by midmorning. Everyone on the flight were fresh troops from the states, had come into Cam Ranh Bay, as a group and were going to Pleiku as a group. All that I remember seeing were young, mostly kids, they had on brand new uniforms and all their equipment was brand new. They kept looking at me, but if I returned the look they quickly looked away, they didn't want to be staring. I was likely a candidate for a picture post card home, blood in my hair, on my face, down between my eyebrows and around my nose and around the corners of my mouth and on over my chin and down my neck inside my shirt. I had a couple of days beard, was dirty, smears of blood on my fatigues, and the left pants leg soaked in blood, now dried. I had no chance to clean up and wasn't even aware of some of it. Eventually I looked in a mirror and did laugh, no wonder they had been staring at me. I guess I would have seemed to be part of the real war. I still had my since of humor and could laugh at myself. I know that somebody had to do it. This was a cargo plane, no seats, just straps across and you set behind the straps and leaned over with your arms hooked over the straps so you didn't slide, on take off or landing. When I got back to Pleiku, at the airport I got a ride with a combat engineer, that I knew, and he took me right to the 330th. I got there about 12:00 noon and the First Sargent was there to meet me outside of the Orderly Room. He said "I didn't think I would ever say this but I am glad to see you". "Well I didn't think I would ever say, 'Well I'm glad to see this place', but right now I am". He wanted to know where I had been and what had happened. I had been listed as "Missing in Action" for 26 hours. So I told him of my experiences and what I knew. I didn't know about Mark. Mark had later been taken to the hospital, I believe by jeep, and we had never seen each other. He then went to our detachment, down the road from the hospital, and spent the night. He returned to the 330th the next morning, also, but I didn't see him right away. MSG Lamb, from Goodland, Kansas, was in charge of our detachment and gave me a bad time, later, about not coming there and spending the night like Mark. MSG Lamb and I had been friends before Viet Nam. My left knee wouldn't hold my weight if I tried to walk and bend it, so I walked keeping my knee straight and only bending it a little bit. Most people didn't realize that I wasn't bending it, when walking. I used a cane some of the time, and some days it was better than others. My hearing got better but has been bad ever since, the ringing got less after a while but has never gone away. It's like a door buzzer, all the time, and interferes with normal hearing. And it varies, and is effected by the weather. I suppose the atmospheric conditions or pressure effects it most. I was, originally, suppose to be presented my Purple Heart by President Johnson, when he was there for a visit, but they decided that it was to dangerous for him to come to Pleiku and he stayed at Cam Ranh Bay and they had plenty of awards to present there. I was never disappointed by this, I wasn't a big fan of President Johnson. They sent me my Purple Heart in the mail. The Purple Heart never was actually presented to me but this was probably appropriate, given everything that happen along the way.

When we went to Viet Nam we were ask to fill out a number of forms, one of which is if something happens to you, other than death , do you want your family or next of kin notified. I filled mine out that I did not want them notified. So when we hit the land mine I did not tell Mom and Dad about it. I had a friend who was from Salina, Ks. He came over in Sept. 1967, his name was Jim Hayes. And along in December, about Christmas time, he got a call from the Red Cross that he needed to go home and get married, and then come back. Emergency Leave was set up, granted, and he took off for home. He flew into Denver and then caught a bus to Salina, with a meal stop in Phillipsburg, Ks. When he got into Phillipsburg the first thing he did was call my Mom and Dad. They were thrilled that he called and he was talking to Mom and said that I was doing okay, now. Silence, "What do you mean, NOW?" And Jim thought "Oh no I didn't say that". Well he wasn't going to lie to her, so he told her "Ralph had gotten hurt in a truck accident". "What kind of a truck accident?" "Welllllll, they had hit a land mine, but I was fine." Right, try explaining that to an upset Mother. I never told her/them that I went on convoys, this one or others. She was unhappy with Jim and more than a little with me. She and Dad went down and had supper with Jim at Martha's Café. They had an okay visit, not sure what all they talked about though. I got the only less than nice letter from her, ever, in just a couple of days. What else had I not told her/them about, oh never mind, I probably wouldn't tell her the truth anyway. And so on and so on and so on. She went on for awhile then quit and I got a nice letter the next day saying she was sorry and to try and keep them better informed. And of course I didn't do any better. I've still been bad a long time.

We paid a given fee each payday and this covered the workers for the kitchen, house girls, and grounds maintenance. I think that is all the extra help we had, but operations were working pretty regular, 12 hours on 12 hours off, 7 days a week. And didn't have a lot of time for anything extra, like filling and stacking sandbags. Also, the nature of our work was also mentally stressful and took its toll.

After I was getting around better, and we were through with the buildings. I started working on the crew that was getting sandbags filled out at the rock quarry by the Montagnard Indians. Due to the treaty with South Viet Nam, these people were not allowed on a Military Reservation. They filled sandbags, loaded them on trucks for a per day wage. They had to be paid each day, as you would not always have the same people the next day. We came out to the village at about 8:00am in the morning. We picked a crew of 30, from the available people waiting for a job. Then they loaded on a truck and were transported to the rock quarry where they filled sandbags and loaded them on trucks for the rest of the day. We had the workers get on the last loaded truck and returned to the village about 4:00pm and a representative from the 330th was suppose to be there, by 4:30pm, and pay the workers for that day. We got to know some of these people pretty well, working with them every day. Sometimes we would have the same people each day, although a few changed nearly everyday. We would usually have 10-15 women, 6 to 8 men, and the rest were kids. The women and kids were some of the best workers, as a rule, you would have individuals in the men who were good workers, also. They were a very industrious people, as a whole.

On the 30th of January 1968 we were doing as usual, however on this date, and we didn't really discuss it till later, there were no men that showed up for the work crew. When we returned to the village between 4 and 4:30, no one was there from the 330th to pay the crew so we waited. When 4:30 had come and gone, we were getting a little irritated and concerned. The crew were a little disgruntled and a few wondered away into the village. Time passed slowly, the other soldier with me was Pat Blewitt, and we talked and waited. Now in times past I had been invited to stay in the village, as had Pat. On this day Pat said he would just stay the night in the village. What was I going to do? Usually I would have stayed, about 9 times out of 10, but not on this day for whatever the reason. Something was telling me to get out of there. I'm going to walk out of here at 5:30, if no one shows up. He told me that was stupid and that he wasn't walking anywhere. "Your choice, but I'm walking." We then talked about other things while we waited. When 5:30 came most or all of the workers had already left and went into the village. I stood up and was going to start walking. Pat said "You're really going". "Yes I am." He said "If you're going to walk so am I". When I had taken 1 or 2 steps I reached up and jacked a round into the chamber of my rifle. We carried M-14's, and they were in 7.62 Nato caliber, that was the military equivalent of the civilian 308 Win. Caliber. I had 2 magazines taped together, called banana clipped, in the rifle. I had 2 more on pouches on by belt. We carried them without a round in the chamber so if someone grabbed or got a hold of the rifle they would have to put a round in the chamber and take the safety off, before they could fire it. Theory was that maybe this would be enough of a delay that you could take some kind of defensive action. Pat said "Why did you do that?" "So I will be ready if I need to shoot." We did argue about this for a little while and I told him he could just walk out in front, so he wouldn't be close to me if I started something. He thought about this and decided that it wasn't such a good idea. He was concerned that if I shot at somebody that they might shoot back. I hoped that they would not be able to. We walked a few more steps and he reached up and jacked a round into the chamber on his rifle.

I'm not sure anymore but I think it was about 3 miles or a little more to the blacktop road back toward Engineer Hill and Pleiku. We were about a ½ mile from the road when the last truck from the rock quarry went by. We didn't know this until no more came by. We got to the blacktop road and continued walking back. After awhile a "dong cart" came along. A dong cart is like a Vespa scooter with a covered box on the back that had 2 benches that would seat 6 to 8 people. We got to the main intersection where the highways crossed and he was going straight or to Pleiku and we were going left to Engineer Hill. We started to walk again and got a ride from an engineer truck that took us on to our post gate. We were very glad to walk the rest of the way. When we got to the company I went to the Officer/NCO Club and kicked the door open and walked in, looking around. I was still carrying my rifle. My boss was 1st Lt Iverson and he was there. He knew that I was upset and looking for someone. I'm sure he knew who I was looking for. I still remember the face of the SSG that I was looking for. When he asked what was wrong, I told him. I was looking for SSG ......, who will remain nameless. He said he wasn't there and he hadn't seen him since earlier in the afternoon. I told him he hadn't shown up to pay the workers and pick us up. How did we get back, and I told him. He said "Then you missed supper". I said "Yes we had, but I am more interested in finding SSG ....". He said he would take care of that but we needed to eat and we were going to the mess hall. Lt. Iverson was also the Mess Officer. We went to the Mess Hall and the cook said they were closed. The Lt. said they were now open and he was to fix us a steak and whatever else we wanted, now. They always seemed to have steaks on hand for visiting VIPs. So he did fix us a steak with trimmings and I'm sure that this accomplished what the Lt. had wanted. A little time to cool off. While we were eating the Lt. came back and said the SSG was passed out in his bunk and would be dealt with later and to stay away from him. I did, but it was somewhat difficult. We had gotten back about 7:30pm and at around 11:00pm everything in the area, except the Military Bases, were overrun and taken possession of or held by the Viet Cong and/or NVA (North Vietnamese Army).

At this time I was still walking without bending my left knee and the right one was still tender and they both hurt. We found out later that the VC were in the village when we were there. They just didn't want 2 guys, and were probably afraid if we didn't show up, that we would be missed and the military would be put on alert and ruin their surprise. Likely no one would of missed us until later, when it was to late. That has always been a comforting thought and I have often wondered what Pat thought about it, since he was going to stay and I kind of talked him out of it. I never really talked with him again and he went home before the end of February.

We went on alert about dark, we, meaning the 330th. Suspecting something was going to happen. The higher up commanders did not believe anything was going to happen and didn't do anything until it started, for us, about eleven o'clock that night. We were on continuous alert for awhile. For these situations I was in the Command Bunker and I was the backup radio operator. Lots of times this meant that I didn't do much but sit and wait. In the following days I sat and listen to the radios and the progression of the war and the taking back of Pleiku and the surrounding area. When they were going back into Pleiku and retaking the city, we listened to the action and progress, on the radios. The tanks were leading the way and they were meeting with stubborn resistance. I guess this could be called exciting, now, or from the comfort of a fortified bunker, if not, it was interesting. The tanks were taking small arms fire and some other forms of attack. When they were reaching the center of the town, shoulder mounted rockets were fired at them. Several took hits and one tank that we had been following, on the radio, and listening to, was hit. This tank was in the lead of the attacking force. It was hit in the track and disabled. The radio man on this tank was young, you could tell by his voice, but was cool and calm. Where they had been disabled was forward and he had good visibility and set there and directed fire over him and into the positions of the snipers. Also where the rockets were coming from. He directed fire power into these positions and either wiped them out or made them untenable and the VC moved out. This went on for a time period that I can't define now. As our forces were going around his position he went quiet and could not be raised on the radio. When they finally got to him, he had bled to death. He was literally cut into near the waist and the whole time he was directing fire and spotting for others, he was slowly bleeding to death. I have wondered for a long time if he knew or not that he was bleeding to death. We'll never know. He was 17 at the time, and I know I will always remember his slow, cool, calm voice directing the fire into those positions. I have often wondered how many lives he saved that day by doing what he did. With time the area was taken back and returned to, more or less, the same as it was before the 30th of January. I did go check on the orphanage, that I have written about, but it was gone.

Taiwan: A Different World

This story is one that I have hesitated on, but in talking with Mary Lynn, she had never heard any of it, didn't know that I had went to Taiwan China and wanted me to write it, so I did. Kate knew most of this but I doubt that I ever told her the whole story. As I have told Mom and others, Kate was somewhat jealousy of my encounters with other women. Understood. But they all did happen before I ever knew her, and nothing ever would have been considered or have taken place after I met her, enough said. So here it is, as best as I remember it, please remember that this is the first time I have ever spoken of this, to anyone but Kate, and this was in a different time and place, life was completely different than anything most of you have ever experienced.

When I was in Viet Nam, we got to go on R & R, rest and recuperation some would call it. We got the rest of the first day and then 5 nights and 4 days to do whatever we wanted and it should be at least considered legal. Although there were several locations available, Bangkok, Thailand, was very popular, Australia, Japan they were always booked full in advance and several others that I'm not remembering now. I had chosen Taiwan, China. Sounded like a nice place to visit. As I remember there were 4 of us from the 330th, that went at the same time, together. We got there and checked into our hotel and then the next order of business was, uh lets see now oh yeah, girls, women, members of the opposite sex, something like that. Now things were somewhat different there than most of us ever encountered anywhere else. The service men from Viet Nam were big business, and the government wanted control and to have their piece of the action. So the girl business or legalized prostitution was a very serious business. The places and girls were all licensed and regulated. This was good in that they were taken care of, medically speaking, and health concerns were a priority. You went to an establishment, not sure if they were bars or what they were called. They had women there that were available and it did speed up the act of getting everyone together quickly. They were there and dressed to go out, lounging around, talking or whatever, waiting for the U.S. Servicemen. That means that you would be spending money that much quicker and in larger amounts than if you were just out looking on your own. Like I said this was very big business for them. When you had made your selection you would then sign a contract for the amount of time and the terms that you agreed upon, the amount was set by the government, you paid in advance. Then you were free to go with whichever girl you had selected and that you and she had agreed. Needless to say that these transactions were lots of time very quick, as most of the men had been out of circulation, so to speak, for sometime and were in somewhat of a hurry to get back to the hotel, and rest up. Now everything was explained in detail and probably in writing, also.There were times when things wouldn't work out and then had to be worked out by the parties. So they had procedures set up and in place to handle these situations and you were so informed before hand. They wanted the men happy and spending money, not unhappy and arguing, or sitting in a bar somewhere drinking or whatever alone. Two could spend more than one. We did make it to one of these establishments, somewhat quickly, as they were located near the approved hotels. We made our selections and signed the necessary contracts and left. We actually went and ate at a nightclub, bar, dance hall or whatever it was called, and partied, dancing and a floor show, for awhile before returning to the hotel. Things went well for me until the next morning when said girl started telling me what our schedule for the day was going to be and what I was going to buy for her. Nope, this was not the way it was going to work, so back we went to the pick up place and I explained the situation and that there would have to be a change made. In trying to resolve the problem we discussed options and they had several people involved, there were at least 1 man and 2 women, with possibly a second man. They said to just pick another girl and they would change the contract accordingly. Now things weren't as pressing, maybe, as they had been the day before and I think I was probably a little more picky on my selection. I had not found or picked anyone and might have been getting a little thin on possibilities. I don't know or remember for sure, but they said pick a girl, any girl, and so I picked the girl who was a kind of trouble shooter or problem solver for them. I don't think she was actually available for selection, because the people exchanged looks and said "welllllll???" They looked to this girl/woman and she said "wellll, OK". I do believe this girl was above the norm, she spoke 10 different languages and 15 or 16 dialects. She was a little older, dressed more conservative, and had on a lot less makeup than the other girls. And she was very sharp on about everything you could think of. She told me in our conversations that she had a 8th grade education and that she had done the rest by reading and studying on her own. What a display of what a person can do my applying themselves and trying to achieve a better education and better themselves. Yes I was impressed, and it's probably just as well that I wasn't around her any longer than I was. She was very big on saving me as much money as she could and anywhere we went you never paid the asking price. She would tell me or them what a reasonable price was and we paid accordingly. She could even get me to talking with her and we had some good conversations, very unusual for me in those days. I think it was the first night we were together, but could have been the second, we went to a very nice, to read, an expensive restaurant. There were the original four of us, with 4 girls, and we had picked up 4 more Americans with three more girls. The fourth guy was married and hadn't picked up a girl. In wanting to experience all the different foods, we were discussing the menu and all the possibilities. Wanting to try as many different dishes or foods as possible, we discussed ordering different things and trading back and forth so everyone could sample the different dishes and foods. Now I don't remember this girls name, I wished I did. She had been studying the menu, part of it was in English and some of it was in Chinese (?). She told me that they had an offer on the menu for a buffet that included about everything that they offered on the menu. It would be placed out and you served yourself and could eat anything and everything you wanted and as much as you wanted. She said, that the drinks and deserts were included. Having done the arithmetic, we would not spend anymore and it would maybe even be less, and we would get more food than we could ever possibly eat. Well, this sounded very good to me and I asked the others what they thought. We all agreed that this was the way to go. So she took care of ordering this and getting it all arranged. Like I have said, she was pretty sharp. The restaurant was really happy about this and went out of their way to accommodate us. This was a big sale and they probably got rid of prepared food that they wouldn't have sold otherwise. A guess would be that it was over $50.00 for each of us or over $400.00 total, as we split it equally between the 8 of us. In waiting for the food to start arriving, I noticed a young couple that had just come in, and were a little out of place. I ask her about them and she said that they were probably married and were splurging on a night out and were stretching their budget to eat there. "Hmmm". I asked her "If it would be okay if I asked them to join us?" She said "It would be okay, but I don't know if they will accept". So I said "I'm going to go ask them". She laughed and said "I better go with you, as they would not understand a word you are saying". I laughed too. I said "It would probably be a good idea". We approached them and I introduced myself and the girl, and then she started interpreting for me and explained the situation and asked them to join us for dinner. They were hesitant, and I asked them "Please, be our guests, as we were guests in their country". She interpreted this and they looked at each other, shrugged and accepted. They came to our table and set across from us and while we couldn't converse directly, she did a very good job of explaining and translating between all of us. This idea maybe got a little carried away, for us as a group, we wound up inviting and having join us about everyone in the place. I don't remember inviting anyone else personally,. There were some who did not join us but most were people who had already gotten their food. Needless to say we had a party and a good time was enjoyed by all, and we not only fed ourselves but at least 12 or more, extra people for the same amount of money.

We went to a lot of shops and businesses while we were there, looking or buying, and she always got us a better price. I had a pair of boots made, as in cowboy boots. They had no idea what a cowboy boot was, so we went to a book store, they had magazines too. We picked up a magazine with pictures of cowboy boots in it, took it to them, and yes, they could make them. They were definitely dress boots, and they fit like a glove. After I came home my feet changed, spread or something, and I couldn't wear them anymore and gave them to my nephew, Lance Smith, when he came and lived with us, for awhile, in about 1982. We went to a china factory (in China?), with my intent of buying a 12 place setting of China with all the matching serving dishes and utensils. They usually had them made up, but due to some kind of a labor problem, the china was not in production at the time. Usually you would buy them and they were shipped right then and there to your home in the States. They were going to take my 'prepaid' order and ship them to me whenever they got them made. I wasn't sure and she wasn't sold on the idea, either, so I passed, still regret not doing it. I believe I left 2 to 3 hundred dollars in the hotel safe when I left. I could have thrown the money away on that just as easily and might have gotten the china, too.

This girl was from up in the mountains. I don't know anything about the geography there, so I'm not sure what would qualify as a mountain there. She was suppose to go on vacation on the last full day of my stay. She had planned on going home to spend a couple of days with her family. She was not going to go. We discussed all of this, and I said she could go. She said no, she had accepted the contract and would honor it, and stay. I said I would let her out of her contract, so she could go. She still said "No". She would honor the contract. She did ask me to accompany her, but I would need an another day and a night to be able to do this and there was no way to get them. I would have gone in a minute, if I could have. Don't know what I would have been getting into, but I was willing to find out. I would guess this situation could have been a little more intense than having to go with Kate to meet Mom and Dad the first time. They could have been a little more violent. Mom and Dad weren't violent. We would have been in the middle of nowhere, but I did trust her and don't think I would be in any more danger that some of the other things I have managed to get in to over the years. Of course some of those were life threatening. But it was a mute point as I couldn't go. I did not let her out of her contract, but told her she was going. After talking to the officials at the pickup place, I decided that I would not release her from her contract and would not ask for a refund. By not letting her out of her contract they couldn't have her do anything else at work, because she was still fulfilling her contract with me. She was required to do whatever I wanted her to do. She just wasn't where I was. On the morning when she left to go home, I took her to the bus or train station, not sure which anymore, and put her on some kind of vehicle that was to transport her to her destination. She did recommend a replacement for the my last afternoon and night. Because I was on my way back to Viet Nam, I accepted her replacement recommendation and did have a long/short night and overslept and was late. I had to hurry to make my plane, probably why I forgot the moncy in the hotel safe. Before you go jumping to conclusions, we went bar hopping, we would go to a bar, restaurant, night club, theater, or where ever they served drinks. We would have 1 drink and go on to the next one, I used to know how many places we patronized that night, but have forgotten now. It was more than 3.

Now I know that some people might not approve of me, what I did, and maybe of the people that I met and dealt with in this situation. That's okay, but please reserve judgment on, I guess , all of us. Until you have been there and walked a mile in all of these people's moccasins. I'm not asking for you to join us or even approve, just hold your judgment. It was a different time and place and a whole world away from the life we live today. People adapt and live in the world that they find themselves in. Good, bad or something else, I don't know. I was there and I lived it and tried to do my best in whatever I did. And yes it would have been different had I met Kate before this happened but I didn't and don't apologize to anyone for my actions. There were only 2 that were in line for it, one said I didn't need to, to her, and the other has been taken care of long since. My believes might be something different but I am not discussing them here. When I got back to the States, alive and somewhat still intact I met and married Kate and don't know if I was a different person or not, but I did at least conduct myself in a different manner. Maybe I was just adapting to a new environment, I don't know. I guess I'm in over my head again, so I will bail out.

I finally moved into the special assignment that I had come all this way to do, after the Tet Offensive was over and things settled down. I worked at this for the rest of the time that I was there.

Having never been too smart, I did make several trips or convoys to Qui Nhon to bring back much needed supplies for the 330th. As I remember, I was something of a specialist, I hauled Budweiser beer and hard liquor for the EM and NCO/Officer clubs. Now what I learned on the first trip, that I actually made it all the way, was you are allowed 1 broken bottle in each case of liquor, so you only had to account for 9 bottles instead of 10. If you took a broken pallet of beer, you could load single cases to make up for the missing ones in the pallet. They didn't care or count how many you took, just so you got enough. Now I do know that there are 144 cases of beer in a pallet, might be useful information sometime, but if you take 40 or 50 extra cases it surely makes up for the missing ones. I know I don't have a degree in mathematics so I operated on the safe side of making sure I got enough to make up for the missing cases. Now before you go jumping to conclusions, I never did take a bottle or a case for my own use. But there were a lot of soldiers who were happy to drink warm beer, as opposed to no beer, because of those broken pallets. And some of them even enjoyed a bottle of liquor that, of course, was from a broken bottle. Now how was this possible, you ask? Well, when you had all this extra weight on your truck and in an attempt to lighten your load, you stop at bridges along the way and toss off those loose cases of beer, to the guys who are stuck out there guarding those bridges. You just naturally lighten your load as you head toward those hills that are very steep and hard pulling, in the central highlands. On some of the bigger bridges, with more guards, you might also lose a bottle, that of course was already broken. They never even seemed to care what it was or what had been in them, because they were already broken, don't you know. You might have been surprised at how many GI's knew the 330th trucks, when they came through, and they always waved when they saw you, if you were driving one of those trucks. Now I'm sure the Statute of Limitations has run out so I can, maybe, admit to these things now. It was rewarding, when someone you didn't know, would come up and say "you don't remember me, but I sure enjoyed that beer that you dropped off at bridge (such and such), back in April of 68". I guess I was just practicing for the times in the future when I, or someone, would do something for someone else, who was in need.

I also used some of these extra items to trade for things for the company back in Pleiku. I traded a bottle, for each truck load of plywood for dividing the buildings into rooms, or a case of beer for a dump truck load of sand, or whatever we needed and didn't have. I did do some trading, at times. And I guess if you were in Viet Nam in the first half of 68 and drank warm beer or whiskey at a bridge, that someone dropped off for you, then you might still, maybe, owe me a thanks, because it might have been me or someone I taught my bad habits to.

Three times I was to go to Khe Sanh, for something, twice we got to the staging area for the forming of the convoys and we were sent back. Only combat unit vehicles were allowed to go. The other time we didn't even get to the staging area before they told us to go or stay home. This happened when they knew the convoy was going to run into trouble. One time Charlie was suppose to have ditches dug across the road and armed combatants were waiting in those ditches. Charlie was a slang term to identify the enemy, Viet Cong or North Vietnamese Army combatants. We stayed for the briefing. You were to keep driving, no matter what happened, the trucks would and could cross the ditches, might have been a little bouncing around, but just keep going and if a truck was disabled, you were not to stop and try to help, that was left to the Military Police guards with the convoy. Then we had to go back to the company because we weren't a combat designated unit.

We were in direct support of Khe Sanh, it was a supply point for the VC and NVA. They could come to Khe Sanh and resupply with whatever was available. It was a kind of a wide spot in the road or trail, or holes in the ground, at first. Someone in a high up position decided if we took Khe Sanh out or occupied it we could shorten the war. There never was any doubt that we could take and hold Khe

Sanh. We took it and Charlie wanted it back and an all out effort was made to take it back. I forget how long this waged but seems like it was 6 to 8 weeks, 77 days actually. The bodies were piled up outside the perimeter fence, and the rats were feeding on the bodies and Bubonic Plague broke out among the Vietnamese. Finally Charlie decided that they were not going to succeed and called off the effort to take it back, and moved to a new location to start a new supply point. After we showed we could take and hold Khe Sanh and Charlie went else where, we pulled out and gave it back to them. Without destroying the whole place. There was a air strip built for the Caribou's, they could land and take off on a football field. I know that at one time this strip was still intact, don't know if it stayed that way or not. This was where they lost me as far as supporting the war went, when and if I went home, I wasn't coming back.

Sometime in March of 68 we had some new people come in, as replacements. One individual went out to one of the villages and was drinking rice wine with the people there. As usual they asked questions and he answered them, too well, and then diagrammed our company area and placed us on the post. We had been listed as a light amour unit, because we had APCs, Armored Personnel Carriers, on their battle plan, now we were listed as communications. Would you like to take a guess at how long it took us to get hit? Try less than 12 hours at 3:00am, that next morning. I was working in operations. We started taking in coming rounds, I think there was about 15. When the rounds are incoming you know instantly the difference. Artillery shot rounds over us all the time, but you know when they are coming the other way. The first one hit and my feet hit the floor and I was standing. The 2nd one and I was intently listening and on the 3rd I was moving. I went into the next room and told Ronnie and Hank that those were incoming and lets get out of here. Hank was moving but Ronnie said "just a minute", he wanted to finished what he was doing, number 4 had just hit, I grabbed Ronnie by his shirt collar and yanked him out of his chair and we both went to the floor. Number 5 hit right beside us, about 10 feet, luckily we were on the floor, shrapnel went over us and a piece about the size of your fist went through Ronnie's chair backrest. It would of cut his spine in two. He had been setting in a swivel chair and when he came out of it, it turned back to a normal position as if he had been setting at his table. I would think that my eyes were as big as his, and his were quite large. We crawled out and got to the most protected place we could find and waited until the barrage or salvo was over. We got up and dusted ourselves off and started checking for injured and damages. The trick chief took hits but his flak jacket, which he had just put on, stopped all of them, none penetrated the jacket, this was from Number 5. Number 4 had hit a Quonset hut and there should have been 4 men working right there but 3 were gone and the fourth was injured pretty bad, but he lived. He was flown to Japan for medical treatment and recovered there. He was the worst casualty we had, luckily, for the rest of us. We actually were very lucky in our casualties and damages also. The individual that started all of this, with his big mouth, was removed and taken else where.

It was sometime around this time that one night I was standing out of the buildings, just inside the gates into the compound at operations. I was talking to Sgt Richard 'Flakey' Knight of C Team Special Forces. In the course of our conversation we happened to look up over our heads and there were tracers going right over our heads. We looked at each other and turned and looked behind us, it was a bare hillside. We continued to talk but were watching the tracers and decided to move over to see what would happen. They moved with us, we moved again and they moved with us again There would be a stream and then they would stop. The shooter would lower his aim to hit us and would shoot into the dirt berm around the compound. Then he would raise up to clear the berm he would go over our heads. We decided, some what quickly, to go else where to finish our conversation. We figured he had a spotter higher then he was and the spotter was directing his shooting and luckily we could not be hit from where the shooter was at.

Flakey told me about some things that happened at his home base. They had lost 8 or 9 men, on base. I think that all had their throats cut, and were found in out of the way places. There wasn't blood or enough blood to support the fact that they were killed in that location. Eventually they caught the responsible people. One was a barber, at the barbershop on base, and another was a shoe shine boy who worked at the barber shop. The shoe shine boy would act as a look out for the barber and when they got the chance, with only one person in the shop and no one else around, the barber would cut the soldier's throat, probably with a straight razor, and use towels to cover the wound and soak up the blood, a rolled up towel pulled over the wound would also help hold the man down until he was dead. He could cover his face with a towel or towels, if anyone came around, like he was getting a shave or something. They had a store room or another room available that they could store the body in until they could dispose of the body, else where on the base. Not sure how this was accomplished. The shoe shine boy could also delay someone wanting to come into the shop. There could of been others involved also, not remembering now if there was more people involved or if I ever heard. Unable to remember now how they caught them but thankfully they did and put a stop to these assaults against the young American soldiers.

Another thing that happened was that they had several guys that seemed to blow themselves up with there own hand grenades. What was happening was that someone was wiring the pins on the grenades to the nails that the flak jacket, suspenders, and pistol belts, with all the gear on, were hung on the wall with. Then when you grabbed up your gear and went to leave the wires would pull the pins out and you would self destruct. The pins would be removed and straightened and oiled so that they would come out very easily and you wouldn't feel it. The wire was thin copper wire and hard to see. Most of the soldiers put 2 nails in the studs, in the wall, spaced about shoulder width or a little more apart and then hang the flak jacket or vest on the nails through the arm holes, outside to inside. Then you came up and put your arm through the arm hole, on both sides and slide into the vest and you had it on and away you would go. Fasten you pistol belt and zip up your flak jacket (vest), put on your steel helmet, grab your rifle and you were ready. This could be done very quickly, with a little practice, and you were off to the alert or whatever was going on. They figured out what was going on but not who as yet. They had barracks or buildings like we had and they were divided into rooms with doors so you could lock the door when you weren't there. You were either to let the house girl in to clean and pick up your laundry or put the laundry out in the hall and clean yourself. Flakey had opened his door for his house girl and then left to go do something. She left the door unlocked and went and did his laundry and then came back and put it away. She left leaving the door unlocked. Before he came back they were put on alert. He ran to get his gear and the door was unlocked. When he went in, put his arms through the vest, pulled it on and started to leave and thought "the door was unlocked". He stopped and slid the vest back on the nails and looked. He had 3 grenades wired. This was pretty close. He just stopped and set down on the cot and thought about it for a while. He took the wires off and pulled the pins, re-bent them and replaced them. He checked everything over and then put it back on and went to his assigned place for the alert. Oh and he locked his door when he left. He never forgot again, I'm sure.

I had a acquaintance who was in the Air Force and worked on a command dispatch plane. Which picked and assigned targets for air strikes against the enemy. After they thought they were through one night, having given all aircraft a target or assignment, they set back to relax, or take a break, and a voice came on the radio, "This is War Eagle 1, do you have a target for me"? WHAT and WHO is War Eagle 1? "Stand by War Eagle 1". They scrambled and could not find any War Eagle 1 on the code or call sign sheets for this day. A quick discussion solved nothing. In stalling they ask him to identify his aircraft and armament, which he did, it was a Korean War Era fighter plane. Planes of this type had been given to the South Vietnamese Air Force and were not being used by US Forces. He had, in addition to his normal machine gun type armament, carrying one 500 pound bomb. There were quite a few, quick, discussions and opinions about this, but they decided that they would give him a target and see what happened. They had not seen an aircraft and ask his location. Right off your left wing. Sure enough there was a plane out there. "OK, we have a target for you". It was a river crossing that was a thorn in the side of the US Forces. Where supplies and reinforcements could be brought in from across the border, and into the war zone. They flew over the crossing and dropped flares, to light up the area. They backed off and waited, the plane flew over the crossing and then told them to back off about 4 or 5 more klicks, for safety's sake. He made his run and there was a large explosion. They flew over the area and dropped more flares, then made another pass and looked at the damage. Where the crossing had been, there was a very large hole in the river and it was filling with water. In the past, they had tried to take it out with the smaller bombs that had been available but had not been unsuccessful. The VC would have the previous holes filled back in, by hand, using bamboo baskets to carry the dirt and rock to fill back in the holes in the crossing. Not this time, he didn't know, and I sure didn't, if they ever got it filled back in and back in use or not. My friend did some checking and investigating and over time tracked this man down, information wise. He was a pilot that had been forced to start flying a desk, because of age and medical reasons. He did not want to hang up his wings yet. He was going out on his own and with the help of friends in the South Vietnamese Air Force, was able to get a plane and armament, on occasion. He would make his private flights into the war. He continued to make these flights, as far as we know, for the rest of the time he was in country. They got so they looked forward to the nights when "War Eagle 1" would come on the radio and ask for a target, and most of the people involved continued to wonder who "that Masked Man was". I maybe on deep reflection could remember the name but for now he is just some Air Force pilot who was not ready to retire and fly a desk, instead of an aircraft. Whoever this man is, I do admire and respect him. I always thought I wanted to meet him, and I guess I still do. I hope he is around and still flying those flights, where ever he is, and do wish the legend of "War Eagle 1" to be on going and be remembered. Colonel, I Salute You, you are one of my heroes.

One time we located a company of NVA in between us and the Air Force Base. They were only active at night, but we pinpointed them with the use of direction finding. When we notified the appropriate department, they scoffed at the idea. We did get conformation the next night and the military looked during the day. We confirmed the next night and they decided we were right. Night time aerial photos showed some of the active and so on about the 4th day they were bombed and their tunnels collapsed. I don't think there were any survivors.

In about August 1967 while on perimeter guard duty we watched as the reportedly, first, Puff the Magic Dragon got shot down. This was a twin engine plane that only carried ammunition and was feared by the VC and NVA. They were awesome, total fire power, and just about wiped out anything in their spot light (s). They were shooting at something on the mountain side and then fire was returned by a, suspected by us, 50 caliber machine gun. They continued flying and then the plane started down and slowly rolled over, upside down with guns still firing, and went into the mountainside this way. There was a very large explosion and fire. Ground troops went in and retrieved whatever was retrievable the next day.

Another friend was a LuRP, this was a forward observer, who at times was behind enemy lines, and on their own. The lived and existed on their own and by their wits, however they could, where ever they could. They scouted places and enemy positions and the enemy. They had a radio that they could report information, major troop movements, direct fire on to positions or call to be picked up, if they needed it. They didn't have to be crazy, but it helped. They lived off the land, at times, and as was necessary, they could and did subsist on very little, as far as carried food went. It was also a plus if you liked bugs, lizards, snakes, and the like. At times they stayed in holes, caves, or even in trees, inside and out. They could have there choice of weapons, and for a rifle most of them, that I knew about, chose the AK47, ammunition was readily available from the enemy and was considered by some to be more reliable than other choices.

I remember Bill Ansel, a quiet unassuming man. Nothing really remarkable about him, except for what he did. He was assigned to one of our outposts, a spot out in the bush, so to speak. Once when they were coming under a major attack, a patrol was ambushed right outside the perimeter fence and most were killed. There were 2 of these men still alive, but wounded. While they were under attack, no one wanted to go and try and retrieve the wounded men. Bill volunteered to go and bring them in, he went through the perimeter wire. He made 2 trips, while under fire, crawling and carrying the men on his back. As I remember, both of them lived. As was his nature Bill down played the whole thing. He was put in for a Silver Star with V Device, for Valor. It was down graded to a Bronze Star with V, because no officer, in the immediate command had a Silver Star (this was unofficial, of course). After this happened Bill was transferred to the 330th and was to be presented his Bronze Star there in an awards ceremony. Bill told them no, not to hold a ceremony for him, he did not want to be awarded anything. They went ahead with the planned ceremony anyway and he refused to show up and didn't go. I don't remember if anything came from this, not showing up, or not.

Mark Harbin was sent to Bambi Tuwee (spelling), after it was overrun and to reestablish the detachment, that we had there. I don't remember to much about it now except that they were overrun and he went down tdy (temporary duty) and when it was back functioning he came back. He was eventually put on as permanent Sargent of the Guard. And was doing that when I came home.

After I got back and checked in at Two Rock Ranch Station, in Petaluma, Calif. I was sent to Walter Reed Army Hospital in Washington, D.C., by way of Letterman Hospital, at the Presidio of San Francisco, and Travis AFB. When at Travis I was put in an 8 man Hospital room with 7 marines who were returning wounded from Viet Nam. The officer was a Major, and had been wounded along with the other 6 in an ambush. He had requested to remain in a room with his men. Normally he would have been given a private room. They had lots of stories about life in the Marine Corp. Life expectancy of a 2nd Lt., arriving in country was less than 30 days. A lot were shot my "snipers", in the back of the head, some people just have to learn, the hard way. That 2nd Lt.'s don't know everything and aren't even very important, except to themselves, as far a war zone is concerned. A lot of people could die very quickly if someone didn't know what they were doing and started giving orders that were not in the best interests of the whole group. If he survived the first 30 days then it jumped to 4 or 5 months, and if you survived that. Then after 6 months you were pulled off the line and given desk or office duty. Life expectancy jumped to, I think, 11 months and then you got to go home. Now this captain, at the time, had made it his 6 months but there were no Officer to relieve him so he stayed with his platoon, maybe a company. They would get him a relief as soon as possible, 7 months, 8 months, 9 months and still no relief, 10 months (got promoted to Major at just over 10 months as I remember) and was working on11, when they were ambushed coming back in off of patrol. He must of established a pattern, unbeknown to him or his men. Because "Charlie" was waiting and they still got out of it pretty good, everything considered. I don't think that they had any dead, which was lucky. They told a lot of stories about the war. I have forgotten, most likely I wanted to forget, a lot of what I was told about. I have been 40 plus years trying to forget, but it comes back, sometimes in bits and pieces. So if it seems a bit choppy, that is why, I will continue to add to and update this as time goes on. There are some things that I'm not ready to put down yet.

I don't remember when we first saw this Country and Western Band. The band had been formed over there, by a civilian contractor. He started the band with 3 other civilians and I think one guy from the Air Force. To make up the 5 piece band, they had a lead guitar, a base guitar, rhythm guitar, a steel guitar, and drums. They had a female singer who was French-Vietnamese and her name was Miss Mai. I started going to all of their performances, that I could. Miss Mai sang half of each set and she started setting at our table, when she wasn't on stage. We became friends with her and the band. Mark Harbin and I were usually together at these shows. There may have been others but seems like he and I were always there together. Miss Mai was engaged to a 1st Lieutenant, seems like he was in the Army, might have been the Air Force. I don't remember ever meeting him. They were up to one of the Combat Engineers enlisted men's clubs for a show. She had just got some new outfits, these were pants and blouse type outfits, that were really sharp. She had always worn tops, before, that went up on her neck and her skin was covered. These were a modestly lowered neckline and fit fairly tight. The first one she wore was yellow, I would say canary yellow, and she and it looked really good. She was some what self-conscious, but was putting on a good show. Someone threw an ice cube and hit her, on the bare skin, on her upper left chest. She was hurt, but not physically, and started crying and left the stage. Our table was front row center and she came down to our table. I/we tried to console her, I had actually put my arms around her and held her while she cried. I kept talking to her. She was really upset, and after a while we did set down and I kept my arm around her shoulders and she kept her head on my shoulder. When she started worrying about my shirt being and getting wet I knew she would be okay. The leader of the band ask who ever threw the ice cube to come up on stage and he would personally kick his ... butt, all over the stage. Of course no one accepted, the show was not going to continue until something was resolved. The guy was not known, unless it was to the guys he was setting with, but his nerve broke and he jumped up and ran for the door. A big engineer stood up and took a full round house swing and caught him behind the ear and knocked him out threw the door. The latch broke and he was out, not only outside but as in not being conscious. The door was closed and he was removed. The band started playing and one of the guys was singing. I/we were still talking to her and she had quit crying and I was kidding and teasing her. She finally said "OK, I'll go back on stage and try to sing". So after the man's song was finished she returned to the stage and started to sing, but was tentative. I kept talking to her and got her smiling and she started singing and putting on a show. Like she was capable of. We stayed friends up until my leaving of the country.

When I got down to short time left, we planned a party and the band agreed to come and play a 3 hour set. Now when we had a party, we had a party, and this was no exception. I did win a $20.00 bet at the party, for drinking a whole case of beer (24 cans of Budweiser) in the 3 hours of the party. I was walking, after it was over, thank you. I was looking forward to putting this country behind me.

As long as BD was under my bed I never had a problem with rats. When I had 2 days left in Pleiku and no BD, a rat jumped up on the foot of my bed, while I was asleep. It ran up over me, right over my face, his tail drug on my nose. I didn't sleep again in that bed or much of anywhere else in Pleiku.

When clearing country and I went to the 313th in Nha Trang, the personnel clerk couldn't find my 201 (personal) file and had to go ask a supervisor what to do. The supervisor came back and went to the bottom drawer in the cabinet and clear in the back was my file. When I asked about this, I was told I had been misfiled. Because of the situation of being sent where I wasn't suppose to be and injured, I just seized to exist, as far as any paperwork went. The 330th couldn't justify my being there and rather than have to explain it, just ignored it and me, on paper. Going on to the 509th(Group), I ran into some of the guys I had worked with before and was congratulated. I thought it was for getting out alive and said so. No, this was on my promotion and why wasn't I wearing my E-6 stripes? Because I am not an E-6. Oh yes you are. They had seen the orders posted on the bulletin board. No, I wasn't. Yes you were. So at 10 at night, we went and they got a clerk out of bed and had him open the Personnel Office up. They had him find a copy of my orders. Yes, I had been promoted but not notified. Because no paperwork went though the 313th. The orders were returned "EM was not located". This started a whole new line of thinking. We now had to celebrate my promotion, they said at my expense. We hooked up with an all girl Country and Western Band, from Portland, Oregon. They were there to perform for the troops. We did celebrate most of the night, as I remember, and I'm right sure we had a good time. American Girls and all. No, Mom, I don't remember anything other than the celebrating, as far as the girls are concerned. One was a red head, fuzzy details now, at best, if its not poor memory, its at least good sense.

In actually leaving the country, we went to Than Son Nhut Air Base, outside of Saigon and boarded. Then we got the special announcement, the VC were off the end of the runway and shooting at the planes with mortars. Great news, planes would be using unusual takeoffs methods for this reason. It was explained that the planes were going to stay on the taxi way, then when it was their turn they would run up their engines, and start their take off from there. Instead of starting on the runway, the take off would start on the taxiway and then onto the approach ramp and onto the runway. By doing this the planes would have additional speed to get airborne quicker and could get started on evasive maneuvers faster with the increased altitude. This was before reaching the end of the runway and the perimeter fence. This was a somewhat sobering thought and might even be considered serious. We just pulled a short way from the gate and waited. I was next to the window so had a good view of the other planes taking off. I got to see 3, 707's, take off in front of us. Really WOW. The planes would start moving on the taxiway and be accelerating, while turning on to the approach ramp and actually power slide on to the runway, with tires smoking, the pilot (s) would straighten the plane using power and brakes and used maximum acceleration to get airborne as soon as possible. This was a sight, not soon forgotten, and has never been forgotten by me. And then it was our turn, the run up of the engines and the release of the brakes. We were moving, down the taxiway, on to the approach ramp, this was a wide sweeping turn, picking up speed along the way. You could feel the thrust of the engines on the approach ramp, and then the power slide on to the runway. You could feel the plane sliding, the slipping of the tires on the tarmac or surface of the runway. Then the sensation of the straightening of the plane, all the while under power and accelerating . I have flown enough to know that we seemed to be under as much power, for takeoff, as I ever remember. Possibly this was do to the heightened awareness, because of the situation. Could be called an adrenalin rush do to the circumstances, at the time and place. But was very much aware of the sensations experienced and it was good when we were airborne and while waiting for the acknowledgement that we had made it and had not been hit. I guess this is how you spell relief. I know, very funny. I was smiling when the announcement was made that we were up and away, with no new holes. It was the 4th of July 1968 and I was on my way home. With crossing the International Date Line we were back on the 3rd of July and got to the U.S. on an early hour of the 4th of July.

When going through customs, we had been told how extensive the checks would be. So I had not tried to bring any of my handguns home with me, but had put in some of my carpenter tools, as a check. We went through about 3 to 4 in the early morning hours. I was asked "Do you have any plants, drugs, open alcohol, or fresh fruit?" "No". "Next". "That's it?" "Yep, you're out of here." "You sorry, mumble, mumble." "What's that all about?" "Never mind." No x-ray and no open bag checks. I could have brought my handguns or some of them, that irritated me.

Ronnie Rooker and I went to an establishment to have a beer, while we were waiting for our flights They wouldn't serve him because he wasn't 21, he lacked a couple of months. He had served 2 years in Viet Nam and they wouldn't serve him a beer. They brought both and then asked us for ID's. They served mine but took his back and we got up and left, and I didn't pay for or drink mine either.

Ronnie died in a car accident before he reported to Fort Bliss, Texas, for his new duty assignment. He was still not 21 years old.

I flew to Denver and he went to Kansas City. I contacted Aunt Lil (Gulley) when I got into Denver, to let her know that I was back and maybe I could see them while I was waiting for the bus, to get on home to Phillipsburg, Ks. She was glad to hear from me and came to the Air Port to pick me up and insisted on taking be on home to Kansas. Would not even hear any arguments about not doing it, so we went on to Phillipsburg and I was home on the 4th of July. I was cutting wheat the next day on my birthday. While at home I had a sore open up on the outside of my left knee. This was an open sore, that kept draining and would not scab over. Every morning I checked it and it was the same. I was getting scared. Again I didn't tell anyone at home about this. Finally I decided one more day and I would go to the doctor. The next morning I got up and checked my leg, there was a scab over the sore and it itched very badly. I started scratching around it and looking at the scab. Remember, I was almost a doctor, I had been to 2 weeks of Army Emergency Medical School. I decided that it needed attention. I sterilized a small knife and proceed to remove this dime sized scab. It was metal. It had come several inches through my knee. What a relief, the leg was healed under it. The wound had healed behind the metal as it migrated through the flesh.

Chapter 8:

Life after the War Zone.

We finished cutting wheat and decided to go to Bainbridge Island, Washington and visit Pat and Richard and their 3 boys, Garrett, Lance, and Kyle. We used my pickup and borrowed cousin Walter Jensen's over the cab camper. Dad, Mom, brother Ken, and I went and had a good time visiting and seeing new and different country. After visiting at Pat and Rich's, we headed south to Southern California and Edwards Air Force Base, in the Mojave Desert, to visit brother Tom. Ending my visit there I caught a plane in Los Angles to go north of San Francisco and on to Two Rock Ranch Station in Petaluma, California, an hour north of San Fransisco and the Golden Gate Bridge.

Life in California and in the Army. But there were the motorcycles and I still liked the thrill and challenge of riding and racing. In a short while I was back into racing and went to work for a Yamaha Dealer and got to go to the Yamaha Factory Mechanics School in Los Angeles. I did as much racing as I could and loved riding in the desert. When I first checked in to work at Two Rock Ranch I was assigned to operations as a supervisor. The Personnel Officer decided that I was no longer physically fit to perform my duties and started paper work to pull my MOS (Military Occupational Specialty) and I was assigned to a special duty assignment. While still in operations, I was outside my MOS. After several months of unsettledness and disagreement, I was eventually pulled from Operations and given duty, first in the

Company Orderly Room, and then in Special Services. I was given an MOS in this field, no qualification involved..

The guys I worked with kept after me to start playing sports again or at least get involved. I did, in the form of Slow Pitch Softball, pitching; coaching volleyball, coaching and then playing basketball. I had a real love for basketball, both as a player and also as a coach. When they finally talked me into the basketball coaching job, it was at half time of a game they were loosing to a less talented team. I took over at half time and we did win the game. We had some good players on this team but they needed direction. Wayne Byers, was from Kansas and had a scholarship at Kansas University. As I remember he was about 6 foot 4 or 5 inches and played guard at KU. On this team he jumped center and played forward. They had another forward that was pretty good and a very good shooting guard, with another guard that was a good ball handler. We could use a center but another forward would be good. It just so happened that we had another forward, that played on the Post Team, and was eligible to play on our team, but wouldn't play on this team. His name was Joe Carvalho and he had been my roommate at Ft. Devens. He had spent the previous 4 years playing basketball all over Europe on an all Army Team. He had had a scholarship at Bradley University, before Army life caught up with him. He had married his girl friend from Hawaii and was living happily, off post, enjoying married life. When I asked him to play with us, he said he would as long as I was going to coach. We had a good team and it was made better with the addition of Joe. The Officers had a good team also, Captain Bergman was a pro caliber player, who was a 6 foot 7 inch center. They had a good forward, who was a Captain but I don't remember his name, but do remember both him and his wife. They had 1 good guard, Lt. R. James Fisher. They had some other players that filled in around these 3. When we played this team they were undefeated and we had lost 1 game, from before I started coaching. I played them with a box and one, this was a 4 man zone defense and a one man, man to man. I played the hatchet man or the one, man to man, on Captain Bill Bergman. He had never seen this defense before and was very frustrated when he didn't get the ball. We held him to just a few points in the whole game and he was upset with me. At one point he grabbed me and threw me away from him and on to the floor. Of course this drew him an intentional foul and I shot 2 free throws. After the game, which we won, he came and shook hands and apologized for his behavior. He wanted to know where I had learned that defense and to not, please, tell anyone else about it. I told him I had learned it from my High School coach, Curtis Tarrant, who had been in the Air Force and played all over Europe on an all Air Force All Star Team in the 50's. He acknowledged that it was very effective, when played with a defender like me, who knew how to play it. He had 9 inches of height on me and probably an additional 6 more inches of reach, but I had almost shut him down completely. I did have Wayne and Joe playing behind him and were really huge factors in the effectiveness of this defense.

I continued to race motorcycles all during my stay in California and rode in the Mojave Desert as often as I could. I really liked riding in the desert and chasing Jack Rabbits. It was fun and helped to improve your reflexes. I liked any kind of racing but was really drawn to the Flat Tracking events that were all over California. I rode in several events called Motorcycle Rodeos, where you competed in fun events that took riding skill. With the competition being in each event and then an overall, decided by how you did in each individual event and you had to compete in all the events. These include carrying an egg on a spoon in your mouth, over a set course against the clock. Another was pushing a barrel with you front tire, supposedly in a straight line, for a given distance, this was run against the clock or if enough room was available then were run with the bikes side by side. Another one was riding on a 2 x 4, or 2 x 6, for a given distance and decided by who got the furthest or who went all the way in the least amount of time. Another one was a cross country race where you went from point A to point B, everyone started at the same time and the first one there was the winner. There were several more events that were used by the different clubs that put these on. Still another one involved carrying a container, holding water, and you had to navigate a closed course and not spill any water, then if water was spilled, and almost always was, then it was decided by who had the most water left and if a tie then who got there the fastest. A number of obstacle courses were also employed in these events. We held one on Post at Two Rock Ranch and since it was a fun event, I made all the Trophies from used motor parts. These were functional and some were made to be a desk set to hold pens and or papers, using springs spread to make slots or a place to put a pen, at least they were different. This was held with the Two Rock Ranch Sports Car Club whose home was on Two Rock Ranch and was made up of Military people wanting something to do and having to do, primarily, with Sports Cars.

We ran a number of events in this group that included; Auto Crosses, Rallies, Poker Runs, and this type of events. I helped set up and run a couple of these Rally type events. They were run from a starting point to a finishing point, obeying all traffic laws and directions. You had written instructions and were to follow them. You might be directed to pull into a rest area, and to follow given instructions, exactly as written. This might include pulling into the parking area and parking in a certain way, the passenger would get out and stand at the water hydrant and then the driver would get out and walk around the car two times, get back in and call the passenger (or navigator). He would then get back into the car and they would proceed with the written directions. Usually on these points there would be a hidden observer who scored the entry on how they followed the instructions, with points given or taken away accordingly. It was all in fun and made for some hilarious stories. One being that the course took the cars into a mountain area and the instructions said to, at a certain point, pull off on a "pull out area", park and the passenger got out and went and looked out over the look out point, without turning to watch the driver get out and walk around the car twice, get back in and call the passenger, who got back in and they drove off. We had an observer up on the side of the mountain where he could not be seen and scored the situation accordingly. Some followed the instructions and some did not or only followed them partially. While this was going on a couple of guys came a long who I will describe as "California Hippy types of the 60's". They set down a short distance away on the opposite side of the rode and proceeded to smoke their pipe (s), of a substance that was most likely not tobacco. They set and watch these going ons with much wonder and were questioning, something or somebody, as to the sanity of these proceedings. They set through almost the whole set of cars that participated in this event. When the observer came down off the mountain, when the tail car came through the course and picked him up, these gentlemen came over and wondered what was going on, as they were starting to question the strength of their smoking material. John Heintz, the observer, had been observing these individuals all day and laughing accordingly, as they were very animated and vocal in their observations. He could hear at least some of their comments about the actions of these drivers (?) (their question mark) and they announced that they were the ones smoking "the weed". He explained what was going on, much to their relief, and they all had a good laugh. And so did all of us, at the social gathering after everyone had completed the event and made it in. Made for an interesting memory of a Sunday in Rural Northern California, in 1969. A nice Sunday afternoon, John said he would not have traded for anything, it was a fun memory.

John was an artist, by desire, if not by profession. He had painted my Motorcycle Helmet with Snoopy flying his dog house, complete with bullet holes, and Snoopy shaking his fist and saying "Curse you Bultaco" on one side. The other side was him just flying with his white scarf blowing in the wind. This helmet was stolen out of my pick up in early 1970 at a race somewhere in Northern California.

When I had been there a short time and in about December of 1968 I found and purchased, from a used car lot in Petaluma, Cal., a 1964 Chevrolet Impala Super Sport, 2 door hard top, metallic tan in color, with beige leather interior and luxurious bucket seats. This was, I believe, the most comfortable riding car I ever owned. It was comfortable doing about anything you can do in a car. When Kate and I started going out together we would on occasion go to the drive in movies, yes they still had them in that ancient time, and after the first time decided that we would try the back seat for watching the movie. And it was roomy and comfortable. Of course, with her there I thought the beach was roomy and comfortable, also the hard rocky ground, for a picnic, in the mountains, was roomy and comfortable, but do think that the back seat of that car was the best, of the mentioned options. We kept the 64 Chevy until just before we left for Ethiopia in July of 1970.

When I traded my Chevy Pickup in on the 64 Chevy, I needed another pickup to haul my bike around so I was looking for another one and found an ad in the Petaluma newspaper, for a 1955 Studebaker pickup, $200.00. So I called the number and the lady said to come look, and I did. The pickup ran great, was a narrow long bed, a dull black in color, and no chrome. She and her ex husband had gotten a divorce and she had gotten the car and the pickup. She didn't want the pickup. I never met her husband, but the guy knew what he was doing. He started out with a pickup, not sure what year, and put a 289 Golden Hawk engine in it, a brand new engine. It had a Pontiac 4 speed automatic transmission, the weak point of the whole drive train. I am not sure what the rear end was but was high geared. He did suspension work and widened the wheel base. The interior while not fancy was put together from 51 through 55 year model pickups. It had a monster 4 barrel Holly carburetor and got about 8 miles to the gallon, but oh would it run. This pickup went up to 150 MPH and was still climbing when I chickened out and backed out of it. My friend John Cunningham, from Arizona, had a Jaguar that paced me up to the 150 and that was faster than I wanted to go in a pickup. I changed the carb to a large 4 barrel and the mileage jumped to 15 MPG. We had a lot of fun and many miles in this pickup and oh, yes, I did buy it that night, on the spot for $200.00, cash. That way nobody changed their mind about selling it.

Chapter 9:

Kate

Around the first of May 1970, I don't remember the exact date. I either met Rocky Hergenrader at his girl friend's, Julie Broadwell house or I went with him to the house, in Cotati, California. While we were there one of Julie's 2 room mates walked by, it was Kate. I didn't even know her name and she never even looked our way. I did notice her, she was attractive and had good legs, she was wearing a short mini-skirt, as was her habit in those days. I know, but I am a trained observer. Nothing was said by any of the people there, but Julie and/or Rocky must have noticed my interest. Rocky had a sense of humor, he printed his name Roc3ky, the 3 was down about a half a line. When he was asked , he would say "the 3 was silent". He signed his name without the 3. A few days later on Post, Two Rock Ranch Station, Petaluma, Ca., Rocky ask if I wanted to go to supper with him and Julie. No, I don't think so. Well, we're going to ask Julie's room mate, Kate, to go along and we'll make it a foursome. I took about 2 seconds to think it over. I knew this was the girl I had seen a couple of days before, and said "Okay, I'll go". We met at the house in Cotati, we were introduced and we all went to supper. We had a good time and I really liked her. There was something different about her, I was immediately comfortable around her. After we returned back to the house, Rocky and Julie went on into the house and we stayed on the porch and set and talked. Now this in its self was unusual for me, to just sit and talk with a girl alone was not the norm. This was a week night and I asked her to go to the movies on Friday night and she accepted. I guess I could be described as floating along above the ground. We went to the movies on Friday night and had a good time, this was the time when we set in the front on my 64 Chevy, bucket seats with a center console, I was positive I didn't like the center console any more. I think we also went some where on the weekend but am not sure where now. I was trying to not push to hard but if it had been entirely up to me, we would have been together everyday. I think it was probably a whole week, after that first night of going to the movies, before I knew I was in love with her. This was something completely different for me. I liked girls but this was way beyond anything I had ever experienced. I won't say I was out of my head or anything, I still had some common sense left. But I did want to be with her all the time and do anything she wanted to do. Yes I know, I had it bad, but while not being stupid, I was infatuated and in love. I knew very quickly that she was the one, for ever and always. In not trying to rush things and push her to hard, I did use some restraint. We continued to go out at least 2 or 3 times a week and on most other nights I would be at her house and we would set out front, in the car or on the porch and talk. We went for drives, movies, to eat, to the beach, north into the mountains for at least one picnic, into San Francisco, at least a couple of trips to the Mojave Desert to ride motorcycles. She accompanied me to a couple of races, as I was still racing motorcycles. In the middle of June I was slated to go home to Kansas and help Dad cut wheat. I did this but pretty sure my heart was still in California. I called her every night when we got in from work. With the 2 hour difference in time it worked pretty good because we worked fairly late most nights. Mom and Dad knew something special or out of the ordinary was going on, for me to call anyone, especially a girl, every night was completely out of character for me. She was there every night to answer the phone. I had asked her if she would like to have her own motorcycle and she said "Yes, that would be nice". I located a 175cc Yamaha Enduro dirt bike that was either new or almost new, and they agreed to hold it for me, without a down payment, until I got there to pick it up on my way back to California. It would be after the first of July. As soon as we got through cutting wheat I was off to California. I don't remember where the bike was but it was west of Phillipsburg. When I got there to pick it up they had already sold it, supposedly a misunderstanding between the salesmen. They would get me another one, real quick, and they were so sorry. In 5 minutes? Well, no. Bye. I was going to California, just as quick as I could get there and as fast as I could. I drove straight through, 1600 miles, to get back to see her. As I remember it was evening, maybe 7 or 8, when I got there. It seems like she met me at the door and we went into the living room. Something was going on as there was a room full of people setting around talking and probably drinking, something. Kate wasn't drinking anything and was quiet as per her usual. All the seats were taken so I set down on the floor, with my back to the wall, and she at first went back to her chair. In just a little while I lay down on the floor, with an elbow on the floor and my head in my hand. I was tired, I had been up for about 32 hours and had driven over 1600 miles. I wasn't really talking and sure didn't need any alcohol to drink. Kate got up and came over and set down on the floor, with her back to the wall, and put my head in her lap. As I remember she was wearing a fairly short mini-skirt. Now, I was really comfortable, and with her hands on my head, hair, and maybe shoulders I wasn't moving for anything. I don't know how long it was, not to long I'm sure, and I was asleep. I'm also sure there never was any better pillow. I did tell her about her bike and she said that it was okay, and "what was I going to do with the money, now?" "Well, I think I might as well buy you a ring." She just said "That's okay". That was as close as I think I ever came to verbally proposing to her. She never ask anything more about the ring and I assumed she knew what I was talking about. But I have wondered ever since, because we went shopping the next day, in Santa Rosa, in a large department store and when we eventually wound up in the Jewelry Department and when the Sales Lady asked if she could help us. I said "I want to see the Engagement Rings". Kate did a double take at me with a look of surprise on her face. She did go ahead and pick out the set that she wanted, in white gold, and that the engagement ring and wedding ring interlocked when both were put on. She knew her ring size and when I put it on her finger it fit and she never took it off. So I guess that meant she accepted. I figured that also meant that I had to pay for it. She insisted that we get me a white gold wedding band for later use. I think that I was still floating. We returned home and really for the first time talked about the actual getting married. We had talked around it but I still don't remember ever talking about the actual getting married part. I think it was understood between us that we were going to be together, for sure for me. We were going to be together and that meant getting married. And for her too, but it was never actually stated. With talking about it she said this was very fast, because I told her we needed to get married right away, as I was going overseas before long. The Army authorized me one wife and she was it. If we didn't get married she was going to have to ride in my duffel bag, because she was going with me, one way or another. She was concerned that it might not work out, so I told her we would give it a trial, say 50 years, and if it didn't work we would call it quits and go our separate ways. She started laughing and said under those conditions she accepted and would marry me right away. I never intended to let her go after 50 years or for ever. This was on either Wednesday, the 8th, or Thursday, the 9th. We would go to the Mojave Desert on Friday night, we had already planned the trip to ride in the desert. We would go to Las Vegas, Nevada on Saturday night and get married. She didn't bring an ID, and couldn't prove who she was, so we couldn't get married. I did tease her about they didn't think she was old enough. But the license guy said "I don't care how old she is, but I don't know who she is". We had a wedding cake and we had a small party. We did everything but actually get married. We rode motorcycles on Sunday and went home to Northern California on Sunday night, we went to work on Monday, July 13th, and after work went to Reno, Nevada and got married there in the Chapel of Promise, not the Chapel of the Pines like I said in the Memorial that I wrote for the Sandoval Sun, her family's newspaper. The Chapel of the Pines must have been another wedding, and yes I'm kidding. I only tried to get married 3 times and none of them were at the Chapel of the Pines. All 3 were to the same beautiful girl, I liked practicing, especially with her. Her roommate Julie Broadwell and Frank McCoy, a friend of mine that I worked with, went with us. Rocky had to work and couldn't go. We returned home and both of us went to work the next day. My orders were cut, dated, on Thursday, July 16th, and we were going to Ethiopia in August. I had still not met any of her family, and she would not let me go with her to tell Mom and Dad that she or we had gotten married. She went to see them and during the conversation casually mentioned that "Oh yeah, I got married on Monday". None of the parties to this conversation has ever told me of the rest of the conversation. But it must have been okay, as we went to their home for dinner and they didn't throw me out of their home. I met her siblings for the first time. This was when I met 3 year old Julie, it is mentioned elsewhere. We were getting ready to leave and still getting to know each other better. A couple of times we took Julie with us when we were running errands. She and I both enjoyed having her with us and I was thinking she should just go with us to Ethiopia. Before we left I told Kate that we should just go kidnap Julie and take her with us. Kate said that Mom would not like that and we had better not do it. I think she was afraid that I was serious about this and of course I was serious about wanting to, but with no intentions of doing it. We had them over for dinner, Dad and Mom with the kids, Julie, Lisa, Paul, and Sue. Margie and Tom Reese came with there new baby boy, Tom or Tommy. Grandma Eileen, Dad's mother, also came with Dad and Mom. It was a very informal dinner and we got acquainted better, we were leaving in just a few days..

In very short order we were closing out our affairs and saying goodbye to family and friends. We traveled to Kansas and stayed with my Mom and Dad for a few days before going on to New York City.

Chapter 10:

Memories of Kate

When we first met I was still racing motorcycles in California, I had been working for a Yamaha dealer, part time, in the Sonoma, Ca. area, he had 2 shops 1 in Sonoma, and the other one (?), (my mind is blank) his name was Park(s). I had gotten a factory 125cc Yamaha motocross racer, only 2000 were made, in 1969 and then a 250cc Yamaha motocross racer, again only 2000 made, in 1970, these was the first years that both of them had been offered to the public. These were special machines and really ran good. When Kate and I started going together I was going to the Mojave Desert about once a month to ride. Stayed with my brother Tom on Edwards Air Force Base. Kate started riding right away and rode with us in the desert. We went down there several times before we were married, had actually planned on getting married when we went down there on July 11, 1970, in Las Vegas, Nev. She didn't bring an ID so we couldn't, she couldn't prove who she was. The first time we went down I believe she stayed in the bedroom with Tom daughters. The next time she was suppose to, but after everyone had gone to bed she showed up at the couch, where I was trying to sleep, and wanted to know if there was enough room for her. I always thought that was one of those "That's a dumb question". Of course there was, even if it was narrow. And yes Mom we both slept there, as in 2 people in the same place but not as sleeping together. I had to hold on to her real tight, so she wouldn't fall off, she got the outside. I must have been doing a pretty good job as she ask if I would give her a little slack so she could breath, as least part of the time, which I did but still held on to her reasonably tight, we had to stay very close together to be able to fit on that couch. Maybe that's why for the rest of her life I had to be touching her when I slept, if she was there. She told me that if I went to bed and went to sleep before she got in bed, I would usually have a hand on her side of the bed or when she got into bed I would reach a hand over to touch her, while I was still asleep, if she moved it back over, then in a little bit it would be back touching her. I wasn't to selective where this hand went, face, head, arm, body, where ever it landed. I know that this went on for at least the first 20 years we were married, actually this went on for always. When we came home from KC, when she was sick, I would set in the rocking chair by her bed and keep a hand touching her all the time. And when I couldn't sleep in the chair I would lay on the floor beside her bed and stick my hand up through the rail and touch her, if she moved or spoke or anything, I would wake up and check on her or do what ever she needed. We have over the years slept in some strange places and configurations, but as long as she was there it was okay and it worked.

Probably the most upset I ever got with her was when we went riding in the desert on one of the trips to Tom's, before we were married. I let her have my 250 and I rode the 125, this in itself was quite a concession because that 250 was my pride and joy and she was about the only one I let ride it, with me riding something else. This didn't happen with anyone else. We had gone out riding, Tom, Mitch Mitchell, Kate and I. We had got out about 6 miles from the house, as I remember, and I was so worried about her. I should have been paying more attention to myself, she was doing fine. I fouled the spark plug, on the 125, you had to keep the motor running at a higher rpm or it would do this. I knew it, but just didn't pay close enough attention to what I was doing. She could be a distracting influence on me too. So when it fouled out and the motor quit, I was riding last in line and the others just kept going. Tom or Mitch was up in front, the other one second and then Kate. No one ever looked back and they just kept going and completed the circuit and wound up back at the house before they missed me. I stopped and tried to get the bike going but no luck, and the tools and extra plug were on my 250, which was now else where. I waited for awhile then decided to follow the trail, because they would surely be coming back before long. They fooled me. After about a mile and a half and since we were going in a circular direction, to the house, I gave up on them coming back and cut across country, in a straight line, for the house. Now is was getting warm and I had on full leather, pants, jacket, boots, gloves, and helmet. I was starting to sweat pretty good. I was over half way back, from the trail we had been on, when I spotted them coming back looking for me. They were strung out and covering a wider area to have a better chance of seeing me, because it was now obvious that something had happened to me. I quit walking and waited. Kate was the closest to me and just knew she was going to rescue me. Wrong again, she rode by me and never saw me. I didn't realize until she was a breast of me that she didn't see me, and rode right on by. I tried yelling but she didn't hear me either. I watched as they rode on out of sight. I wasn't going after them. I knew I couldn't catch them, so I turned and went on to the house. I got something to drink when I got there and set down out front to wait for them, they finally came in and wandered where I had been, "Oh right here, setting in the shade". I told them they had ridden right by me and I didn't realize that they didn't see me until they were completely by me. I told Kate that she did it because she just wanted me to have to walk home. She didn't think so and was a little upset with me for saying that. She learned later to not get upset when I started teasing her, but she hadn't reached that point yet. So she got upset and I got upset, because she was upset and that I had caused it by trying to tease her. It didn't last long and we were soon back on better terms and she rode behind me back out to get the 125. When riding behind me I always told her she had to put her arms around me and hang on tight. Now she has done all kinds of things while riding and didn't hang on tight, but if her hands weren't otherwise occupied she needed to be hanging on tight. I would try to tell you that this was a safety factor, but probably wouldn't expect anyone to believe it. I changed the spark plug and we rode some more and came back home. I didn't worry so much about her and paid more attention to what I was doing and didn't foul anymore spark plugs.

Tom's 4 kids were always trying to give me a hard time and then Kate, because of her association with me, fell into line to receive some of it, too. Like in the almost wedding pictures they were trying to tease us, mostly her because it didn't do much good on me, and she was easier. On one of these trips, maybe the same one because it was still the same 4 riders as I remember it. They had been giving me, or all of us, a hard time about actually catching the jack rabbits that we were catching, then letting them go. They didn't believe that we were actually catching, or catching as many as we said, and so we started bringing them the tails, they are attached by cartilage, and they pop right off. When the rabbits would go in a hole you could take a short, forked branch off the brush, trim it so you had a Y on the end with the legs about 3 inches long, and stick in down into the hole. When you touched the rabbit's skin, you would twist or turn the branch and this would roll up in the rabbits skin and you could pull them out of the hole. This didn't hurt them and then we would let them go. You could do the same thing with a piece of barbed wire by bending the end into a Y and then use it the same way. But then they decided we were trying to fool them some way and still wouldn't believe us. They were giving me a bad time about this and so I told them I would just load them up in the pickup and park it out on one of the hills and they could just watch. Everyone agreed that this was okay, to do, so I loaded my bike, in the back, and the kids in front with me, and we headed out to the desert. We had decided to go to the area near the hospital as there were usually more rabbits in this area and the kids would be able to see more action, in a closer area. The rabbits were more condensed in this area because the hospital put out leftover food for them to eat. The others rode their bikes out and I drove the pickup with the kids and my bike. On the way out we continued with our discussion about catching rabbits, they were not about to let up on me. I told them that as soon as I kicked up a rabbit close to the pickup I would run him right to the pickup and I would actually jump over the pickup bed. I wanted them to dive on to the floor when they saw me getting close. Right, they didn't thing so. OK but you better get down on that floor so they didn't get hit when I went over them. We got to the hill and I parked the pickup to the best advantage that I could and then unloaded my bike and went to find the others. The kids got to see some action in the distance but finally we jumped a rabbit in the area of the pickup and as luck would have it the rabbit ran right for the pickup, and I mean right at it, you would think the rabbit had read the script. We were getting close to the pickup and headed right for the bed and the kids. The look on their faces was priceless, when we got close, they dove for the floor, an I don't remember if the rabbit went under the pickup or behind it, but I went behind it and looked in to the bed as I went by and all 4 kids were face down with their hands and arms over their heads. I started laughing, this was to good to be true, but he who laughs last, laughs best. I went on after the rabbit and over a small hump we went, following a trail. We went over the top and I don't remember if I left the ground or not but there in front of me in the trail was a cone of rock about 15-16 inches tall, the path actually went around it to the right. I tried to go to the left, the rabbit went to the right. I was probably running about 50 mph and when I went to the left I missed the rock with my front tire but hit the right front corner of the motor. I almost made it, that counts in horseshoes and hand grenades. This motor had an oil pump there with a cover on the case. I had eliminated the oil pump and hand mixed my gas and oil, but the cover was still there and I hit the rock with this cover. It then slid back along the side of the motor and frame. It put me side ways and I kept the power on and was trying to bring the bike back, in what was about the same thing as a full lock power slide. I was using power and body English to try and bring it back up, the rear tire was unable to grab traction and was digging a hole about 8 inches deep and about 28 to 30 inches wide and also pushing sand in front of the tire sidewall. I'm not sure how far we went like this but the rear tire finally pushed enough sand up that it flipped me sideways, to the left. I went down hard, on my left side, I also hit the end of the handle bar in coming off the bike near the point of the hip. The bike went ahead and rolled sideways and flipped end over end once or twice. I hit so hard that it pretty well knocked the wind out of me, and was having trouble drawing a full breath. Tom got there first and was wanting to help me, and I told him "Don't touch me, I'll be OK, go check on my bike". I wanted to proceed at my own pace. I was able to get to my feet and go look at my bike. Tom had picked it up, the oil pump cover was broken, the right foot peg was smashed and smeared back along the frame, the gear shift lever bent back and around behind the motor. The front forks were turned in the triple clamp, but could be straightened, don't remember about the handle bars. All fixable, this was good anyway. I had hit on my left side, most of the blow on the point of my pelvis, it was very sore, bruised for sure, hopefully not broken. It did hurt pretty good. I was already purple from the point of the hip, about 4 to 5 inches wide, to my belly button, about 3 inches wide, and from the point of the hip to my spine, about 3 to 4 inches wide. We decided we were already near the hospital so I might as well go to the Emergency Room. They would load my bike and go home and I would ride Tom's bike and go to the Emergency Room. Kate didn't say to much, she did kiss me before I went to the hospital and said she was glad I wasn't hurt. I was tempted to ask if we were talking about the same thing. But I didn't. I had my military ID with me so I was off to the ER. They x-rayed me and examined me and said I was bruised and not broken, so I had a very stiff ride on a motorcycle back to Tom's house. We lounged around for awhile and then got ready to head back to Northern Calif. I soon found out that I wasn't going to be sitting in the seat and driving. It worked out that I could sit on the floor across in front of the seat, Mitch would drive and Kate would set on the right side. Her right leg was my back rest, and her left leg was over me, I put my head kind of in her lap or on top of her thighs and could put my right arm over her left leg, I was comfortable. She said that if she didn't know better she would say that I had done this on purpose, just so I could ride home like that. She did smile. I said if I had only thought of if before. It was better than the couch, if only it didn't hurt so bad when I breathed. She did tease me all the way home and I would just smile and make my head more comfortable. We finally got home and I was pretty stiff and sore but it was good to be home, and no, I'm not going to tell you where or how I slept for the rest of the night. Sometimes the imagination is simply better and some things left untold. And if you really want to know, then don't ask. Actually I don't remember but I can tell you where I wasn't.

When we first started going out, I still had my 64 Chevy Impala Super Sport 2 door hard top. I really liked that car, it was probably the most comfortable riding car I have ever had, super large leather covered bucket seats in the front, you could almost get lost in those seats. The interior was leather and the back seat was very spacious also, of course I don't think I ever rode back there, but I guess I may have set back there some time or other. The only thing that I learned to dislike about this car was the center console with the floor shift, it never bothered me until we started going together. She would sit in the bucket seat and that put her way over there on the other side of the car. And I preferred that she set a lot closer than that. One time for some reason, I don't remember if someone else was with us or what, but she set in the drivers seat with me and while this was a little tight it was much preferable to the other way. I'm not sure if she would have agreed with that or not, but I thought so. I was always wanting to be holding her hand and sitting close enough to be touching her, sometimes this was okay with her and sometimes not. Then when we did get married she was the other way, she wanted to be always holding hands, setting close together, and be touching somewhere. More than she had been before. It was pretty rough but I could tough it out and do it, actually it was pretty easy for me to endure all of this affection and displays of affection. I should have been making those quarters in those days, wow what a lot of money I would have been making. (Explained in a later chapter).

Chapter11:

More of Kate from Ethiopia

W e got married and went to Asmara, Ethiopia, this turned in to quite a honeymoon for us, I guess now that the honeymoon actually lasted at least 2 years. We spent a little time in California and then a little in Kansas, with my Mom and Dad, and then flew to New York City. We spent a full day and 2 nights there, then part of another day. Then flew to Germany, just spent a couple of hours there. Next was Athens, Greece where we spend most of a day sight seeing, we got to go to the Acropolis. This was truly an amazing viewing of history. We were with some kind of a tour group and got to visit a lot of places, they were all interesting. I would like to say here that while I did enjoy seeing these things, I can honestly say that being with her was more important to me than the sight seeing and playing tourist. Although she was enjoying the sight seeing, I was enjoying being with her. It gave me great satisfaction to be able to share this together. We spent the night at a really nice hotel and went on to Rome, Italy the next day. We spent the rest of the day there and a night also. In trying to put this in to perspective, you would need to understand that I was quiet, shy, private, and normally not outwardly a very expressive person. And here I was sharing everything with someone whom I had fallen completely in love with, and as I have stated before I could never get enough of her in any way. There were so many ways that I did enjoy her. Going from being somewhat of a loner, yes I did things with other people but if I wanted to do something, I did it by myself. When there was no one else to do it with. This was being 2 as in 1, not sure that this makes sense, know what I mean but not sure if am able to convey it to you. This meant that I did not ever have to be alone again, even when we were apart. She was always there, and was with me to do things with, even when it was something that she wouldn't have done otherwise. She now did because I wanted to, she was a part of me. Such a new experience for me, as I'm sure it is for many when they first meet and marry someone like this. It was like opening and reading a new book, with all of the new and fascinating things that were contained within. What a way to get to know someone, everything was new and different for both of us and we were able to enjoy these things and each other. I would wake up at night and just lay and watch her sleep, and marvel at the fact that she was there with me and was mine to have and to hold. Not that I owned her, because I didn't think like that, but we were together because we wanted to be. I loved her and was rightfully proud of her in who and what she was. And for this time period no friends, family, work, or anything to interfere or interrupt us. Maybe this is what honeymoons are suppose to be, I don't know and hadn't really thought about it this way before. It was just being with Kate, on our way to a new and different life for both of us. I knew that shortly after we met for the first time that this was what I wanted and that I wanted her, in all ways. I was a different person then and would never have said anything like this to anyone, except her. As we came to know each other, I could always share anything with her and did. It was during this time that I first became aware that she was possessive and jealous of me. This was somewhat hard for me to understand, because I was so completely engrossed with her that while I could see other people, I guess to read other women, there was no one else but her, even open for consideration. As far as possessive goes that was fine with me because I was hers for whatever she wanted that to mean. And I think she knew this, I told her often enough, and appreciated it for what it was. And I have become aware, at this late date, that she didn't really share me with others in most any way. And I think that for a long time I thought that to love someone else, in most any capacity, would take away from my love for her, and it took a long time for me to realize that nothing could take away from my love for her. When the kids came along they did not fit into this, because I guess it was okay, because they were a part of her so I could love them and not be taking away from my love for her. Because it was long after the kids came along before I came to this realization about my love for her. And I think that because of this, I didn't need anyone else, but her, and for a long time did not let anyone else in because of it. Because of this feeling I think now that this is why I am having such a hard time of dealing with her loss. Because in times past, no matter what the situation, I always turned to her for everything that I needed and wanted. And when in the normal course of events, in life, you have trials and the loss of friends and family, I always turned to her and needed no one else. In this time of my greatest loss possible she was not there and I am/was completely lost in dealing with this.

As I have stated else where, I have been in some degree of pain for a long time, and in what I have seen in relation to people using or actually misusing drugs, I do not like to take pain killers or other drugs, for that matter. As you get older I guess you accept this, taking of drugs, more readily. When I first came home from Viet Nam I was given loads of pain pills, that seems to be the Military answer for things, but I usually didn't take them until I would be hurting so bad I couldn't sleep or it got bad enough that I would take one just to gain some relief. I did not take them on a regular basis. After we were married I usually had pain pills around but didn't take them very often. When I would get to hurting Kate would set with me, or lay down with me, or hold me and this was so much better in dealing with the pain. She could actually hold me and make the pain lessen and I would be able to go to sleep, maybe this was her prayers or maybe it was her love, but it worked. My left knee would get to hurting and she would try to do anything to make it better, and a lot of time anything you did made it hurt worse or hurt more. After several attempts she learned how to put her leg over my left knee and hold it there, without making it hurt worse, and in doing this would actually make it better, with her leg over mine and her arms around me I could go to sleep and she would extract herself with out waking me up, usually, but sometimes she would continue to lay against me because she knew that when I became aware that she was not there, I would in my sleep, starting searching and reaching for her and wake myself up. I guess this could be called having the best of 2 worlds, pain relief and her with her love right there.

We went on to Ethiopia, and checked in to the Nyala Hotel where we lived for, three months or more before we finally got a house off base in Asmara. We moved in to our new house, number two, and started making our home. Along with our house we were furnished a watch dog by our landlord. Now this dog had been on a chain all its life and didn't like people. When we first moved in the landlady had to come feed it or we would have to put its food down and use a broom or something long to push the food close enough for the dog to be able to eat. After we got to know the dog and could actually feed it without fear of bodily harm, it bothered us that this dog had been chained up all its life. So, first me and then Kate made friends with the dog and then turned it loose, off the chain, so it had the run of our compound and up the stairs and on the roof of the house. This dog was so happy it didn't t know whether to lick our hands, jump up and down, or just run around. This went on for days but the dog finally settled into life off the chain. She would not let anyone in, unless we let them in, through our locked gates. She turned in to quite a companion for Kate while I was working and I didn't t worry quite as much about being gone.

While in Asmara we did a lot things, some new for me and some not, I think most everything was new for her. She set up and made a home for us, and I think this was somewhat new for her, but as with most things she did, she handled this with an ease and manner that was a marvel to me. Maybe it was because to me whatever she did was pretty much right. She still rode motorcycles, played softball, went swimming, got into ceramics , and did some volunteer work. And took care of me, that was almost a full time job. I have a number of things that I want to tell about from this time period so will start with the telling of the local wedding that we went to, it was mentioned in the Sandoval Sun but in a shortened version. I will try to recount it here in all the details that I can remember.

In the course of my work, I worked in Special Services, I had working for me 4 local men who did maintenance work and also mechanical work on vehicles. One of these men not only worked for me but became a friend, his name was Waldu. I won't even attempt to spell his last name. And as friends do I would buy him, and the others, lunch on occasion, or get soft drinks or something to drink on breaks at and from work. They would bring me samples of local foods to try. I was always interested in the local food, customs, and the people. Now the local native food was spicy, as in Spanish and Mexican type food, only more so. As a rule this food was to hot, spice wise, for me, but I would still sample it, much to their amusement. I would take some of these samples home to Kate and of course she would eat it and enjoy telling me that "it wasn't to hot". She was always getting even with me for my teasing and kidding her. Of course I didn't do this very often. I limited myself to 20 or 25 per day, but not required on a per day basis. When Waldu was telling me of an upcoming wedding in his village, his father was an elder in the village. I started asking questions about the whole wedding process and what all was involved. He took great pains in trying to answer my questions and inform me of everything that would take place and be done concerning this event. The wedding actually lasts for 8 days, Sunday through Sunday inclusive. And in this case 2 brothers, from his village, were marrying 2 sisters, from another village. In talking about this and the overall of the wedding, I got the idea that if they had light, as in electrical lights, they could have a much more enjoyable wedding. That would interpret to party, because the wedding was an 8 day long party for the people. Everyone seems to have to have an excuse to party and have a good time. I had the means to get an Army generator to supply the power for the electric lights, for the festivities. I'm sure that this raised his status in the village, and I was happy to do it. I got the generator and picked up gas for it, on base, without the local taxes, took it out to the village, about 8 miles from town and helped him get it situated and set up. Running wires to the community tent, this was like a circus tent that was used for village functions or ceremonies. They wanted me to attend any and all of the wedding functions, I guess this meant the ceremony or the partying, not sure that I was or would be welcome at anything else. I also took them additional gas at least once during the week. And it was completely understood that any place I went, Kate went with me, or I didn't go. In telling Kate about this she wasn't sure about participating in this big event. I could understand her concerns, but not for me, of course. I had done some checking and asking about this type event from local sources and had something of an idea about it. When the second Sunday rolled around and we still had not been to any of the events, a group from the village showed up at our house in the late afternoon and informed us we were going to the wedding. Now a number of the village members knew me and Kate had met some of them. I believe that they did view her as different from the other American women that they had come into contact with. She was always polite, friendly, and courteous of all of these people, and if she wasn't respected for herself, which she was, she was respected because she was my wife, which she also was. While not bragging, I was liked and respected by most, if not all, of these people. I brought light to the party and this made it a lot easier to party all night. We all have our means to fame. I was also know as Number 7, all over the area, from my motorcycle racing exploits. I was the highest standing rider most of the time we were there, and I had the rights to the number one plate, for 2 years, but never displayed it on my bike for racing. My numbers were 7 and 87, the 87 in honor of Mark Brelsford, of California, of motorcycle racing fame, later he was also number 7. Anyway, Kate was wearing blue jeans, a red shirt, had curlers in her hair with a red bandanna over them, and had sandals on, she wanted to change clothes but they said no, she looked OK. She looked at me, for support, and I said that "you look good to me", as always. Now I was always helpful and in this case very truthful, so she reluctantly said "OK". We headed for the village. We took our VW Bus, and we loaded Waldu's bike and he rode with us, the others rode their bikes back..

We got there and were taken into the big tent and they had seats for us, almost, if not actually on the dance floor. That we drew a lot of attention would be an understatement. We were seated and I was presented with a 'cold' Budweiser beer, which they knew that I drank, if I drank anything. Kate declined anything, her wishes were respected and no one tried to push anything on her, she said nothing and nothing was it, for the rest of the night. She might of have taken a sip of my beer, I don't remember, which she did once in awhile.

After I had drank most of this beer it hit me, where did this 'cold' beer come from, there were no means in the village to have cold beer. I was almost finished and another one was placed in front of me, hmmm, where were they coming from. Now we were enjoying the people, dancing, and explanations about things from people who were most happy to tell us of the customs, people, and happenings. She still wasn't overly happy with her attire, for a wedding, and I was on occasion made known of this. Her elbow was the most remembered reminder, it was also very pointed. If I happened to meet with her elbow, she would look at me and smile and I did smile back. About half way through the second beer I got Waldu's attention and he came over and I asked him "where the beer was coming from?" He said "why, is there a problem?" "No, but where is it coming from?" His reply was "Well, all the small boys are lined up all the way to town, and when we think its time to order another beer, we give enough money to the first boy and he runs to the second boy and they relay the money all the way to town, the last boy, in line, goes into the store and buys the beer and runs back and the relay process is repeated back to the village". Now you want to talk about feeling bad and embarrassed. I was. Wow. I said "No more beer". He said "I would have to drink one more because it was already on the way". "OK, but no more." They were having to pay a premium for this beer on the local market, not to mention all the trouble to relay it out to the village. Must be because of my local racing fame. I really felt bad about this. I think Kate rather enjoyed my discomfort, remember the curlers. The village people were drinking 2 local drinks, the first was Suwa, not sure of the spelling, but that is the way it sounds. It was a rice based drink and they called it beer, this looked like muddy coffee with a little milk in it. The second one was Swis and it was a honey based liquor that they considered very potent and they didn't drink much of it at a time, it looked like watered down orange pop. I got the third beer and started drinking it. I telling them we needed to be getting home, old married folks and stuff like that,. "No way, you haven't eaten yet". Well we looked at each other, hmmm what do you do, of course you eat. We were taken to a house, also lighted, to eat with the wedding party, 2 grooms, 2 brides, 2 fathers, 2 village chiefs, and of course us. The brides were supposed to be to embarrassed to eat, had to keep their eyes down cast and not meet anyone's eyes, with their hands folded in their laps. They did set there and giggle with each other all night long, but no one blamed them. We were seated at the table, and Waldu informed us we were the Guests of Honor, for the wedding. Oh Boy, and I thought I was in trouble before. She was not happy with me, for not telling her and not letting her change clothes. This was not her idea of the proper attire for a wedding and a "Guest of Honor ???" I had no idea about what was going on, but that didn't matter. Shortly the food was served, good thing I still had my beer. The food arrived on a large platter, about 4 foot in diameter. There would be a layer of local bread, this was whole wheat bread and looked like a sponge, very porous, about 5/16 of an inch thick, it was good eating. Then there would be a layer of food on top of it, beef, pork, chicken, eggs, potatoes, yams, onions, and so on. I'm not sure of what all the different layers were, that were on the platter. Some of them would be combinations of different foods and maybe I didn't want to know about some of them. Now we had switched places, right and left wise, and she now was on my left side and had new ribs to work on, with that elbow. Actually she got to switch elbows too. She was still not to happy, with the progression of events, she was now leaning over to me and whispering, in my ear, "why didn't you tell me", this without opening her teeth. I tried to tell her 'I didn't know either' but she was not listening to me and it did occur to me to be worried about my ear, but she wasn't opening her teeth. I could still smile, she could too, just not to much at me. The food on this platter was piled over 40 inches high, maybe more, for me to reach the top I would have had to stand up and maybe stretch. The way you would eat was to slide your fingers under the layer of bread and fold over and tear off what you wanted, or could handle, and then eat it with your fingers. Now my embarrassment was not over, knowing that I couldn't or didn't like to eat the hot/spicy food that they ate, they had taken portions of the different foods before seasoning them and placed them on a separate plate, in layers, just like the big one, only not seasoned so much, just for us. After bringing in the large platter, here came our little one, it was set down between us and Kate gently pushed it over in front of me. "I think this is yours." She did know how to get even. I did try to move it back between us, but no, she moved it back directly in front of me, and informed me that "she was eating off the large platter, along with EVERYONE else, who could handle regular food". Oh well, I did eat, all by myself off the small plate or platter. She did enjoy the food and my part was good and she said that the other platter was very good. I wouldn't know. We did eat our fill or all we wanted, whatever applied. We were then was able to thank our hosts and got to go home. She was in a better mood for the drive home and did ask about my ribs, I said they were very sore, and I would need special care and attention that night. She said she was sorry and kissed me, I had to be driving, and said she would take care of me, and did, when we got home.

In talking about this and telling people about it, in the following days, some people on post found out and contacted me about our little adventure into local culture. Asked me about the whole thing and thought it was something of an honor to be included in the wedding party. When I told them Kate really enjoyed it too, they asked if she was seated and ate at the wedding feast. Yes, she was and did. I was told that this was indeed a very high honor for us and especially for her, because women are not seated at the wedding feast and do not eat with the men, normally. This was the equivalent of a Head of State or a very high diplomat, who was a woman, to be seated and eat at that table. I really thought that this was appropriate, but then I was, maybe, just slightly, prejudiced in things concerning her. Really, I was somewhat humbled by this, but also highly honored for myself and especially for my beautiful wife, even if she was in curlers and a red bandanna, of course the red went with my eyes.

And whenever she asked about an outfit she would be wearing or trying on, I always liked her in it, and when asked if I really like it, I would reply that I liked what was in it, oh and the outfit was okay. I'm pretty sure that she knew this but she liked to hear it anyway and I liked saying it to her..

Chapter 12:

More from Ethiopia:

When we went to Ethiopia, I went there for important work. They wound up sending 2 of us for the same job, with the guy we were to replace still being there for 9 months. Sometimes I think the most important thing that I did was build motorcycle race tracks. I built 7 different tracks while I was there, and 2 softball fields. I was in Special Services, this included the gym, auto hobby shop, ceramics and crafts, ball fields and sports. I got the primary job of the auto hobby shop, we did get some vehicles to get ready and then maintain and rent out to the military personnel. We got 3 Dodge 2 ton trucks, 1 Ford 1 1/2 ton truck, 5 Dodge ½ ton pickups, 3 Ford Broncos, and 4 Jeeps. This did sometimes get involved when they broke down, in some distant place and we had to go fix and/or retrieve them. There are a couple of stories there. I continued to race motorcycles while we were there, also got to go on a search for a down aircraft, was in charge of the motorcycle license riding test, got a broken pelvis and back, and played, coached, and officiated sports events. Also got to do and go to a lot of things with my beautiful wife.

I was in charge of the Riding Test for Motorcycle Licenses. We had to take the applicants out and give them a road test. I tried to make all of these tests, but had several assistants that could fill in for me or assist me when I was not there. We had a class out one night and we were returning to Kagnew Station. With the class and testers riding single file on the highway through Asmara. I was leading the procession. I had a Land Rover turn across in front of me and stop. This was in the middle of the street, length wise, no driveway or intersection. I never did get a reason for him doing this. It was so close that I couldn't get stopped, so I put the bike sideways and laid it down on the asphalt, with the intent of getting off. The center stand caught and turned me around backwards and I was unable to push away from the bike and went into the Land Rover backwards, I took the front hub just below where the kidney is, on the right side. I bounced off the Land Rover and stayed on the road and the bike turned and went back into the Land Rover and wound up with the front wheel under the vehicle. I would have gotten up but enough of the people with me wanted me to stay down, that they convinced me to stay down. An ambulance came and took me to the hospital on Kagnew Station. Someone took my 650cc Yamaha motorcycle to the Auto Hobby Shop where my office was. They started checking me out when we got to the hospital. Something, I assume, in the blood test, convinced them that I had broken bones somewhere. My back was very badly bruised and very sore. I was taken to x-ray and the first time I moved myself over on to the x-ray table and they did a complete set of x-rays. When it was time to move back over onto the gurney, they said I couldn't move myself. They would have to pick me up and set me over. Well, OK. And they dropped me, it felt so good. "Oh, sorry." Right, next time, I'll move myself. They then wheeled me back to the exam room. Someone, I presume a doctor, looked at the x-rays and couldn't find anything. Back we went, this went on for a long time. After the third set they just left me on the gurney, in x-ray. That way they didn't have to wheel me back and forth. They eventually put a blanket over me, I did have my underwear on, I was getting cold, maybe shock (?). No one seemed concerned. They took 7 complete sets of x-rays, and they only dropped me twice more. When they dropped me on the 7th set of x-rays, going in, I told them, no more, if we have to do this again I will move myself or I don't move. On the 4th set, the head x-ray technician, Morris Brown, showed them the crack in my pelvis.. The doctor(?) or doctors(?), said he wasn't qualified to read the x-rays, so to do them again, and the doctor finally found it on the 7th set. You would think that the priority would be the patient, not egos or positions. My pelvis was cracked from the right hip socket across towards the left one but not all the way. They didn't catch my broken back until the x-rays were sent to Germany, standard procedure. The doctor(s) in Germany wanted to know what they had done about the broken back and they had to tell them nothing, that they had missed it. Really inspires confidence. I didn't know this until later. One of the doctors came in and talked to me and said that I should be put in a full body cast, but they would have to send me to Germany for that. My first question was whether Kate would be going with me? They didn't know, so I told them if she didn't go, I didn't go, they would check. He came back and said he didn't have an answer yet but we had an alternative. I could stay in Asmara, but would have to stay in the bed for 4 months. After several days, the doctor ask if I had had a bowl movement? "Well, yes", "How come its not on your chart?" "I'm suppose to tell someone when I go to the bathroom?" Doctor "Yes, you are not suppose to go to the bathroom." "OH". Doctor "What I mean is you are not to get out of bed to go to the bathroom, you are to call for a bedpan, you are not to put your feet over the side of the bed, period." "Ohhhh, okay." Doctor "I didn't say anything because I thought you knew". "Nope, I do now". After about 5-6 weeks the doctor came by and asked if I would like to go home for the weekend. Now that was for sure one of those "That's a dumb question". Go home and be with Kate, yep, that was dumb. I had to stay in bed and if I got up, no weight on my right leg, crutches or whatever to support my weight. Sure I was ready, so on Friday night Kate came with the VW Bus and took me home. Now I had to stay in bed and I 'really' had to have constant attention, the whole weekend. I even had all my meals in bed, if I remember correctly. I think I made it to the couch in the living room, once. When I returned to the hospital on Monday, the medics or aids were unhappy because they had to give me special attention, because I was still suppose to stay in bed all the time. And they had to carry me my meals from the cafeteria. They got together and discussed it with each other and then went to the doctor. He came and talked to me, the aids were unhappy because I could go home and spend the weekend with my wife but they still had to look after me and I had to stay in bed. I had stayed in bed all weekend at home. How much of the time was your wife there with you? A lot, I was suppose to stay in bed, and I did. What did you expect? That she would stay in the living room and kitchen, get real. Any way it was decided that I could return home and stay in bed for another month, no walking and no weight bearing on my right leg. OK, what a time I had at home with a full time nurse, who just happened to love me and I'm sure was more than overjoyed at having me there to take care of. And she did an outstanding job, in all areas. You may have heard the term, "being spoiled rotten", I'm sure I was, and I loved it and her.

One thing that happened when I was in the hospital, with my broken pelvis and back, really sticks in my mind. While in the hospital I was not suppose to get out of bed for anything. We were in an eight bed room. With 1,2,3,4 being on one side and 5,6,7,8 being on the other, beds 4 and 5 were across from each other. I was in bed 3, Jack was in bed 4, another guy was in bed 7 and I don't remember his name anymore. Now the guy in bed 7 was one of these people who has done everything, knows everything, has everything, and is better at everything than anyone else. And annoying, very annoying. He's the guy who flies across the United States on a commercial airliner and has slept with all the female attendants by the time they get across. Being unable to escape him, we had to endure him for over a week before I really got upset with him. He started talking about motorcycles and he had the fastest bike in the city. "OK, fastest at doing what?" I responded. "Anything you want to do". "Oh really, I guess that includes drag racing?" And he said "Yep I can out run any bike around here and already have". I came back with "Nope you haven't outrun mine yet". "Well I can do it." And I tried to set the hook "OK would you like to make a little bet?" His answer was "sure how much do you want to bet?" Well I just happened to have 600 or 700 dollars with me, not sure why Kate hadn't taken it home but there must have been a reason. I always carried money in my shirt pocket and had a shirt on with a pocket. So I pulled it out and said "I've got a thousand dollars here that says you can't beat my 360cc Yamaha dirt bike". Boy was he stuttering and stammering. So I said "What's the matter not enough to be worth your while?" I added "I can get whatever amount you want covered, just say how much you want to run for, because it will be covered" Well he hedged and never would agree to a bet and an actual race. It did shut him up for about a day, and then he was back at it. One of the Americans that worked in Special Services for or with me was Tom Hess, from Omaha, Neb. His wife Pat worked at the hospital, in some capacity. We were all friends. Kate and Pat played softball together and the four of us had gone out together. They had some kind of visiting hours rule so that there were times that Kate couldn't visit me. Pat worked at the hospital and could, when she had time and when she was free. She came and visited me a lot when Kate couldn't be there, nice to have company and friends. She was up and down the halls a lot doing her job. Now I would like to point out that Pat was very well developed and on the well muscled, athletic side, blonde and was really a very attractive woman. She had been in to see me and then was doing something as far as work went and went by and down the hall. This guy pops off, something about her looks or build and not exactly in a complimentary manner. I was looking at the ceiling and Jack says to him "Why don't you shut up, that's Ralph's wife, you know". I about fell out of bed and was having trouble keeping a straight face. I had no idea this was coming, and I just continued to stare at the ceiling. They argued back and forth about this for awhile and I continued to stare at the ceiling, thinking, all the while. Jack told him if he didn't think so, to just ask me. So he did, and I told him he was lucky I was confined to this bed or I'd come over there and kick his ....ah ... butt. Oh she's not either you wife, your wife is the cute dark haired girl that comes in all the time. "What, you don't think I know my own wife?" So all three of us kicked this around for about an hour. Time flies when you're having fun. Then he ask me again about Kate, I said "No, that's my girl friend, and don't you be opening your mouth to anyone about anything and messing anything up or when I get out of here I will find you and fix you good." Well this went on till Kate came in, and then stopped. I had her pull the curtain around my bed and told her what was going on. At first she wasn't exactly overjoyed with this, but she didn't care for this guy and his mouth, at all, either. We talked about it for awhile and she said "OK, I'll go along with it". Kate just continued like she had been doing, and about all we ever did in public, was, she would kiss me when she got there and then again when she left and hold hands and talk. Quite appropriate for a girl friend I thought. I think she got into this more than a little, once started, and Pat still didn't know anything about it. She still came around and we talked and joked around like always. But Jack and I never let up on this guy. After about 2 weeks, we had been telling him to ask Pat or ask Kate, and he wouldn't do it. So on this day Pat came by to see me and had her back to him and I said to her, "Pat do me a favor and tell (whatever his name was) that you're my wife, he doesn't believe me", she was looking at me very intently, trying to figure out what was going on, knowing me, she was sure something. She kind hunched her shoulders and tightened her muscles like she was mad or something, turned around, cocked her hip up, put her hand on her hip, and with a kind of sneer said "What's the matter, don't you like his taste in women" and stomped out. Beautiful, it couldn't have been better if she had practiced. This guy was all over himself trying to apologize to me and later her. Every time she went by or came by to see me. She just ignored him, no matter what he said, she just ignored him. If she looked at him, she just glared, and he got no sympathy, anywhere. A couple of days later she came by at noon, when she knew everyone else would be in the cafeteria. I finally got the chance to talk to Pat in private and she was cracking up. She said that the first day she hoped she got far enough down the hall when she started laughing, so he couldn't hear her. She told Tom and he thought it was hilarious also. This went on for a little over 3 weeks, total, and then he left the hospital. We never did let him off the hook. We all laughed about that for as long as we were there and when ever we remembered it. He never made anymore comments about women while we were still around him. Jack was still in the hospital when I got out, he had blood poisoning from the coral down on the Red Sea, it was rare and they were having trouble treating it, he may have been evacuated to Germany, eventually, not sure any more. This was not the Jack Contoleon that I rode motorcycles with.

When I got out and around, at the first race I worked the flags on my crutches and of course got my picture in the paper, and maybe on TV also. The price you pay for fame. I was known by almost everybody around, because of sports and motorcycles, and just because I was such a nice guy. I know, I know, you can quit laughing anytime. By the second race I was about to climb the wall. So in all my wisdom, I figured I could run the flat track race and not ever put my right foot down and put no weight on it, its nice to be always right. Kate protested and was against it but when she realized I was going to do it, she did support me in my efforts. I never took my right foot off the foot peg, and I won the race, of course. At the end I was racing with Tony Gage, of the Kawasaki team. I caught and edged him at the finish, by going inside of him coming into and out of the last turn. We were lapping a slower rider at the finish line and the rule on the track is you take one more lap after you get the checkered flag. He decided to go straight off the track. We were there and going into and around the first turn like we were suppose to. We were going very fast and he ran into me and trapped me between him and Tony. So we went down in a stack with me in the middle. I could do nothing but set there. I wasn't hurt but it scared some people, not me of course. didn't have time to be scared and by the time I got time, I knew I was fine. I just had to wait until they got the bike off of me and stood me up, still on the bike. I started it up and rode to the pits. The gas that leaked out of Tony's gas tank, of course didn't bother me either, when it was dripping on me. it did cross my mind that it was not a good situation but it came out okay and I didn't mention it to anyone, until now. Of course they had to be taping this for a television sports show and the news and sports. In knowing the TV crew I went and ask them to just leave my name out of things because I was not suppose to be racing yet. Sure they would do that, they would not mention my name. So I was watching the sports that night and they didn't mention my name. The race was won by the 'rider with no name', and the 'no name rider' was in a 3 bike pile up after the race ended, complete with video of the wreck. Thanks for not mentioning my name. I got more publicity with the no name rider thing then if they would have used my name. This made everyone look at the video, and there was number 7 in the middle of it, and everyone who knew anything about the motor-cycle racing in Asmara knew who number 7 was. I went in to see the doctor that week and he asked how it was going and I told him OK. I was using my crutches and trying to keep weight off my right leg. "That's good" he said, "anything else going on". "Nope". "OK, just be careful". When I was leaving he said "Try not to be in anymore wrecks and be careful on that bike". "OK, thanks".

When we got there in September, actually I think it was the end of August, of 1970. The first race was just after we had arrived (September 15, 1970) and I didn't have a bike or anything but my helmet and leathers. We went to the race and it was a hill climb. We already had our VW Bus, so we had transportation. All the proceeds, from this race, were going to charity. Some of the guys who worked for me were there, and were entered. Since it was one at a time against the clock, if you actually made it to the top, they offered me a couple of bikes to use. Bob Moorehead had a 250 Yamaha similar to what I had been riding, so I took him up on it. It cost you so much for each attempt, I watched for awhile and decide the best way was to just go up over a big rock, in the path of a straight on approach. A couple of guys had tried this early on but couldn't make it. So everyone one was trying to go around the rock and not making it to the top. It was late in the day before I tried and I went straight up and over the face of the rock, like I had planned. I only made one run and won it on my very first attempt. I was in the paper and on TV my very first race in the new place, a good start we thought.

We were very involved on the motorcycle scene while we were there. Kate served as the Treasurer in the club for 2 terms. I was the Competition Chairman for 2 terms. I didn't want any other position, I helped direct the direction of the competition in the club.

As an example of my nature to respond to a challenge, I offer this episode. A friend of ours was Ed Johnson, U.S. Navy. We were friends with him and his wife and 2 kids. He had a 600cc BMW touring road bike. He trail rode this bike along with riding it to work. He had some friends, in the Navy, younger unmarried guys, that were lieutenants or JG's. They went trail riding with Ed. They were giving him a bad time about his choice of bikes, 1 of them rode a 250cc Yamaha, 1 a 250cc Suzuki, and 1 a 250cc Kawasaki, all trail bikes. Then in the process challenged him to a race, on the club race track, he said "No". If they just wanted to race against his bike, he had someone who would ride it for him. They said "Sure, because they didn't have anything against him personally". He came to me with the challenge and wanted a special grudge race at the next regular race. Okay, I think I can handle the race part of it. He also wanted me to ride his bike. I started thinking, always dangerous, if I could reduce the top end weight thus the overall weight, maybe. I told Ed lets take a ride out to the track. We went to the track and I got on his bike and started getting the feel for it. This was a BMW road bike, the engine cylinders are 180 degrees apposed, making the overall width of the bike wider than other bikes. It had a 6 ½ gallon gas tank, a large padded comfortable seat, flared road fenders, factory saddle bags, and street tires. I liked the feel of the bike and the low end torque power. If I could do something about the weight and high center of balance, maybe it could be made competitive, and not just against the navy juveniles. We talked about it and we decided it was a go, he would bring the bike to our house and I would start working on it. I took off the seat and gas tank, the front fender and the back part of the rear fender, the back fender was mounted in 2 pieces, so that helped. Nothing could be done about the width of the engine, so I would live with that. In talking with Kate about this project, I would replace the gas tank with one of our Yamaha tanks, but what about the seat. We came up with the idea of a pillow wrapped up in a laundry bag, shaped and then taped, then taped into place on the frame. A very innovative idea and approach, we thought. I took the mirrors and accessories off and anything else that we could do without and wasn't needed. The headlight had to stay because the wiring all went through it, the sealed beam of course came out. We worked on this for several evenings. Our house had double exterior doors on every room except the bedroom. We had one room set up for working on bikes. We wheeled the BMW into this room and I did the necessary work inside the house. By the weekend I was ready to try it out. Early on Saturday morning I took it out to the track and tried it out. The reduction in weight and lowering of the center a gravity did wonders for the performance and handling of the bike. After practicing some, I took some laps and Ed caught some of my lap times. With the flying start, my lap times were up there with the track records, as far as recorded times go. We quit early so as not to spoil our surprise, no one else was around. The Navy boys showed up later and did some practicing and left saying they would see us tomorrow. We pushed the grudge race to the public, via advertising and we were ready on Sunday afternoon. The Navy boys never showed, I never did get an excuse and if Ed did he never shared it with us. We were faced with all the work for nothing, but the open class was there, soooo, we entered the open class. We did get some chuckles and outright laughs but that's okay, we came to race and give it our best shot. We were running a scramble type race this day with motocross scoring. This means that it is a dirt track with mostly a hard packed dirt surface, right and left turns, moderate jumps, a boundary enclosed track, 3 races are run and used to determine the winner. On the start of the first race I was apprehensive. I have forgotten to mention the clutch on the BMW, it was a dry type clutch, like on a car. This being different than the wet clutch that is used on the Japanese bikes that most were riding. I was not sure of how this would effect the start. It should not matter but it was different than what I was used to, more solid and positive, I think. Maybe less forgiving than the wet type clutch I was used to. On the start line I was setting there rapping the engine and the torque would pull the bike over and I would let the throttle off and it would come back, this proved to be a big Psyche out for the other riders. I rapped the engine, for the start, and dropped the clutch rather than maybe slipping it like I would have on a wet clutch. I came off the line so hard and fast that I thought that I had maybe jumped the flag for the start, I looked back and no it was go. I had pulled a hole shot and was in the lead, so away I went and lead start to finish, one down. As it turned out I had dug a trench with the rear tire about 4 inched deep, 5 to 6 inches wide and about 6 feet long and then tapering off to nothing on the start. On the second race it wasn't quite as successful but I did take second. On the third race I didn't get the good start, but worked up through traffic and managed to win it and took the overall win. No one was chuckling or laughing any more. It was a display of what could be done when you put your mind to it and with the help of others, we were able to overcome supposed handicaps and obstacles to achieve a goal or success that others deemed unobtainable. It does help to start and maintain a frame of mind that you can do it. It also effects the mental game of your competition in later encounters. And I did win the 250 class that day also.

If you want it then try. This is something that Kate brought to and did for me. If I wanted or decided to try for something, she was there supporting me and doing whatever she could to help. Even when she maybe thought I was more that a little crazy. "You can do that" was a phrase often heard by me from her. She had that belief, if I wanted to try then I could do it. She was there supporting what ever idea I had come up with to try. She always told me she didn't worry when I was out late working for the Sheriff's Office or working in a blizzard or on a fire somewhere. Because she KNEW I would be home safe when we were finished with whatever we were doing. Even when I was a whole day late and I was unable to call. She knew God was watching out for me and would see that I got home safely to her. Sometimes this was a hard expectation to live up to. But with help, I always did.

I rebuilt a used 250, that I bought, into a 360. I lowered the motor and moved it back to change the point of balance. This motor, which I tore down and completely rebuilt, with a different clutch, was a high torque-low rpm motor and was completely usable but with extra horsepower. It was so manageable that Kate could and did ride it, this was her favorite bike, I think, I know. Of all the ones she rode she liked this one the best. This was the bike that I was willing to bet $1000.00 on in the proposed drag race mentioned before. I was willing and did take on all comers, at the races, with this bike. Especially the drag races, dirt track, for 1/8 of a mile. I out ran all bikes, any and all. The 500cc three cylinder Kawasaki street bikes had been the most competition for this bike before I lowered and moved the engine back, then it was no contest. I about had to quit running in the drags so others would enter and race, because no one wanted to take on this bike. Yes here in the states this would be different but at the time and place it was the ultimate available. This bike would go from 10 to 40 mph in 10 to 15 feet, it would give you whip lash if you were not prepared for it. If you didn't know what you were doing it could get you in a lot of trouble and hurt you. And I trusted it and her. When Kate rode it, she rode it to her ability and didn't try to do things she was not ready for.

I was riding it in a motocross race and won the first moto and took 2nd in the second one. On the third moto I was running second and had to only finish 6th or better to win overall. So I wasn't pushing first place very hard. I was right behind first place, Geo Flores from Guam, and as we crossed the finish line and we were given the white flag, for 1 more lap. We had a straight away, then a hard left, a short straight then a tight S curve, right left right, when we were going in to the S curve we caught and were lapping another rider, he panicked, I think, and when going into the left turn decide to pull off of the track and ran into Geo. Geo kept the power on and rode out of the wreck, this guy grabbed his front brake and hit the bank and flipped end over end. He was thrown over the handle bars and landed face down on the ground. The bike came straight down, front wheel first in the middle of his back. He and the bike bounced and did another complete flip and he landed face down again and the bike came down the same way in the middle of his back, again. He stayed on the ground this time and the bike bounced away. I was right there and put my bike down to get to him, my throttle stuck wide open and eventually blew my engine. I got to him and he was completely out. The ambulance got there and we got him on a back board, with a neck brace, and they transported him to the hospital. Some one picked up my bike, put it in neutral, and pushed it to the pits. We all made it back to the pits. They had stopped the race and it was backed up to the last lap finished and was over. So I did win first, but we had to wait for the ambulance to get back to continue. We had a 1/8 mile flat track race to run yet, but things kind of had a damper on them. We all agreed that we were going to go ahead and finish the day. I had the flat track race lined up and ready to go, starting positions were determined by a one lap, flying start, for time, everyone else was finished, so I went to get my bike and found out that I had blown my engine. The piston came a part from the ring grooves down and it twisted and bent the rod. I found this out when I tore it down. OK, I'll set this one out. John Kohler came up and offered me his 100cc Kawasaki, for the 360 class. Now this got a lot of laughs and remarks. Opinions were that I wouldn't have a chance. I wasn't going to do it, but with the offer of John's bike, and then the remarks about Johns bike. I thought it over, quickly, and with John's encouragement I decided to go for it. For my time trial I was third fastest qualifier, laughter had dried up along with the comments. The ambulance had returned, before we started the time trials, with no word on the rider. There were 4 or 5 classes by engine size. Number of entries in each class decided the number of heat races. In the 360cc class we had 2 heats, 20 to 24 bikes. We would run 6 lap heat races, the 2 winners went straight to the main, everyone else went to a semi main, 8 or 10 laps, starting positions by finishing places in the heat races. Then to the main, starting positions decided by where you finished in the semi, the main I think was 12 laps. Short and sweet. In the heat race I had the second slot from the pole in the first race. I asked for and got permission to move to the number 7 position, we started 6 abreast and in 2 rows, this way I would be, hopefully, out of the way of the bigger bikes. On the start I was left behind as expected, 12th into the first turn but I moved up steadily and finished 4th, this moved me into the number 5 position in the semi, as ours was the faster heat race. In the semi I again moved out to the number 7 position, was slow to the first turn, last again, but moved up to 2nd place and this got me the number 4 position in the main. In the main I moved to number 7 position, I was last into the first turn. I again moved up steadily and was running 2nd behind my Yamaha Team Partner, Dan Daniel, from Mt. Vernon, Mo. I took a position off his outside shoulder and anyone trying to pass would have go outside of me to get a round, no one did and he won, with me getting 2nd place. This was some what of an eye opener for most of us. I could go wide open on the throttle all around the track when others were slowing down for the turns, I kept going the same speed. Acceleration didn't come into it because I was going as fast as I could go. Although others did try, they just didn't have the ability to go around the turns at the higher speed. Another good day and memory except I lost maybe the best motor I ever had and I had built it. I did have a new 360cc factory racer coming, since I still worked for Yamaha I got first chance and a better price than the others did.

The rider from the wreck was okay except for a lot of bruises, nothing broke, and was let out of the hospital that same night and went home to the barracks.

Another time we had an airplane go down with 4 Americans on board and they couldn't find the plane. An all out search was on and they were using any and all means to find this plane. I had volunteered but was told no, the motorcycles were no good. Well later in the morning I heard that the local saddle club got permission to help. I went back to post headquarters and ask again and said that I could go any place a horse could go and then some and my bike didn't get tired. Well they reconsidered and said OK. I could take a radio and 5 other riders with me and we would try it, and if we worked out they would let me increase our numbers. We went and covered the areas, by grid, that they gave us, and were back asking for more. They got serious then and gave us rougher and better possible areas, and doubled the number of bikes to me and 10. We found several planes, old crashes, that they already knew about but this let them know we were doing the job. We found one plane they didn't know about but there was nothing in it, either. All information about this plane was turned in, location, numbers, description, and etc., I never heard anything further on it. One place that we went to, we went up the face of a mountain, it was rough but we were able to find a way to the top, the other side was worse and we all agreed that it would be very hard to get down. No one wanted to try but I had to try. I was going down, so I could look in the places we could not see, from the top. I went off the top and went down, mostly sideways sliding. One wash that I went into and was following, had a turn so tight that I had to ride up the side and the let the bike fall sideways and pull it down to make the turn. I eventually made it down covering the side of the mountain, the others rode the long way around, maybe 6 or 7 miles. We helped for 2 or 3 days and they finally found the plane, by air search, about 150 miles off course, all four were dead. There was some talk of smuggling something but never did hear anything more about any of it. We proved again that the motorcycles could make a valuable contribution, we just needed the chance.

We decided to go on a camping trip to Masawa, it was on the coast, on the Red Sea. It was something of a resort town and a lot of vacations were taken there. I think it was called or qualified as a resort town because it was there and there was nothing else available. We took a regular caravan with about 15 motorcycles hauled on a truck, I drove it. Kate brought our VW Bus and there were about 6 or 7 other cars that went along. Some motorcycles that were ridden down. We had to drop down about 8000 feet, on a tight winding road that was designed by an Italian woman. She did not have tractor-trailer rigs in mind when she designed it. It was better suited to tandem axle trucks. There were 6 or 7 wives along and maybe a couple of girls friends. Only 1 wife for me and no girl friends. We camped on the beach with our vehicles circled and each couple or single having there own sleeping area and a common cooking area. This was a family type outing, but as I remember none of us had kids. Or else we locked them up at home and went alone. I don't remember to much about the cooking part, I did eat regularly so somebody must have been doing something. The women were having a good time at the get together. Getting to know each other or getting to know each other better. Some knew the others before, some did not. The guys enjoyed it when they were at the camp. We did ride for part of each day in the desert. Kate did ride out for short rides a couple of times but didn't want to go to far or go with us, to chase whatever we happened to find. As I remember she was the only one of the women that did ride and so she didn't want to if the others didn't. We would have a bonfire in the evening and gather around for the socializing and then we would seek out our beds, out in the darkness away from the fire or fire area if the fire had burnt down. Some went to bed earlier that others and I think that we were some of the early to bed ones. The vehicles were parked in a circle and our sleeping area was on the sand outside of our VW Bus. I considered it quite romantic and can say that I enjoyed her and the setting and got no complains from Kate.

We had 11 serious riders and so when we went out we split in to 2 groups. We were looking for things to chase. We did chase Jackals and Gazelles. Camels don't work, and luckily we didn't find any lions, although they were reported to be in the area. I don't remember chasing anything else or seeing anything else that was of any size. We did kick out a lot of gazelles but they are so fast that they are gone before you could get up to speed, 2 jumps and they are going about 60 mph and would top out over 70 mph. The first day was a day of frustration as far as catching anything went. We saw a lot of country, some flat, some rolling hills and some were fairly sharp hills. And went from bare, as in nothing, to heavy brush and under growth and most everything had big thorns. There were some dry river beds also. At one time, apparently, the rivers ran water, in this desert and there was evidence of farming having taken place at some past time. Fields were still laid out and you could see the boundaries, but it seemed to have been a long time ago but it is hard to tell in the desert. There also was evidence of what appeared to be irrigation ditches, they had filled in very badly by blowing sand. Then we found some areas that seemed to indicate that they at one time were irrigated fields, they had barriers around the fields to hold the water in. In some places I could see patterns and in others I was unable to. It might have been just me but some seemed to have been destroyed by something or nature. We did find some fields (?) that had a 30 to 36 inch high dike around them, these were small, about 2 or 3 acres and there would be several together, never did decide what they were for, but they made good jumps for the bikes.

The second day we did better chasing things, we started getting closer to the gazelles before they blew us away. The jackals were at least kept in sight for awhile. Here the animals tried to run, dodge, hide, when they were fresh and then when they started wearing down they would try to out run you, and they were doing a pretty good job of it. In the Mojave Desert it was the opposite, they tried to out run you first and then run, dodge, hide when they started getting tired. We had a couple of crash and burns and lost a couple of bikes do to broken pieces. On this second afternoon Geo Flores hit something and went down. We got his bike back to camp, pulling and pushing with the other bikes, as I remember, interesting problem solved. I did take Geo into Masawa and as luck would have it there was a visiting doctor there. I helped the doctor put about 15 to 18 stitches in Geo's leg and then bandaged it up and I took him back to camp, he was done. Lets see who was left at this point, Ed Perry, Al Duff, Jack Contoleon, Morris Brown (?), Dicky Lynch , Hugh ...., ..., and me. I can see the faces, but must be getting old can't think of all the names. We went back out, Al Duff chose to watch from the hill tops and try to follow us and keep up as best he could, he could follow the dust. We kicked out several gazelles and then we got one up out on the wing and it ran to the middle. We would usually ride in a V with the fastest bikes in the middle, better chance of getting going and then keeping up. This time it was working like it was suppose to, as it came in, a new rider was there, momentarily at least, to keep it headed in the right direction. Then another rider would pick it up, and then this time I was there and up to a reasonably close speed to keeping up. I was able to keep it in sight and got up to top speed, 70 plus MPH. I was able to maintain this speed and it was slowing a little and I was catching up. We had already gone about 5 miles. I was riding a straight line and it was weaving and dodging so I was able to stay up for a change. I went through brush with thorns, bushes with thorns, weeds with thorns, I think there were thorns where there wasn't even plants. The only thing that I did, other than ride right through was to turn my head down so that the top of the helmet took some of the thorns. They penetrated my gloves, sometimes my sleeves, sometimes my heavy leather pants , if the big thorns hit 90 degrees to, then they penetrated the leather, this smarts, sooner or later. We went off into a dry river bed, it was about 10 feet down and I was going to say, 50 to 60 feet across, but think maybe it was farther than that because I was still going 60 to 70 mph. I broke out of the brush and there it was, so off the bank I went and landed just short of the other side, with my suspension compressed and a 10 foot bank to go up and over. I was close enough behind the gazelle that I saw how easily it jumped from the bank and landed about 3/4 of the way across and then leaped again and was up on the other side and disappearing into the brush I landed and then I was on the bank going up. I threw myself up between the handlebars as far as I could and broke over the bank came down and was into the brush after the gazelle. Wow really Wow. I'm not sure how I made it, but I did, and without time to think, I was still on the chase. After about another 3 miles we repeated this dry river crossing but was a little slower, but it was about the same as the first time. I didn't have time to think, just do, and I made this one also. I'm guessing that we had gone 12 to 15 miles by this time and the gazelle was tiring and decided to take me out on a large flat bowl that was bare of vegetation and a mile or more across, and was going to out run me. I don't think so, now. We made one circle around the bowl and the doe, I could now tell that it was a young female, was tiring and I was down on speed, maybe 45 to 50, and we went around again, almost in the same tracks. By now I was getting ready for it to stop, I didn't realize how tired she was but she went to jump a 1 ½ inch deep run off ditch and didn't make it. Drug her feet on the lip and went down, head over heels. I had my bike killed and the side stand down. I was off and had my hand on her neck and she just dropped back on the ground. I had approached her from the opposite side of her legs or her spine side, so she couldn't kick me, she just lay back and seemed to relax and I was petting her on her neck. She was hyper-ventilating so I held her mouth and blew into her nostrils to slow down her breathing, and it did. She was content to just lay there. The other guys had been catching up about the time that she went down and were there watching as I did this. Al Duff caught up and had a canteen of pink lemonade. I would pour some into my hand and let it run and drip off my fingers into her mouth, she was dry, it would hit her tongue and gums and be instantly absorbed. After we had given her some, she was starting to like this, probably the sugar, and she wasn't nearly as dry as she had been and her breathing was back to normal. I stepped away from her and she just lay there. So I picked her up and set her on her feet, she walked a few steps and went to nibbling on some dry bunch grass. She wouldn't leave us, I liked to think it was my magnetic personality, but would have to guess it was the pink lemonade, with sugar. After all what was there to fear, nothing bad had happened to her so no the big deal. I just knew that when we started those bikes she would blow up, but no she just looked around and walked another step or two and went back to nibbling on some more grass. I was tired, with the action stopped and the relaxing with doe. We headed back to the camp ground, with no more casualties, mainly me. I felt like this was an accomplishment and was glad I survived intact. So was Kate, when she heard the tale later that evening. I think maybe the adrenaline was pumping on this one, too. Don't give up there's more.

The next day we were going to go out in the morning and then come back pack up and get ready to leave for home. We went out and split into 2 groups of 4, the other group after awhile started chasing a Jackal, these wild dogs are about 40 pounds and have 2 inch long teeth. A lot of bite for the bark. They ran him for awhile and were able to stay with him. They actually ran into our group and as they were strung out somewhat, we joined the chase, to help them out. In the process of trying to keep him running straight, one of the guys ran over him. The rear tire flipped him up in the air and he came down on his side, with his eyes closed. I rode up to him and looked, he had his eyes closed. I backed off to the side and waited. Most of the others shut there bikes off and put them on the stands and went up to look at him. Ed Perry saw what I was doing and didn't know why but figured there was a good reason and did the same on the other side. Here they are leaning over him and looking at his big teeth, He opens his one eye, that I could see, and kind of looks around. Then he lifts his head and looks around some more. He jumps up and runs for the hills. Ed and I were on him and figured we needed to run him down in case he was hurt. He tried to outrun me and that wasn't going to happen. We did pull away from Ed. We went out on a bare bowl like plain and went in a circle. Like the gazelle did. He kept trying to cut to the right, so I ran my front wheel up beside him and with staying under power, my front wheel had no weight on it. I turned my handle bars and slapped him with my front wheel. He did a roll to the side and came back on his feet running. This must have done something to him in relation to the lights running on the spokes in the wheel, because now he stayed the same distance from the wheel, in-out-forward or back. When I realized this I took him around to Jack Contoleon, who had broke down, maybe his throttle cable. I yelled at him that I would take him in a circle and bring him back and to kick him, knocking him off his feet. OK, it worked very well until he went to kick him, he decided that when he stepped towards the dog he would move away so he took a step closer and about kicked me off my bike. He seemed to not even see Jack and did not move away from him, he just watched that wheel. The dog, Jack, the dog. We went around again and he did get the dog this time and we were finally able to put the dog down. I don't know if we killed him or he just gave up and died. We patched up Jack's bike and head back to the camp ground. When we got back, there was a Sgt. from Stratcom there and when he heard about the Jackal he wanted it. He wanted to have it mounted and to take it home with him. So we went back and got him. When we were coming back from picking up the dog we ran into some of the 3 ft. high banks and were jumping over them. Luckily we were getting strung out with Jack and I in the lead. Jack was just a little in front of me, he hit one of these 3 ft high banks and was coming down when I was going up. I knew I had a problem as I watched him disappear below me. While it was 3 feet up on the near side, but it was 13 feet down on the far side. You go up and sail over then you go down, down and down, and by this time you are about straight down with your front wheel, not what you were expecting. I came down on the front wheel, leaned back and came on down on 2 wheels and rode out of it. Jack had done the same, we were glad the others were able to get stopped when they saw us go out of sight. Not sure they would have all been so lucky in riding out of this. But we managed to and delivered the dog back to the Sgt. at camp and we finished loading. The women and the casualties had everything loaded except for us and our bikes so we were soon ready to head back up the 55 miles and 8000 feet elevation trip home.

Kate 1971 Asmara, Ethiopia

Ever since Kate and I first started going together we have always been together, when apart we were together in spirit. All of the things

I have done she has been a part of, whether she was there physically or not. She always supported me and what I was doing, whether it was picking broken thorns out of me and my legs, or visiting me in the hospital, or playing a practical joke on someone, or riding with me in the desert, or camping with me on the beach on the Red Sea, or just being with me, she was always there, we were 2 as 1. I hope everyone understands this and can have that experience themselves because there is nothing else like it.

Chapter 13:

More from Ethiopia-continued

When we were in Ethiopia, Kate had a lot of time on her hands, so along with swimming, softball, and whatever volunteer work she did, she still had time. SSG Berger and his wife, Mary, were in Special Services also. He ran the ceramics and craft shops. They were on the post annex, which was across town from the main post. And right down the street, about 1 block from our house was the Annex entrance. She started getting into ceramics, they had everything there, with lots of molds. She started out and got really good at making things for the house. We had lots of dishes, bowls, platters, mugs, and beer steins. These dishes and bowls lasted for years and probably would have lasted a lot longer, if we had never had kids. I think her big turkey Thanksgiving platter maybe in the basement somewhere, it is chipped but still functional. When I was home for a month plus, recovering from my broken pelvis and back, she decided I needed something to do, besides bothering her. Well maybe not bothering, just giving her more attention than she wanted, 22 ½ hours a day. So we came up with the idea of giving beer steins for Participation Trophies in the Motorcycle Club. She poured the mugs, I don't remember if they had more than one mold for the 48 oz. steins or not. We needed at least 40. I hand engraved all of them with the club information, dates, Participation Trophy, and I think maybe the names of those that we knew were going to get them. Some extras for the people who we didn't know if they were going to make it or not. We also made some for trophies, these were smaller and of a different shape. For other things that the club could use, and were made with the hand engraving on them. I'm thinking we made 100 or more altogether. This was a major project for both of us and we really enjoyed the time spent together and working together. The participation trophy steins were brown and had white lettering. The others were various colors as moved by my whims of painting and colors on hand. She coated them and fired them in the kiln. I think they only fired on certain days so when they did she had them ready and put them in the kiln. The night of the banquet those 48 oz steins, Participation Trophies, were big hits. People tried filling them and then drinking them down and filling them again. There were some really big hangovers the next day. I was very glad I drank beer. The guys that filled those 48 oz'ers with mixed drinks, and tried to drink them down, had to have terrific headaches the next day. One guy invited everyone to pour in the extra mixed drinks, they had, in his. Everyone made an effort to be sure that they were all different and were even ordering extra odd ball drinks, to pour in his mug, it hurt to watch. We still had our 2 steins, years later and they maybe still packed away in the basement, from our last move, to this house. They held a lot of memories of a different time and place when we were young, wild, and reckless. Well she was young and a little reckless, I was a little wild and a little more reckless, with some things, like my body. I really loved her and tried to show her everyday, but don't think I was ever successful in showing her how much. But she knew it was a bunch.

She could talk me into most anything if she put her mind to. You may not believe this but she actually talked me into getting up on stage and singing with a country and western band, on amateurs night, at the NCO Club. Not once, but at least 3 times. Nobody actually laughed, at least not so I could hear. Twice I actually knew the songs and could sing all the words, the third time they got me up there and changed songs on me. I didn't know the new song very well and they gave me a paper with the words. I was told I would do fine, not true, not good, that time I even laughed. We agreed that this was the last time, I think it was, or else I drank enough beer first that I didn't remember. She always assured me she didn't laugh, at least very much and had finished by the time I returned to our table. I did agree to dance more if I didn't have to get up and sing with the amateurs on amateur night. At least she only smiled, and didn't laugh at me, while I could see or hear her. She felt it was our duty to contribute, but it was me that had to make the contribution. That must have been love, it sure wasn't talent, the singing or the dancing.

We had a friend, Dick Bridges, am not remembering his wife's name, she was Kate's friend. They had a son that was about 4 years old, he was very active, and at times he would be with his dad and they would come visit us at home or me at work. This boy was very active and wanted to see and do everything. He was constantly looking at and into things when he wasn't suppose to. We got a nut cracker set, bowl, mallet, and picks, from our landlady, for our first Christmas there in 1970. This was made of hard wood and was very pretty. The bowl had a pedestal in the center, cupped out for breaking the nuts on. The mallet was of a very hard wood. He liked to play with the mallet and would tap on the pedestal, and lots of other things around the house. Never hard and never hurt anything but his parents were always on him to not play with it. They figured that sooner or later he would break something. We thought no big deal but they were the parents. One Saturday morning they were at our house and he started playing with the mallet. The women were in the kitchen. Dick told him to put his finger on the pedestal and hit it with the mallet. Before I could say anything and Dick didn't figure he would actually do it, he put his left index finger on the pedestal and really whacked it hard with that mallet. That hurt. He stuck his left hand in his pocket and laid the mallet down by the bowl. His dad ask if it hurt, at first he shuck his head no, then thought about it and nodded yes, and was trying not to cry. But it got the better of him and he was puckering up so Dick scooped him up and held him and he started crying. The girls came in from the kitchen and wanted to know what happened. Dick told them and the boy finally showed them his finger, it was mashed, it was swollen and red. He quit crying after a while, and he never played with that mallet again, ever.

In the winter of 71-72, I was approached and asked to help coach little league basketball. Pat Page and I were to coach one of the teams. We would draft the kids from the class rosters, we would have 3 grades to draft from. Drafting order was decided by drawing, we got last pick in the 6th grade draft, 2nd in the 7th graders, and 1st pick on the 8th graders. We did good on the draft and started practicing. We had 3 weeks, I believe, to get ready for the first game. We got a small amount of money, to put shirts on our team. We decided, with Kate's help, to go downtown to a sewing shop and have shorts, tops, and warm ups made. This cost us more than the allowance but we picked up the difference. The numbers were made right into the tops and the team name was put on the warm ups. Of course they were red and white in color. And the kids got to keep them when the season was over. We also got warm up sweaters for the coaches, Kate wore mine out over the years since that season, it was soft, warm, and comfortable. We had a good bunch of kids and probably the 2 best players in the league , at least after the season they were the 2 best. We won every game and we played all of our players in every game, don't think the other teams did this. We were able to teach these kids some basketball and they were quite willing students, it helps if they like you and want to learn.

The Emperor of Ethiopia was Haile Selassie. He had been in power before the Italians had taken over the country in 1935-36. He was very pro USA, and figured we were the best bet to help him, his country, and his people. He fled the country and went to Britain and returned in about 1941 when the Italians were overthrown but were not eliminated as a military threat until 1943. At the end of WWII Eritrea was annexed by Ethiopia and remained part of Ethiopia until 1991, when it became a separate country again. We were in Asmara, which had been part of Eritrea, the capital actually. Every year Haile Selassie came to Asmara to see the American Dentists, for his teeth. While there we had 11 men with him at all times, an NCO and 10 men, with another team standing by, where he was going next. Another team would be waiting or moving. I was in charge of one of these teams in 1971 for his visit. I was beside him at all times when my team was with him. He was a small man, in stature, and when I was on this guard detail he was getting stooped over. When he was downtown Asmara the kids all tried to get to him and he gave or threw them candy and or money. The people seemed to like him and he was very popular. It was and is my believe that he had the best interests of his country and its people at heart in whatever he did. He knew that he had to control the expansion of industrialization and modernizing of this country because the people were not ready for it, it had to be slowly and at a pace that they could handle. And I think that he didn't want a great influx of foreigners coming in and taking the jobs that his people needed. I know that there was gold in the country, it may have been low grade and in small quantities. I don't know about that, but it was there. I found some samples once and thought it was gold, so I tried to send the samples home for analyses. They were confiscated and I was told to not do it again, by the US Government. I, as always, explored new country and hard to reach places and saw new things. The gold ore samples came from one of these trips.

As mentioned earlier we had vehicles to rent out to US Service Men stationed at Kagnew station, Asmara, Ethiopia. I don't remember what the rates were but they were very generous to the Service Men. We had Army, Navy, and Air Force personnel stationed there, while we were there. Usually the people wanted the jeeps, or the broncos that we had available, for trips to where ever they wanted to go, usually just exploring or sight seeing. When they were moving or had to take something home they would use the one of pickups or maybe one of the trucks. Once in a while we would have to go and retrieve one of them from some place where they decided to quit, for whatever the reason. We did take a replacement to them at times, so we had to go with the replacement and pickup the one that had broken down or just fix the one that had broken down. One time we had to go to Bahir Dar and pick up a jeep. For this trip my boss 1st Lt. Sunderhaus chose to go along in one of the vehicles, I also took Mesfin one of my local mechanics, and there were 6 other Americans that went along, they just wanted something to do and to see some of the country. As I remember we took 3 vehicles and parts and tools. We got to Bahir Dar and was able to fix the jeep and get it running. I believe this was the only vehicle we picked up and on the way home we had 4 vehicles and 9 people, 2 in each vehicle, except mine with 3. It was late when we finally got done and would have stayed the night in a local hotel but no one had any amount of money with them. I had a couple of dollars but we were very short of funds. Why this happened I don't remember but was not a good situation. The roads close for travel with the coming of sundown or darkness, don't remember which it was now. We decided we would just head back and try to make it through. It was getting dark when we got to the Ethiopian-Eritrean border. Which was still a border and had a gate and guards on the Eritrean side of the bridge. Tthe border was a river with a bridge. There might have been guards on both ends of the bridge but I don't remember anything about the Ethiopian side of the bridge, and we had no trouble. But on the Eritrean side the guards on the gate were of mixed opinions about letting us through. One was very friendly and said sure go on, no problem. But one was not friendly and said we could not pass. He said we would have to wait until morning when the road officially opened again. There were a couple of others who were indifferent and could care less, one way or the other. An argument took place between the 2 of them, and the friendly one told me, privately, they would distract the other one and one of them would open the gate and to take off and get out of there fast. The one who was opposed to our going on was carrying his AK47 type rifle and at one point jacked a round into the chamber, in making his point, at the time. This did make me/us a little nervous but no one ever accused any of us of being overly intelligent. So when the plan to distract him and let us go on, came into being, we all took off and tried to get out of range as quickly as possible. As it worked out, maybe by design, I was last to leave and was watching in my mirror. This man was upset that they and we had done this. I could tell by his actions he was at least, very unhappy. At one point he pointed his rifle in my/ our direction but was distracted by apparent talk and lowered it and turned to his fellow guards and then we were gone, at least around a curve in the road and out of sight. Maybe the whole thing was a joke on their part, I don't know, then or now. I had 2 guys with me and the one setting on the right started ducking under the dash of the Dodge Pickup I was driving. I asked "What are you doing?" He answered "I'm practicing ducking any bullets, that might come our way." "Give me a break." We did laugh, but he kept practicing for awhile. We still had aways to go, from memory, it seems like it was around 50 miles or more. There were a number of towns or villages to go through and as I remember there were 4 or 5 more gates or cross arms that were blocking the road. We stopped and discussed our situation after getting some distance between us and the border. And decided we would try and brazen it through. To try and reach Asmara. If we came into a village and no one was around the gates or cross arms the passenger in the lead vehicle would jump out and raise the gate and the others would just keep moving and get on down the road. The lead vehicle would then drive through and the passenger would lower the gate and get back in and continue after the others. He would then be last in line, so we could rotate this job amongst the passengers. What ever happened we would keep moving if possible. This did work well as when we came into these villages no one was around the gates or in the guard shacks so we just moved on through, like a well oiled machine. We were pretty good at opening the gates and getting through without ever stopping. We never encountered anyone at any of these places. It might be said that the smart people were home in bed, not traipsing around the countryside in the middle of the night. After the last village and before we got to Asmara, we were climbing a long straight stretch of road, up a mountain side, the moon was out and it was a pretty night, I remember this stretch of road from past trips. What a beautiful and peaceful piece of country. We found out the next day that within an hours of our going through here a fire fight took place between the Ethiopian Army and a band of rebels, across this stretch highway. On the left side or west, with our being headed north, was high ground. With it falling away and lower on the right, or east, side. From what we found out it was quite a battle for sometime, with no one winning or losing. And while there were wounded, no one was actually killed, was the information that I received. Its nice to be in the right spot at the right time, lucky doesn't hurt either. And I have said for a long time that I have had a co pilot for a lot of years. It makes you think he has had to work overtime in looking out for me. Fools do go where angels fear to tread. It was well after midnight when we got back dropped everyone off, where they needed to be, and I was able to drive home. Kate was glad to see me and wondered how it had gone, nothing exciting, just routine, a drive in the park, maybe a little long and remind me next time to take money with me. Okay, why didn't you just stay the night, in Bahir Dar, in the hotel? No money, or not enough for all of us to stay. Would have been good if we had, wouldn't have got so sleepy. I didn't add that I didn't have time to get sleepy, this night. But I did tell her, later, all about it. I think she did wonder about me at times and then there were the times that she didn't wonder, she knew. I probably needed looking after a little more closely, which she did, no matter how much I needed it.

We had been going to run in an International Grand Prix car race, as a separate class, and on the track by ourselves, on motorcycles. They wanted us to run at the same time as the cars but I among others would not even consider doing this. Because they were short cars to fill out the race. This would have been a road race through the streets of Asmara. Yamaha wanted me to ride a 350cc road bike and I said I would, but win, lose, or draw the bike was mine when the race was over. They didn't want to do that so I was going to run my 650cc Yamaha Road Bike. I had it ready and was putting a fairing on it. Less than 30 days before the race, we were notified that they had gotten quite a few late entries in and were going to cancel the bike race part of the program. We had been promoting this pretty heavy and there was a lot of interest in an International Motorcycle Race. So we worked it out to have a 400 meter oval race, on cinders, at the Queen of Sheba Stadium. This would be a 75 lap race. This was primarily a soccer field, with the race track around it, in downtown Asmara. We had it all set up and decided to run a practice race on April 9th, 1972. This would be the complete program that would be run on April 23rd. A small entry fee was charged and with donations at the gate for the prize purse. Most of the racers, other than the American Military, said they wouldn't race because the guaranteed purse was not large enough. There were a few who came out and raced, but not many, most of the "International community" talked a good race but did not show. And then after watching the practice races, decided that they didn't want to race anyway. You can make your own decision on the whys of this, my opinions are my own. This went very well and brought out a lot of people, to watch. I was fastest qualifier and won my heat race and went right to the main on the pole position. I lead start to finish and went home with the win.

Come the 23rd, and again I was fastest qualifier and won my heat race, but I got a bad start on the main and went into the first turn in 7th place. I worked my way up through traffic until I was running second behind Danny Mills, he was on the Kawasaki Team but had gotten a 250cc Yamaha and was riding it. There was no doubt that I was faster. He kept blocking me when I would try to pass him. Whether on the inside or outside. It had taken me about 15 laps to make up for the bad start and get into 2nd place. We kept dueling and by 50 laps completed, we had lapped 3rd place 3 times, 4th and 5th 4 times and everyone else at least 5 times and some 7 times. We were flying. I had started getting upset about the blocking and had decided to go under him going into either turn number 1 or turn number 3, whether there was a hole or not. If he came in on me I would continue with full power and take him out and if I went with him, so be it. We came into turn number 1 and were lapping Hobby Wright, who was running either 4th or 5th place. Hobby had set up to take the inside line, so Danny went high or outside him, I started to make my move under or inside Danny. Hobby changed his mind and went outside taking Danny with him, I'm not sure if he knew we were there or not. I ducked underneath and was by both of them. If I had just had a little cooler head it may have helped but I just kept riding as hard as I had been and opened up a half lap lead on Danny in maybe 10 laps. I should have backed out of it a little and maybe I would have made it to the finish. I didn't and when I had opened up almost a whole lap on Danny, I was coming up behind him, coming down the back straight, on lap 67, I lost the bottom end rod bearing on my motor. I grabbed the clutch and got the transmission into neutral and coasted as far as I could and then pushed it across the finished line and still wound up in 7th place. I finished 68 laps and got 7th.. I guess not to bad considering and there was no doubt in anybody's mind who was the fastest rider that day. I just didn't have enough motor to finish. Danny and I met on the finish line and congratulated each other, he had ridden a good race and won. We were still friends and I was happy for him. This is what racing is about, doing the best you can do under all conditions. This was one of my last races in Ethiopia and shortly after this race I stripped my bikes and sent them home in pieces. We had a lot of good times and made a lot of friends.

When I had gotten home from Viet Nam the guys I worked with got me to playing sports again, and had started playing softball with them, as a pitcher, because of not being able to run, or not very well. I was wearing a knee brace to be able to play. I developed a curve ball, this was slow pitch, and it was quite effective against some players. So when I got to Ethiopia I was asked to play with a couple of teams. One was LDS, Latter Day Saints, they had a pretty good team and I pitched and played third base. I think I was the only player who wasn't a Mormon. Don't know if they just felt sorry for me or maybe because of friends in California who were of the Mormon faith. Bill Witt, SFC, was my boss and a Mormon. He knew of my Mormon friends in California and Arizona. I also batted quite well, with a batting average of .500 and an on base percentage of about .700. So after this league I was invited to play on another team and was the all star pitcher for the league. Then I moved on to the company level team, HQ company, where we had a very good team and I was again voted the top pitcher in the league. I batted over .500 and had on base percentage of over .700. I was a lot of the time the lead off hitter on these teams because of my getting on base percentage. I had about 7 different pitches that I threw including the curve ball that people said couldn't be done, but I did it and it worked. Again I was good at starting arguments when I would use this pitch. Batters just couldn't believe that a pitch that looked like it was coming at their head would wind up going across the plate. But, again, it did. We were tied for the league lead with 1 loss, but had the tie breaker, when Kate and I headed for home in 72. One game still sticks out, we played the Military Police team, they were undefeated at the time, also, they were a very good hitting team and batted over .500 as a team, but not this night. I pitched a 5 hit shutout, no one got by first base. I had been good friends with the whole team but for a couple of hours they didn't like me very much, but the next day everything was okay again. They didn't want to play a repeat, either. My last night there, of playing anyway, I pitched a double header and won both games, the first game was the slow pitch game and should of cinched the league win for the team and the second was fast pitch and I was the winner of record. If you played fast pitch you couldn't play slow pitch. I traded off playing the outfield with another guy who could also pitch and the change back and forth bothered the opposing batters. But we won and that was what it was all about. And my number 1 fan was there for both games, and we celebrated afterwards. We were back in the hotel by this time as we had moved out of our house and the movers had taken our household goods for shipment and we were homeless again.

Once when I had Post CQ, Charge of Quarters, with an Officer. It required one Officer and one NCO, Non Commissioned Officer, to fulfill the duties of this charge. We were on I believe for 24 hours, 7:00am to 7:00am. The officer took off for something in the morning and I preformed the duties during the morning. When he was asking about this he asked if I wanted to take off any time, and I said in the afternoon to attend the motorcycle races. OK, great, he would take off in the morning and be back so I could go to the races in the afternoon. I seemed to forget to tell him that I was going to race, just a minor detail. Kate met me at the races with the VW Bus with my bike inside and all my gear. I was riding our 650cc Yamaha. I got to the track, changed into my leathers and unloaded my bike. It was ready to go, so I was ready to race. I did win the race but at the end I was lapping a slower rider and he instead of following the track for 1 more lap, per track rules, he decided to go straight off the straight away, and not around the curve. I was set up and going into the curve, on the outside of him, he hit me and I went side ways and went down on the front of my left calf and was sliding with the front of my leg on the ground and then I was able to come back up and ride away. I felt a burning on the front of my leg. When I got to the VW and parked the bike, I looked at my leg and had a 3 ½ to 4 inch long cut parallel to the bone and ½ inch over from it and about 3/4 of an inch deep, and it was bleeding, considerably. We packed something on it to help stop or control the bleeding. I loaded my bike and stuff in the Bus and I rode to the hospital in my leathers to keep my uniform clean. Kate followed in the Bus. They sewed me up and gave me a tetanus shot and sent me home to rest up. Well they thought I was going home, actually I changed back into my uniform and went back to work at Post Headquarters. I was walking a little funny and the officer wanted to know what was wrong with my leg, so I showed him the bandage and told him of the cut. Then he wanted to know how it happened and was a little upset when he found out that I went to the races to race, not watch, I never told him what I was going for, he just assumed that I was going to watch. Oh well, it was a long night with the leg being sore but I was okay, I won didn't I, and Kate was waiting at home when I got off the next morning. She was used to having to be careful of my injuries. While they may have slowed me down, they didn't stopped me. The only time I had a major delay in getting home was the broken pelvis and back, it just took a little longer, that time, to get there, this was the only time they kept me in the hospital, but I always made it home to her, one way or another.

When we left to come home, we had stops planned in3 countries, Spain, France, and the third I'm not remembering. We were suppose to spend a day and a night in Paris but it was pouring rain with the forecast for a couple of more days of it, we were given the option of staying or continuing on in the same plane. We talked it over for a couple of minutes and both agreed we were ready to go home. And we were off to the US of A.

Chapter 14:

Out of the Military

We flew in to New York City and I rented a car and we were off to Fort Dix, New Jersey. Where I would be discharged from active service. I had been given a report in date, so we had some time to use before I could check in, or so I thought at the time. The car I rented was a brand new Dodge Polaris, and it had 600 miles on it. We had unlimited miles so we decided we would drive down the coast and sight see and visit some friends. We went to Pennsylvania first, and out in the western part of the state we looked up Larry Martin and his family. Larry had been in the Army in Asmara, when we were there. He was another motorcycle racer. We were welcomed and treated like family. His mother and father could not of treated us any better. His siblings were great and we had indeed come home. We stayed a couple of nights with them and was shown around and went sight seeing. We visited the New Holland manufacturing complex and saw where a lot of farm equipment was built. This was very interesting, touring the complex and seeing the steps in the manufacture of a lot of different pieces of farm equipment. Then it was on down the coast and we continued to see and visit a lot of things of interest. We stayed in Washington D.C. a couple of days and did some sight seeing around the nation's capitol. Then we decided to head back to Ft. Dix. We would be a few days early still but I would go ahead and check in. We got back and got a motel room near Fort Dix and the next morning after lounging around in bed and a late breakfast, we head in to the fort and I checked in. The man there was a little put out with me for being late. And I told him that I wasn't due for discharge for a couple of more days. He said it didn't matter, if I wanted out today I would have to hurry and catch up with the others. I could just hand carry my paper work, and since I was an E-6 I could just go by myself, instead of in a group, as usual. I had to catch up with all the others being discharged today. Alright, I was ready to go home after 9 years of playing soldier. So with starting a couple of hours late, and not having to wait on others, I caught up with the group before they were finished and I was there with them for discharge and final pay at finance. And so we were free to go to New York and turn in the car and catch a plane for Kansas. I was a civilian again, with a beautiful wife, whom I was very much in love with, and a whole life in front of us. It looked good for the future.

We made it home to Phillipsburg, Wheat harvest was in full swing just south of us. We moved in with Mom and Dad, in my old room. In with talking with Dad, Kate and I decided I would trade in my old combine and get a new one. Dad had gotten a new one the year before. I went to our dealer, Winchell's Inc. and they didn't have one in stock but looked around and found one in Great Bend, Kansas, about a 120 miles away. I went down there, with Jay Winchell, and drove it home. We got home they went through it and we were ready for the field after one more day. We cut wheat and finished out the summer and went into the fall a milo harvest. We stayed part of the winter with my grandparents, Frank and Edna Morton, in Phillipsburg, and then we purchased a small trailer house that we could live in and also take with us when we were out of town on the harvest trail, as it moved north each year.

It was during this late winter, early spring that Kate told me that she wanted to get married in the Catholic Church. This was fine with me and I actually told her "Fine with me, I'd marry you in the middle of the freeway, if that's what you want". We talked to Father Reif, at the Catholic Church, in Phillipsburg. On May 8, 1973 we were married by Father Robert J. Reif, in the Catholic church. Warner and Mary Margaret Cunningham, long time friends of mine, who were Catholic, as required, stood up with us in a private ceremony. I believe she always wanted to be married in the church and I was more than happy to do this with her. Before we were married she had informed me that we would be expecting a small bundle in the fall. I was overjoyed with the idea of a baby, and it was a happy spring that we shared.

We had been cutting wheat all summer and Dad hadn't been feeling very well. We had moved several times in Nebraska already, and were now at Hemmingford, Neb. Located in the northwestern part of the state, and Dad got very sick. The last day he ran his combine was on his birthday, August 2nd. He wouldn't go to a local Nebraska doctor so we decided to move him home and he could see the doctor at home. I had called my sister Pat Smith and she had flown in to help do anything that she could to do. We loaded up and I took Dad's truck and combine, Pat drove one of the trucks pulling a trailer house and Dad rode with her. Gary Flanigan brought the other truck pulling the other trailer house. Mom brought their pickup with combine header and Kate drove our pickup. We got home and got everyone situated and Kate and I took off back to Nebraska to get our other truck and our combine. Now, this sounds pretty easy, but there was a lot of work and driving involved. So when we were headed back, we got to Interstate 80 highway, Kate was going to drive and I would get a nap. We were west bound and I went to sleep. I was having a dream about Kate driving. She pulled out to pass another vehicle. There was an 18 wheeler right in front of us. I came awake yelling for her to look out for that truck, she looked at me like I had lost my mind. But she had just pulled out, of the right lane, to pass another vehicle and over in the east bound inside lane was an 18 wheeler. Everything was just as I had seen it, in my dream, same vehicles, same colors, everything, only the truck was 1 lane over. Oh wow, what a way to wake up. I told her to pull over and I would drive. I wasn't going to sleep any more today, for sure. I did drive the rest of the way and turned around and drove all the way home without getting sleepy.

Dad was diagnosed with lung cancer and we took him to the KU Med Center, Cancer Unit, in Kansas City. I returned home and Mom stayed in Kansas City, with him. I was able to do some work at home and got a silage cutting job in Garden City, Kansas. This would start after Labor Day weekend, the first Tuesday of September. We got word about the time we were to head to Garden City that Dad was done at KU Med and wanted to come home. The cancer had started between his lungs and had spread into both lungs, eventually this would be the end, when he no longer had lung capacity, to sustain life. He had agreed to take experimental drugs and make any contribution that he could for development of new drugs that would benefit others in the future. Not the best news for a caring family, but so like him, the quiet caring man he was. I went to Kansas City and brought him and Mom home and he would continue with treatment and care at home. He didn't want to be anywhere but home. Mom, with Kate helping, took care of him at home. Kate was 8 to 8 ½ months pregnant but she was doing anything and everything she could. Mom would only leave Dad's bedside, to lay down and maybe sleep, when Kate was there to take her place by Dad's bed. And after the baby was born Dad would not allow this because the baby had to be in the house, so Kate could look after her. Dad felt he was endangering that baby and would not allow it. Brother Ken came home on leave from the Air Force and went to Garden City with me to cut silage. We were there for over a month with only a couple of visits home. I called Kate on the 21st , her birthday and everything was as good as could be expected. She never said a word about her condition and I didn't think she was that close to her date. We were working on the 22nd of September and no new news on anything. On the morning of the 23rd I did get the word to call home. I believe that Mike Gigot brought me the word in the field and he said to stop at the shop and call. When I got to the shop I called home and was referred to the hospital. I had the room number and Kate answered the phone. We had a new baby girl, born the afternoon before. I told her I loved her and the new baby. Everyone had been busy and hadn't gotten word to me the day before. Faye Gobel our next door neighbor had taken Kate to the hospital and stayed with her for the delivery. She saw her to her room before Faye returned home. Kate and the baby were doing fine and she would be going home in another day. She told me not to worry, and to stay working as I would probably just be in the way at home anyway, and oh yeah, she still loved me. I did tell her, again, that "I loved her too, and the new baby also". We talked about names, some more, and she wanted Mary for the first name. That was fine, and we settled on Lynn for the middle name, she had to be named before they would let her leave the hospital. I would called her again when we were finished for the day. When I got to the scales, the girls/women told me I was to call home. They didn't know that Mike had already brought me the message. Okay, so I pulled my truck off the scales and came into the office, they said to just call, dial direct, they were jumping up and down wanting to know. They knew we were expecting at anytime. So I called again and talked to Kate, again. She was a little surprised that I called that quick, it hadn't been 5 minutes. But I was already wanting to talk to her again anyway. So we talked for awhile, again, and I had to say goodbye and would call her tonight. I hung up and started to leave and Dorothy (Adams) said "Welllllll". I turned and said "Well what?" "What was it?" I said "A baby". She was kind of grinding her teeth and trying not to hit me. "Boy or Girl." "Oh, just another girl". She did start for me and I ran out laughing. I came back in and told them all the details, that I had, and they didn't do me any harm and let me leave and go back to work. I didn't get home for 10 days to see that baby and it was really working on me, but I'm tough. We got rained out and Ken and I were homeward bound in about 15 minutes, that trip of 206 miles was made in less that 3 hours. I was so very glad to see Kate, Mary Lynn, and all the others. When I finished with Kate, she made me sit down on the couch and she went and got Mary Lynn and handed her to me for the first time. That was some feeling to hold her for the first time. I could sit and look at her for the longest times. Kate grabbed a camera and got a picture of me holding her for the first time. And she did tease me about it, a little bit, but that was okay, I've already told you, I'm tough. I don't know how long it was but I did eventually take both of them to see Dad and Mom. It was only a short walk to their house. Dad was happy and proud of that baby, but so afraid that she would catch something from him. He hadn't let them put her next to him and had not held her. So I laid her in his arm on the bed and he had to hold his new granddaughter. God how he wanted to. She would just lay there with him and never made a sound. She would look at him and then maybe look around, and then back to looking at him. After awhile he said to pick her up as she might catch something from him, and I said "No". She was fine and wouldn't catch anything. But he was so worried about it and it was apparent that he was really bothered by it, so I finally picked her up and set by the bed holding her and talking to him. But he was still bothered that she was so close and he felt she was in possible danger. Kate took her on home and I stayed and visited with him for awhile . When I was talking with Dad, he said that the experimental drugs were working and the doctor had told him that he would be up and running his combine in the spring. I guess that in wanting to believe it and coming from Dad, I never questioned his word. So Ken and I went back to Garden City with that belief. Mom never said anything when she heard Dad say this because she knew better and never doubted that we did also. But Ken and I wanted to believe it and did. We got to stay that day and went back to Garden City, late on the next day.

Kate put Mary Lynn on formula before she left the hospital and after about 5 days she started throwing it up, with an upset stomach. She consulted the doctor and they changed the formula, but about every 5 days this would be repeated, so they were running out of formulas to try. The doctor said that the problem had to be the dairy or cow's milk. We were down to 2 options, goats milk and soybean milk, milk made from a soy product. We didn't have a goat or a desire to be milking one twice a day, so she/we decided to try the soybean milk first. Kate would have milked that goat with a smile if it would have been needed. That kid went to town on that soybean milk and later down the road finally outgrew her allergy to cow's milk. By the time I got to see her, the first time, she was already starting to sleep all night. Kate would feed her about 10:00pm and then get her ready for bed and she would sleep until 6 in the morning. She was a much appreciated baby over the years. I don't remember her having problems with other things as far as allergies went. That soybean milk tasted and smelled terrible to me but she like it and did very well on it, and that's what counts.

When we returned, Terry Gigot talked to me about staying on and working, at least, through the winter. I talked to Kate and then Dad and we all agreed that I should do that. So I told Terry I would and we would move down as soon as we finished with silage but

I had to have a week or so to combine milo that we had already agreed to do. He said that would be fine, whatever I needed to do, he was flexible.

We were still cutting silage a week later, on October 9, when we got the message, between 5:30 and 6 in the morning. Ken and I were finishing breakfast, at the Conoco Restaurant, and got the message to call Mom at home, right away. Which I did. Dad had quit breathing a little after 5. Mom was dozing in a chair by his bed and around 4 he had woke her up and said he wanted to set up for a while, so they set on the side of the bed together, holding hands and with little or no talking. After about 45 minutes he was getting tired and wanted to lay down and she helped him lay back down. She continued to hold his had and he went to sleep and in a few minutes he quit breathing. His lungs had filled and he was no longer able to breath.

This was an additional shock to Ken and I because of our believing what he had told us. To those that questioned this I just said, I wanted to believe it and Dad said it. Ken was the same as me on this.

This time we made the trip in 2 hours and 20 minutes, Ken was driving his El Camino, and it seemed we were hurrying. I had called Terry and told him what was going on and we were on our way home. He said if I needed anything, to call, I said I would, and I would keep him informed about what was going on and the time frame when I would be back.

It was a bad time, but Kate was there and took care of me and did make things better. You would never know, to see and watch her that she had just delivered a baby. What a woman she was, always there, quietly doing whatever needed to be done. So many people benefited from this beautiful girl's quiet helping manner, and so many never even noticed or realized, or acknowledged, that she was doing these things. And she was always there for me, when things would get to heavy, she was there to hold me and when I needed to talk. She could always make anything better with just her presence.

With things settling down, I cut the milo that I had to. I called Terry and asked "If my employment could possibly be permanent?" He said "Yes and start whenever I was ready". With Dad gone and Mom's half of the equipment going to be sold, I didn't want to even try to continue. I would just move to Garden City and start over. I was able to sell out and pay off what I owed and still had my 2 trucks. This job was to last 32 years and covered many things and new adventures.

Chapter 15:

Garden City

My new job would be running a Grain Storage and Drying facility, Southwest Corn Company, that was being expanded and built. We would live right on sight, in our own trailer house and we would pay for our own phone service, with everything else taken care of. Corn harvest was already in progress when we got there but so far it was the high moisture corn that was being brought in and dry corn had not started coming into the elevator yet.

We had 4 other trailers for close neighbors, the closest, about 100 feet, were Jesse and Virginia Aguilar, daughter Gina, son Jesse Jr., and later son Ralph. I'm not remembering the 2 families in the middle, now, but the 4th was John Hayes and his family, wife and 4 kids, 3 boys and a girl. The girl was the oldest and all four were his wife's from a previous marriage. They did have a little girl later, named Jonna.

I had to go about 130 yards to the office and maybe 100 yards to the first drive way of the elevator. This was being pretty close to work, it had it's good and bad points. We soon got a new, larger trailer to live in. Mostly it was just work for the first 3 months, 7 days a week, and then it slowed down and was more of an 8 to 5 job, the first I'd ever had. We were expanding for the next 2 years and eventually we had a capacity of one and a quarter million bushels of storage. This for a farm operation and was larger than some of the commercial elevators around the country.

When I got home early enough, in those first months, Kate would wait to feed Mary Lynn until I got home and let me feed her. I would then burp her, clean her up, and change her. Then I would put her to sleep, usually without rocking, I did have a big rock. I would just hold her and she would go to sleep. When she was asleep, Kate would come and want to take her and put her to bed. "No" I would tell her she might wake her up and I had better just hold her, usually if I didn't let her have the baby, I would soon be asleep and she would take her and put her to bed. Then she would come and get me and take me and put me to bed , also. She was a woman and a lady and I continued to love her more all the time.

In December of 1973 I started hunting again. I finally had the desire to hunt again, I had hunted anytime that I could, when I was growing up and until I joined the Army in 1963. Then I didn't have time and after Viet Nam I didn't have any desire. I started hunting coyotes with Mike Gigot and by myself. I decided I need a different rifle for coyote hunting and so I purchased a Ruger Model 77 Rifle in 25-06 caliber, for my Christmas present. This was a 30-06 necked down to 25 caliber. I really liked this caliber and shot it a lot and became quite proficient with it. I was quite competent with it on standing deer size game at 500 yards. In 1975 I started shooting with the Sand and Sage Rifle and Pistol Club and joined as a member. This led to expanded shooting opportunities, more and different guns and new experiences. I also started reloading and casting my own bullets, and again I became very proficient and competent at this and did it for a long time. Casting my own bullets was something that I really liked and enjoyed. The hunting was something I enjoyed and the hunting, of edible animals, also put food on the table. I also hunted coyotes and fur bearers for bounties and for their pelts, extra money for the family.

In early1975, Kate again informed me that we were expecting another addition to the family, in the summer. She seemed to have more trouble with this pregnancy than the first, nothing major, just not as easy as the first one.

On August 15, 1975, it was a hot, clear, and not windy day. To clarify the wind comment, this is southwest Kansas and the wind always blows. I was home that evening, by about 6 and we had supper and cleaned up. Mary Lynn was wanting to go outside and play on the swing set. So at about 7:30pm we went out to play and Kate set on the step and watched us. About 8:30 she said she was getting tired and was going in to lay down for a little while. "OK, we would be in shortly." It was almost 9:00 when we went in to check on her and she was up and said "We probably ought to be getting to the hospital as my labor pains are getting pretty close together". She had failed to mention any labor pains before this. Alright, I picked up Lynn, grabbed Lynn's bag and the bag we kept ready for Kate and headed for my pickup. We got to the hospital, about 10-11 miles distance, at about 9:20pm, give or take 30 seconds. I drove up to the ER door and opened her door and she got out and went in. I parked and took the bags and Mary Lynn and went in to the ER. They were already wheeling her out in a wheelchair, heading upstairs, by way of the elevator, to the maternity ward and the delivery room (s). I signed her in and got the paperwork all done and Shirley Tursini, RN, an acquaintance and later friend, came over and said "Let me look after your daughter and you go upstairs and check on your wife". "Okay, thanks." This was okay with both of us because I'm not sure Mary Lynn ever met a stranger, she was a good baby. I went up and no one was around, so I wandered over to the nursery, and was looking at 3 new babies through the glass and another nurse, that I knew, came up behind me and ask "What do you think?" "Well, I think that they are all babies." She came back with "Well, that's good, because", pointing at the one on the right, "That one's yours." WHAT!!! I looked at my watch, 9:40pm, Wow, talk about fast. "Where's Kate?" She gave me her room number, just a little way down the hall, and I went that way pretty quickly. I stuck my head in the door and she was in bed a sleep. What a beautiful woman, lying there asleep already, she had had a full day. I wanted to kiss her very badly, but wasn't going to take a chance on disturbing her, so was content to blow her a kiss, leave her bag and quietly leave. I would be back. I talked with the nurse, on duty, and went to get my daughter. I wasn't there for the birth of either one of our kids, I had really planned on being there for this one, and to be there for her, but I guess she didn't need my help, again. As I keep saying, My God what a woman, she was beautiful, strong, tough, and would have done credit to anything she chose to do, she would have been an awesome pioneer where strong, tough women were needed to settle this country. I took Mary Lynn home, fed her and put her to bed. I had called my Mom, who was expecting the call. She had a new grandson and all the particulars. She was going to head down, right now that night, but I said "No, I was really able to handle things for one night, give me a little credit." She did laugh at me, too, but I was use to it. The next morning I went back to the hospital, and was able to kiss my wife this time. The nurses were giving me a hard time about a name. We had not even talked about a name for this one, I don't know why. She asked if I had anything in mind for a name. I said that I liked Lance, after my nephew, Lance Smith, Pat's son. Kate said that was okay with her. What about a middle name. She had nothing in mind, so I said, "How about Arthur, in honor of her Mom and Dad." She thought about that for a little while and said she liked it. So that was settled, no other names were even considered. She was already worried about getting home to take care of me. I had to tell her, again "I am capable of looking after myself, for at least a couple of days". She laughed and said "I'm sorry, I know that you are, but I just wanted to be there to do it". And again told me how much she loved me and wanted to be with me always. I could only say that "I love you too and I feel the same way, and thanks, for another beautiful baby, just like his mother". I left her to rest and went back home. Mom had left early and was there before I went to the hospital. I'm sure I needed to check on Mom, remember her laughing. Kate came home in a couple of days and Mom stayed for about 2 weeks, by then Kate was very ready to take back over her home and kids. She told Mom, thanks, and to go home and rest up, we would be fine.

This one had the same problem with allergies, with the cows milk, so when he started having problems we just put him on the soybean milk. That solved the problem, temporally, as far as dairy products went. Here's what I had written to his grandparents, Dad (George) and Mom (Teresa) about this after Kate went home to Jesus, in September of 2008:

I have spoken about Mary Lynn's allergies as a baby, well you haven't heard nothing yet.

Poor Lance when he was born, we went through the same baby formula problem we had with Lynn. So we decided to just put him on the soy bean milk and be done with it, and he did real well, the same as Lynn. Although I get by calling her Lynn she doesn't really like it and prefers Mary Lynn, but I'm still bigger that she is so I get by with it. Not only was Lance allergic to milk, to read dairy products, it's far easier to list what he could eat. Beef, chicken, turkey, venison, potatoes, plain rice and green beans. No dairy, citrus, tomatoes, most vegetables, pork, wheat, corn, sugar, corn by products. You have just eliminated at least 80% of all the food in the grocery store, if not more. For years he thought his name was "No Lance". We had to teach him his name all over again. No Lance, No Lance, No Lance, don't even think about it, you can't have that, you know better, what will your mother say, you know the answer, no way, and the list goes on. He's heard them all so much the he didn't even have to listen to know that he wasn't going to get permission to eat anything he wanted . No pop, sodas, or any soft drink that was sweetened with corn syrup. We gave up eating out because usually he couldn't have anything on the menu. I think he was about 39 when he finally out grew his allergies, maybe not quite that old, it just seemed like it. He's only 33 now. One of the things that he really liked was the venison, the other kids didn't get venison so he had something special and different. We had to draw a deer license, some way each year or talk someone out of their license or their deer. Kate was forever trying to find new recipes to try to get him something different to eat. It was pretty tough trying to find things for him to eat. We didn't have milk, pop, candy, ice cream, none of the necessities of life in the house, because none of us would eat them if he couldn't. I just hope he appreciates how much ice cream I missed because of him, just kidding Lance. His life just wasn't always fun, but we did the best we could, and it looks like he managed to eat enough to grow over 4 foot 9 inches tall. He could eat pheasants and quail too, so I just had to hunt more to try and feed him, sometimes it was rough but I kept right on hunting every chance I got.

In late October, 1975, we were in corn harvest and it was in the afternoon, Lynn came over to the elevator and found me and said that something was wrong with Mom. She was crying and couldn't move her (right) hand. I grabbed Lynn up and yelled to Joe Gonzales, who worked for me, that I was going home. I ran home carrying Lynn and went in to check on Kate, she was crying and was having trouble talking, she couldn't use or move her right hand and arm. I told her to wait a minute and I went to my Uncle Herman and Aunt Goldie DeWild's trailer and got Aunt Goldie to come watch the kids. She was there immediately. I picked Kate up and carried her to my Bronco and took off for town and the hospital. The trip was made very fast. I pulled up to the ER door and they came out to meet us but I carried her right on in and took her to an Exam Room and laid her on a table. Dr. Bruno was called, her/our doctor. They started testing and looking for an explanation. They came up with nothing. We wasted 2 days here and learned nothing. I made arrangements to fly her to Wichita, Wesley Medical Center. Where Specialists were available. I had called Mom and she came down that first evening to look after the kids. I stayed with Kate. I flew her to Wichita and they retested and tested more, but came up empty also. We were in Wichita for quite awhile. Uncle Herman and Aunt Goldie brought my Bronco down to me, so I would have transportation. Also some clothes. They had places that I could of stayed but I just stayed in her room. She had all the symptoms of a stroke, but 25 year old women don't have strokes. The doctor finally came to us and gave us his best educated guess. There is a rare virus, it has all the symptoms of a stroke, to be diagnosed 100% it must be checked for in the first 24 hours, after 24 hours the chances of diagnoses drops until after 72 hours the percentage is 0. In Kate's case there were no lasting effects but she never was as physically strong as before.

I have heard others versions of what she had wrong with her on this. People that said they have the inside information. I don't know where they got it but it did not come from her doctors. Unless they talked to others about it and not to me. Other people's theories are I guess their opinions and I am not sure where they got their information. But it was different than mine.

I came on home and got Terry Gigot's van so she could lay down, went back and brought her home. Mom stayed until Kate was sure she could handle both me and the kids and then Mom went home, again.

Chapter 16:

Finney County Sheriff's Posse

In January of 1978 I joined the Finney County Sheriff's Posse, this was, up on completion of training, a fully sworn Law Enforcement Group that functioned as Deputy Sheriffs, and worked under the direction of the Finney County Sheriff, Grover Craig. My training took from the first of February until May 22, 1978, when I was sworn in as a Finney County Deputy Sheriff. I was active in that capacity until 1994, when I officially quit the Posse, but still carried my badge until Grover retired. This was interesting work and was what you made of it. The stories of my adventures as a deputy would fill a book all by it's self. This was an opportunity to help people and also help enforce the law. I was involved in a lot of things, routine patrol, building checks, security at school events, traffic control, funerals, funeral escorts, prisoner transfers, barking dogs, loose live-stock, missing livestock, missing persons, runaway kids, escaped prisoners, domestic disputes, bar fights, burglaries, robberies, armed robberies, accidents, traffic accidents, break ins, homicides, rapes, body guard for celebrities, blizzards, drug raids, personal protec-tion and escorts, stake outs, plane crashes, fires, back up, lost kids, visitation at the jail, courtroom duty, trials, notification of next of kin, training, firearms training and being there for someone to talk to. No doubt I missed somethings on this list. And when I needed someone to talk to, I had but to go home, because there were times when things bothered me, and I had my own personal therapist and she was the best.

One of my favorite Sheriff Department stories, took place around 1990-91, and goes like this: Garden City hosts Beef Empire Days, a 2 week celebration honoring the Beef or Cattle Industry. There are all kinds of events planned and held around and honoring this big event. There are street dances held during this time that take place on Friday and Saturday nights. One will be Country and Western and the other Rock and Roll. We had never done security for these dances and they were a big thorn in side of a lot of people. Maybe the reason to shy away from them. You get that many people together dancing, partying, drinking, and everything that goes with it, you have problems. But they are very popular and make money for the organizers. At the time I was the Commander or Captain for the Posse. We were approached about doing the security and I had some questions for the people running these events. How are we expected to handle these dances? What do you mean? Well are we allowed to handle the security in our own way or are you going to tell us how we have to do it? I was assured we could handle it anyway we wanted, as long as we got the job done. In the past various organizations had taken on this task, with mixed results. I was confident that applying Grover's beliefs and theories to these dances, we could make it work for everyone involved. They wanted us to work on a commission basis rather than pay us a normal hourly fee or lump sum. Okay, the money was actually secondary to me anyway. This money went to the Posse Fund for continued operation of the Posse. To get in to the dance (s) you had to have a Beef Empire Days Pin or Button displayed. If you didn't have one, you could buy one at the gate for $2.00. They wanted to give us $.25 for each one sold at the gate, but we had to have people at the gate helping sell these Pins. No labeled alcoholic beverages were allowed. Okay, but the deputies selling pins or buttons would not be in uniform, we would have Uniformed Officers there but not selling Pins. This would take extra people but we had the people. We would not make people a problem, if they were not a problem. On Friday night things started slow but started picking up as the evening progressed. People came to the gates and were admitted with pins or bought pins and then were admitted.

They were not allowed to bring in labeled bottles of alcohol but a generic cup was not checked. I was not going to taste your Coke or Pepsi to see what was in it, and as long as you conducted yourself in a reasonable manner, you were treated accordingly. People were coming and going, the band was playing and people were dancing and have a good time, with no problems. A few people at the gates were turned away if they had labeled containers of alcohol or they were disorderly or creating a problem, but these were a very few instances. The people learned the rules and followed them and got into having fun. Some would lose there pins and buy new ones. Some made a game of where they wore their pin, on the inside of there blouse, shirt, skirt, or where ever. Some chose to pin it to there bra, I do remember all of these as being girls or women. Some didn't have one on, referring to a bra, again I am referring to the girls or women. Some decided somewhere on their underwear was a good place, but all had to show them when they came in. Yes, they did show their pins, where ever they had them. When these displays were made, I would say "Thank you, ma'am, that was just what I needed to see", meaning the button of course. It might be considered interested viewing, by some, but we were just viewing the pins. I was working with Stacy Regan, chair-person for the dances, we oversaw the whole operation and participated as needed, where needed. But she was enjoying the large crowd and the no trouble scenario, that we had. There were a group of motorcycle people or bikers, that were having a good time and appreciating the no hassle-no problem atmosphere. Several of the women took particular delight in trying to embarrass me with the showing of their pins. Stacy, I think, was amused at their antics toward me or us, because they might have been aimed at her too. Now I like to have fun, and if they thought they could embarrass me this way, then they didn't know me well enough. While I might have been a little uncomfortable with this, I was not embarrassed, so let the games continue. We made it through the first night with1 arrest, a drunk that had a warrant out for him, and this happened when he made himself a problem and pushed the limits. He was treated fairly but didn't think he had to play by the rules. That was why he had a warrant out for him to start with. The second night was even better than the first, the crowd from the first night came back with all the new ones for the different kind of music. The whole block of the street was full of people having a good time, dancing and socializing, and with no problems. And yes there were a number of people who continued to show their pins in all kinds of places and in maybe, by some, in an inappropriate manner, no laws were actually broken to my knowledge and I will reserve my own opinions, as my own. Kate took this as always, in her own way, and said she thought that it was okay, but she would wear her pin on the outside of her shirt, and it was okay to do my job, of just looking at the pins, where ever they were displayed. She laughed and kissed me, when I told her of these going ons and attempts to, maybe, embarrass me.

On Monday morning I received a call from the head of Beef Empire Days, wanting to know "What had I been doing at those Dances"? He had had no complaints but his phone was ringing off the hook with congratulations and compliments of a job well done. And we had to do it again next year. Grover called and said about the same things. He wanted to know " What did I think I was doing?" I told him "I did it the way you would have and the way you wanted it done." He laughed and said "Well put". He thanked me for a job well done and appreciated the fact the he received no complaints from the street dances. Even of loud music, as there normally was. I think that maybe the neighbors were at the dances and so didn't complain about the music. Maybe the only exception was the Police Department, arrests were down considerably.

They had figured that we would make $200.00 dollars, maximum, and our take was over $800.00 dollars. Just for selling pins and watching people have a good time. I think everyone agreed, unless of course, you preferred fighting drunk, making arrests, putting people in jail, and doing paperwork, that this was a better way. I'll take the first every time, I prefer the easy way and having fun.

The next year, I was contacted to do it again, but they said we made to much money the year before and we would only be paid $200.00. We had done such a great job the year before that we just had to do it again. I took this as a slap in the face, first for each quarter we made the year before they had made $1.75. So where we made money so did they. Second, if we did such a great job why did they object to paying for what they got. I didn't care about the money, but the principle was important. I would rather work for nothing than take a 400% cut in pay. But I will take it to the posse as a group. After talking it over we agreed not to take it on their terms, we would be willing to discuss it, though. You would think that somebody could figure out, if we worked on a commission, then they also made 400% more on their share of the gate. I guess I'm not up on this type of economics. Beef Empire Days chose not to talk to us further and to go elsewhere for their security. They had another wreck, in my opinion, and we never did the security again, while I was still around.

During the same time frame we had another job that was at least interesting. Tanya Tucker owned a part of Lobo Feed Yard, east of Garden City, on Highway 50. Bob Lowrance was majority owner and the manager of the feed yard. He, with some others, decided to have a company party, a way of saying thanks to the employees from the feed yard. I don't know if I ever knew how it came about but Tanya Tucker was going to be here to look over the facility, because she was part owner, and said she would perform at the party. I don't know if she was already coming or whether she scheduled to be here just for the party. She was to fly in on Wednesday morning and they wanted a security guard, or body guard, with her at all times. The Posse was contacted about providing the guards for Tanya while she was in Garden City. We talked about it and I was the only one that could be relied on, as far a time off from work went, to be with her during the daytime. Talk about your dirty jobs that somebody has to do. The result of this was that the Posse would take on the job of guarding her body (?), joking again. We had people who could take the different time slots, for outside of her room, in the evening and at night, if I could cover the daytime. I would in essence be with her whenever she was away from the Hilton Inn, name now changed. This was all planned and scheduled and we were set. It was really going to be a rough week, I was going to have to spend 3 and a half days with Tanya Tucker. What happened was she got sick and was feeling poorly and changed her plans. She wouldn't be coming in on Wednesday morning but would fly in on Saturday morning and go straight to the Hilton and her room and stay there. We had deputies scheduled for duty outside her room and she wouldn't be going anywhere and I would not be needed until time for the party. Talk about rough, I could have worn blue jeans, boots, western shirt and hat, with radio and gun, escort Tanya Tucker around, where ever she went until party time, but it didn't happen. We also had the security for the party. On Saturday, in the middle of the afternoon, instead of escorting Tanya Tucker around, I was overseeing the security for the party. I was with Bob Lowrance and taking care of any and all details for the party. He was telling me that no one was to be allowed in the side doors around the area of the convention area and swimming pool, where he had the whole area reserved for the party. OK, I put out the word to all the security guards, who were deputies, about the doors. Within a few minutes a very irate Mrs. Bob Lowrance approached us and proceeded to express her displeasure with the guard on one of the rear or side doors. Bob started laughing and I was embarrassed. She had parked around behind the Hilton Inn and was going to come in the back door, but a very inconsiderate security guard would not let her in the back door. Mr. Lowrance said no one is allowed in the back door and I don't know or care who you say you are. She had to walk clear around to the front of the building. She wasn't exactly overjoyed with Bob for his laughing, either. I tried to apologize, that the guard didn't know her or who she was, but Bob wouldn't have any of that. Rules are rules, even for Mrs. Bob Lowrance. She listened and finally started smiling. She said he was right, and it was okay. She did go and personally apologized to the guard on the door, and thanked him for doing his job the way he was told to do it. She was a very nice lady. I had a little time, with everything ready, so I did something to pass the time until I started guarding Tanya's body for the show.

I went to her room, I think at 7:00pm, and waited outside her door, with the guard that was on duty there at her door. I waited until it was time to go to the backstage area, for her to go on stage to perform. Her mother was with her and I spoke with her a couple of times and with Tanya once, before she came out, and we went to the backstage area. She still wasn't feeling very well but we walked to the backstage area and waited there. When we got there a waitress met us with a glass of clear liquid, for Tanya. I could say that it was water but I really don't think so, there were swirls in the clear liquid that would lead me to believe that there was something else in that glass. But I don't check what ladies are drinking, so I really don't know what was in it. She drank about half of it, in one drink, and we stood and talked quietly until it was time for her to go on stage. When she got the call to go on stage, she drank the other half of the glass of liquid, set the glass down and mentally picked herself up physically. She stood up straighter, put her shoulders back, and took a deep breath, put a smile on her face and walked on stage. Wow, what a transformation, I know something of how she was feeling but none of that audience had any idea. She put on a super show. I watched from the wings, I was impressed. She was feeling so rotten, was putting on a free show in the sense that she was not getting monetary compensation, but that didn't make any difference, she is a performer and did put on the best show that she could, and it was good. After 4 or 5 curtain calls, she walked off and said "Get me the (pause) out of here". We headed back to her room going through the lobby. Bob, his wife, and granddaughter met us in the lobby and we stopped and spoke with them. Bob asked "Could his granddaughter get an autograph?" Of course she said "Sure". She looked at me and I asked "Could I have one for my daughter?" She said "I would be happy to." Then she asked "Would you like to have an autograph?" I said "Yes, I would". She smiled and autographed her picture for me. It's still here with me and Mary Lynn still has hers too. Tanya only gave 3 autographs when she was in Garden City. Here is another one of these women who did so impress me, there must be a lot of them out there or maybe I'm just easily impressed. While I like her music I am much more impressed with her as a performer, it is my opinion that she would be hard to beat as a performer, and she's good looking.

In about 1984, I think, about the 1st of May, I was working on Patrol, for the Sheriff's Department, about 8:00 pm on a Friday night. I made a traffic stop on a car pulling a horse trailer. They were from Arkansas going to Holly, Colo. to pick up a horse at the race track there. The trailer had lost its lights, and I stopped him to see if we could find and fix the problem. The owner and I were in back of the trailer talking about what to do. He asked about nearby motels and I told him about the Best Western Motel. He asked if he could pull on into the Best Western Motel, on the east side of Garden City, until he could get it fixed, and I told him he could, it was about 2 miles. I would follow him so somebody wouldn't run into the back of him. I became aware of a vehicle coming towards us at a very high rate of speed. The hearing may be bad but not that bad. I had made a near text book stop, as far a parking the patrol car, to give us cover from on coming traffic. After telling the man that I would keep somebody from running into the back of his trailer and upon hearing the vehicle coming, I started to turn and was hit by my patrol car, the bumper hit me right below the right knee. When everything stopped moving the patrol car had slid 42 feet, it had hit and pushed the horse trailer 28 feet and the car 26 feet. The patrol car hit me and threw me into the horse trailer, high enough that the patrol car hit below me and pushed the trailer. Then they bounced apart and stopped and I dropped in between them on the ground. Bruce Crawford, Kansas Highway Patrol was coming to back us up and check on our welfare. Bruce eye witnessed the whole thing. The car with the Vietnamese swerved over in front of him and went down in to the left ditch and up into Great Plains Wholesale's parking lot and stopped. I flew through the air, with the greatest of ease, hit the trailer, and rolled up in the fetal position and dropped to the ground. He stopped his Patrol Car in the middle of the road, turned on his emergency lights and called in "Officer Down" and the location. Got out of his car and ran to me and was standing over me looking at me. I wasn't breathing, he thought I was dead. The guy from Arkansas was yelling for help, he was thrown into the ditch on the other side of the trailer. Bruce went on to him because he didn't think there was anything he could do for me. I remember something hitting me and hitting the trailer, then I was on the ground. These oversize boots and blue pant legs with black stripes, were standing beside me. Thinking I must have been out for awhile because the highway patrol has had time to get here. The black stripe on the pants leg being the give away. When Bruce went to help the guy from Arkansas, with me being so intelligent, I knew that I must be okay because he hadn't spoken or helped me. I couldn't breathe but I was trying. After a couple of quick short breaths, I reached up and grabbed the rail around the horse trailer and pulled myself to my feet I stood there leaning against the trailer and trying to get my breath. Hoping my breathing would return to normal. Not sure how long I stood there but the first ambulance got there and they went to the guy in the ditch. He had a broken leg and collar bone, from impacting the trailer and then being thrown about 15 to 18 feet out into the ditch. The second ambulance got there and the attendants went to deputy, Ed Carley, who was riding with me and had stayed in the patrol car trying to communicate with dispatch on our location. He had his door open, on our patrol car, and was ready to get out when the impact occurred, he was thrown forward against the door post and out of the car and into the ditch. Being of high intelligence, as stated earlier, I knew that I for sure I wasn't hurt now, because no one had stopped to help me or ask about me. Actually neither ambulance crew had even seen me. A large number of Emergency Vehicles responded, I remember some but not all. A friend, who ran the Corral Club about a mile and quarter away, heard the Officer Down call. He was listening on a police scanner radio in the bar, and knowing that I had the "East Finney County Beat" that night, came to the scene and was the first one to approach me. He asked if I was alright and I answered, medically speaking I'm sure, "I guess so". I was looking at the ground and searching, with my eyes, for my glasses. He thought that I was maybe a little "out of it" and ask "What you looking for?" "My glasses" I told him. He said that "You just stand there and don't move, I'll find them for you". He proceeded to look for them. About this time the Technicians working on the guy from Arkansas, were trying to split his blue jean pants leg. They needed to get to his broken leg. They were calling for someone with a sharp knife, their scissors would not cut the heavy denim cuff. Of course being unhurt and having a sharp knife, I answered. I walked over to them, pulled up my pants leg and took out my 6 inch, double edged fighting knife, which was sharp enough to shave with, from the boot sheath where I carried it. I handed it to one of them saying "Its very sharp". He proceeded to cut the hem of the pants leg, with the other Tech holding it tight. When he applied the knife, he cut the hem all the way to the man's crotch, luckily he stopped when he did. The patients eyes were very large and his face had turned very white. The Tech looked at the knife and said "Wow, that's sharp". I took my knife and said "You asked for a sharp knife". I stepped back on the asphalt and returned the knife to the sheath in my boot, took a couple of steps and was going to check on the knife and couldn't bend over enough to get a hold of my pants leg, never less pull the knife out. About this time it hit me, my glasses would be back from where everything was setting. My friend Melvin Walker was still looking under the patrol car and everywhere else. He saw me walking, okay maybe hobbling, back and wanted to know where I was going. I told him my glasses would be back here somewhere. He said don't walk, I'll find them for you. Of course I didn't listen to him. I walked back and saw them on the asphalt and tried to bend over to pick them up off the asphalt where they were laying. I couldn't bend over to pick them up. He picked them up and handed them to me and I put them on. They were okay, untouched. I was trying to figure out why I couldn't bend over to pick them up, very strange I thought. The third ambulance got there and Melvin, grabbed one of the attendants and said he needed to check me out. When the attendant got to me, he asked "Are you hurt?" It seems I have been asked that question numerous times over the years and I still don't have a good answer. He said I needed to come back to the ambulance and "sit down". I told him I could stand or lay down, there was nothing in between. "Okay, come on back to the ambulance". Upon arriving at the ambulance he told me to "Sit down in the ambulance". I told him again, " I'll just stand, as there is no sitting going to happen." They wound up having me lay down and transported me to the hospital. Melvin and his wife Doris were good and appreciated friends.

The left rear tire of our patrol car had stopped up near the steering wheel. The doubled reinforced frame was L shaped. The car was totaled. It had driven the tongue of the trailer off the ball hitch and into the trunk of the towing car. Two juveniles were in the impact car and had been chasing 3 people, Vietnamese, and shooting at them with a 410 shotgun. They had fired at least 10 rounds, at the Vietnamese car, with 5 confirmed hits on it. They thought that we were a road block and deliberately drove in to the back of our patrol car. Impact speed was set at 90 mph plus, calculated by the Kansas Highway Patrol who worked the accident. All 3 of us were transported to the hospital, the Arkansas vehicle driver, Ed Carley, and myself. The lady and child in the car were shaken up but not hurt, is what I was told. I never got to see any of the 3 from Arkansas again. Ed Carly was battered and bruised but not otherwise hurt, but later complained of whip lash.

At the hospital I walked into the treatment room and was told to sit up on the table. They never learn. I told them I would just stand, there was still no sitting allowed. Finally a doctor(?) arrived and told me to "Sit down on the exam table". I told him "It was either stand or lay down, nothing in between". He said "Okay, but get up on the table and sit there". Talk about never learning. I said "I'll stand". He told me to take off my shirt, which I did. He was asking questions while I was taking off my shirt. He got out a pair of scissors and I asked what he was going to do? He said "I'm going to cut off your vest". As in bullet proof vest. "Oh no you're not" He said "You don't have anything to say in the matter". Now I was, for some reason, getting irritated with these medical people, and said "NO YOU'RE NOT". He said "I'll make the decisions around here tonight". I replied "You're not cutting my vest". "It had just saved me great bodily harm, I have a 44 magnum and you have a very small pair of scissors". He did see the logic in this (I didn't say he was stupid) and left the room. With help, we took my vest off, over my head. The doctor returned and said that "You have to give up your gun". "No, I'll just keep it, maybe it will help you with your future decisions." They eventually took x-rays and decided I had nothing wrong and could go home. I still couldn't bend, but I guess that is nothing. When they were almost finished with me, Donnie Diehl, Deputy Sheriff's, showed up and ask if I wanted him to take my gun and gun belt? Said the doctor was worried about me. I said "I know, yeah you can take it". I also explained to him what had happened. So he understood where I was coming from. I didn't realize they were going to let me go home, at this point. Shortly I was told to go home. As in times before, I got a lot better care at home anyway. I told Kate all of this and she took care of me, as always. The next morning I couldn't get out of bed and she had to help me get up. I then could navigate, at least move, to make it to the bathroom and around the house and back to bed. Through all of this Donnie Diehl was the only one that ever came to check on me or called, while I was at home. He didn't return my gun and belt for about a week. I needed it when I was going to the FBI instructor training school. He had put it in the armory at the Sheriff's Office. I did go to work on Monday morning but didn't move very fast. I was running a loader at the time, cleaning pens and loading manure trucks over in Gigot Feeders, the feed yard that was next door. I would climb up in the loader in the morning, and I didn't get out until time to go home. The guys I worked with serviced it for me all that week. It took major effort to climb that ladder up into that loader.

Oh, you remember the 2 kids that were in the car that ran into us? When they went to court, the judge, found them guilty of careless driving but suspended a $25.00 fine and they would have to pay $10.00 court costs. Justice, I'm sure. The inside of both knees were very purple, about 8 inches in diameter. I know, the knees are not 8 inches across but are up and down.. The marks on my uniform shirt, where I hit the rail on the trailer, are still in my shirt. The imprint marks in my bullet proof vest stayed for over a year before finally disappearing. Only hurt when I laughed or breathed. My vest had at least saved me a broken shoulder blade, maybe a broken spine/back and possibly my life.

Ten days later, from the date of the accident, I was to start the FBI Firearms Instructors class. Someone at the sheriff's department decided to cancel me out, when informed of this I said "No way I'm going". The Sheriff, Grover Craig, said "Yes and that person would get me re-instated", and they did. Up on showing up for class, Monday morning at 8:00am, we were asked if we had brought at least 800 rounds of 38 special ammunition. Three of us said "No". "Then had we brought 357 magnum ammunition?" Two said "Yes". I said "No". "Well, what did you bring?" "I brought 44 magnum ammo." Instructor "Oh, can you get a 38 or 357?" "Yes, but my duty gun is a 44 magnum and that's what I am going to shoot." Instructor "No one has ever made it through the course and passed with a 44 mag, You had better reconsider". "Nope, I'll make it". Instructor "Okay, but you'll have to shoot the minimum score to pass". "No problem." We practiced and trained until Thursday afternoon and then they ran us through the qualification course . If we passed we didn't have do it again on Friday, but if we didn't, we had another chance on Friday. Minimum score was 94.0%, I scored a 96.8% and top score was 98.0%, Donnie Diehl from Finney County SO, shooting a 38 special. I was in. The class practiced a little with 12 gauge Riot Shotguns. I declined the practice. The head instructor said I didn't need to practice and probably didn't need a shotgun either. The way I shot that 44 Magnum. I didn't need the battering on my back. At the end of practice they shot the qualification course, for practice. They recorded the scores, just in case. Everyone qualified but me, who didn't shoot, and one other guy who couldn't shoot very well. As luck would have it, it was raining on Friday. They took the scores from Thursday for the guys who shot and qualified. That left 2 of us to shoot in the rain, no problem. I maxed the course with the shotgun and the other guy finally made it, with help. After lunch we were to meet back at the GCCC classroom. After a change to dry clothes, I went back to the classroom for graduation. At the start, the head instructor from the FBI, called me up in front of the class. He offered his hand and an apology for questioning my ability, the first day. I told him that it was okay, I hadn't believed him the first day anyway. The apology was accepted but not necessary. He stated that I had made it and that every one of my shots, while not scoring a perfect score , would have taken a man out, every time. That if he ever came back to Kansas, on assignment, he would request that I be assigned to the FBI, for whatever purpose they came to Kansas for. He would be proud to have me for a partner and his backup for whatever we had to do. Another good memory.

The next week I was booked for 5 days of bear hunting in the Colorado Mountains at Gunnison, Colo. And while I was still hobbling and sore, I was still going. On the first day it was snowing, and was cloudy and dark, not the best weather for the hunter. The second day it was just raining, again not the best weather. On the third day the sun came out and I went trout fishing in the morning and mid day. We went to our stands about 3:30 in the afternoon. Everything looked different in the sun light. About 5:00pm I noticed a black spot up on the mountain side. As it was quite a ways off and I couldn't tell for sure what it was. Or if it was really something or just my imagination. Maybe a shadow that seemed to move and change positions, caused by the sun moving and the shadows changing. Possible when I was trying so hard to see a bear, whether there was one there or not. Finally there were 2 spots, one larger than the other and then at times it seemed that they were both the same size. They were in and out of the trees and working closer. They were grazing on the green grass like cattle. I first noticed them at about 3/4 of a mile and it took forever for them to get closer. After about an hour I could tell that this was a bear and she had 1 or 2 cubs, but I was sure that there were 2 cubs. These were yearling cubs and while legal to shoot were not what I had in mind. I was in no doubt but that there was a grown bear also. They were coming in. Since I was already standing, I stayed standing. I was up in the trees, in a tree stand, that you could stand or sit in. I was using a 44 magnum Smith and Wesson Revolver, model 629, 6 inch barrel, stainless steel and open sights. When they were getting closer and behind a hump or mound of dirt I drew my gun, from the cross draw holster I was using. When they were about 40 or 50 yards out they went out of sight again. I cocked the hammer on my gun and waited. They took for ever coming in closer and the light was getting darker by the time they actually got to my stand area. They circled me, around to the front, staying in the trees. Never giving me a clear view of them. Momma was suspicious and not coming in. One of the cubs decided to and came right on in. Momma was talking to it and not liking the fact that the cub came on to the stand area. I had the cub at about 3 yards and 10 feet down, but I was not going to shoot a cub. The sow kept working around an arc, of about 150 to 160 degrees, in front of me and about 30 to 40 yards out in the trees . She set down, centered on a 10 inch aspen tree, looking straight at me, her middle line completely covered. I do think that this was completely intentional. We had an agreement that the guide, who was to pick me up, after dark, would not come in to get me, but would wait on the road, some distance away. The other cub was out there, somewhere out in the trees. The first one was down below me eating green grass and some of the stuff on the bait pile. The sow heard the vehicle coming before I did and I could watch her track it, coming around the mountain. She was still setting centered on the aspen, but was turning her head and tracking the vehicle. After awhile I could hear it, too. To say that this was exciting and nerve racking would have to be an understatement. I had been watching them and anticipating a possible shot for over 2 and a half hours. The vehicle stopped and the motor was turned off. It was so quiet and clear that you could hear things for a very long distance. I could actually see Gunnison, when the sun went down and you still had light. When the sun was out and shining, I could not see the town but after the sun set, I could. I was expecting to hear a door slam and so when I heard a loud noise that was what I heard, but was actually the guide stepping over a log and then dragging his foot and kicking it as he stepped over it. The sow was tracking him all the time and I was zeroed in on her. Now the cubs were old enough to survive on their own and we had been told that this was a legal bear to shoot. I was fixing to try, if I ever got the opportunity. When the guide kicked that log the bear came to her feet, turned and started to leave, all in one motion. My gun came up, I swung on her and I fired when I swung by her on a line with her heart. I fired after I passed the heart area, in trying to lead her. I should also state that although we could only hunt till dark, and being sure it was before that, I couldn't say that I remember seeing my sights but was possibly shooting instinctively which I was also competent at doing. I had the instant flash sight picture of being on her belly line, low for shot placement, but about right front to rear. My estimated yardage was 15 yards. The bear went into high gear. I didn't see either of the cubs. The guide about had a heart attack or at least coronary failure when that shot went off. Because it was nearly dark, especially in the trees. He had a flashlight and it did come on shortly there after. He was shining it all over trying to find the bear that he knew I would have been firing at. He also knew he had screwed up by leaving the car. In the dark there was nothing to do but go on out and come back in the morning, to look and hope-fully find something or have something to track. I came down out of my stand and was making my way out to the road and the vehicle. When the guide over took me. Whispering, he wanted to know what had happened? I told him to wait until we got out to the road. In not wanting to make any more noise than we had too. When we reached the vehicle I explained everything that had happened and that I thought we should wait until we got light, in the morning. He agreed and we headed back to the outfitters house. Where everyone was waiting for us to get in. I then had to tell the story in complete detail and answer everyone's questions. The outfitter, 4 guides, and about 13 other hunters. Not to mention Daniele, who was a hunter and the wife of Mike Grosse, the outfitter. Mike said that there was a sow with 2 yearling cubs in that area and had been seen there before. So this was likely them. It was late by the time this broke up and we all wondered off to our cabins, with the plan of going back the next morning, early. Mike Grosse, the guide, and I were the only ones that went back the next morning. We walked in and looked over the stand area, everything was as I recalled except that the bear had been at 25 yards instead of the 15 yards that I had called. Why 15 yards, I don't know now, but was my call at the time. It would seem that 25 was more consistent but things had gone into high gear. The tracks were there. The other thing that was different was that there was a mound of dirt that I didn't remember being there before and the bear had ran uphill on it. When I made my very hurried shot, my sight picture had been correct, I was on her belly line when the gun went off. No blood or hair or anything. We tracked them for as far as we could, but no she was not hit and I had missed. Mike was impressed with the details that I had supplied and the accuracy of everything that I had relayed to them. We were all disappointed with the end result, my missed shot. But such is hunting.

That day, one of the other hunters from Garden City, Ks. did get a shot and wounded a bear. Which we looked for the next morning and tracked it for 2 and a half miles. Some of it on our hands and knees.. We never found this bear either. We decided that the bear was hit in the leg and that was where the piece of bone came from instead of the body and the wound was not a lethal hit. Bears hit in the leg will usually survive.

On the last day of the hunt another of the hunters from Garden City did take one of the cubs that I had seen, on another stand about 3 miles away from the stand where I had taken my shot. This was the only bear taken by the 14 hunters that were in camp for this week. Not very good and was not even close to the normal for Mike's hunting camps, but like I said this is hunting.

We were all given the chance to come back later and try again. And we were also given the chance to buy a share of Mikes hunting operation. Don't know if any of the others did or not. In talking with him about it, the shares sold for $2500.00 each and when I told him that I couldn't do that much. He wanted to know what I could do or had in mind. I told him that I had saved about $1000.00 from my bonus's at work, for hunting. He said he would sell me my share for that amount. We got 25% return, per year, to be used for hunting and after 4 years he would buy back the share at face value. If we wanted to sell it back, or we could just let it ride and could continue to build up credit, for hunting. Mine has been going all this time and in 1999 I went on a buffalo or American Bison hunt in south Texas. I will cover that at a later time.

In writing some of these things down over the past weeks, in trying to share with Kate's family about us, I have learned that a number of my family members haven't heard some of these things or only heard maybe pieces. And they never asked. So I am continuing to write for not only Kate's side of the family but for mine also, or better put would be for all of my family.

Kate worked at the Emmaus House from a early date, after our moving to Garden City. When both the kids were very young, she started volunteering there. It is a homeless shelter and a food kitchen, to put up and feed people in need. They also dispense food to needy people.

One time when she was working there she gave away my sleeping bag to a homeless man, who had stayed there. He had gotten a job, and they supplied him with a room for sleeping, as part of the pay for his job. He needed something for bedding and she decided my sleeping bag would fit the bill. Now I don't know if she had my sleeping bag in her car or she came home and got it. When I came home from work this day, she was fixing supper. She knew the second best way to my heart (you'll have to use your imagination for number 1). When I came in the house, she turned and said "I did something today and you're going to be mad at me". I responded with "OK, it won't be the first time, what did you do this time?". She said "I gave away your sleeping bag". At first I was irritated, but as she told me the circumstances and as I came to understand, it was okay. I told her "It's okay, but there is a catch". She wanted to know "What is the catch". "Well, without a sleeping bag to keep me warm, you will have to keep me warm." She said "I can handle that". She laughed and kissed me. When the time came she did keep me warm, as always.

Over the years she did many things in helping those that needed it, vegetables from the garden, food from the house, meat from the freezer, meat from game that I had taken or whatever we had available. She volunteered, helped, and ministered to whomever she came across that needed it. And she was always there to love and take care of me. And I was there to return that love for and to her.

In the 1980's sometime she was told by a Catholic Priest that she had to do something in relation to the kids. I'm not sure what it was anymore. She said "Excuse me?" He repeated that she HAD to do whatever this was. "NO, I'll decide what my kids HAVE to do, not you". The priest repeated that she HAD to do this. "NO" She had fire and steel in her. She turned and walked out of the Catholic Church and never went back. She could get mad, although it was rare. She started attending the Plymell Church, about 4 miles from home, with the kids. She continued going to church there until there was some kind of big disagreement that split the church. I'm not sure she was on either side but didn't want the hassle either. She then started attending the Word Of Life Church, in Garden City, where she continued as a member until the time of her passing.

It was sometime in this time frame that she had her gall bladder taken out. It was bothering her and Dr. Bruno did some tests and diagnosed it and did the surgery. She recovered and didn't wear a bikini anymore, after that surgery. She never wore one before the surgery either. In about 1987 she wasn't feeling very well. She couldn't eat very much, and with a few bites she would feel full and was losing weight. She finally agreed to go see Dr. Bruno and he ran the tests and determined that she had a tumor on her stomach. She had to have surgery to remove the tumor. While they were in there they did a modified hysterectomy. The tumor when Dr. Bruno removed it, was the size of a basketball, with a softball sized one under it. Which they did not even suspect being there but removed it as well. The surgery went well and she was out and in recovery

very quickly. I was there when she woke up and ask how she was feeling, right after I kissed her. I was teasing her about not wearing a bikini anymore and when she laughed, it hurt to laugh. She said not to make her laugh anymore, because it hurt to much. I agreed to wait for a while before I teased her or told anymore jokes. She was in the hospital for about 5 days, as I remember, and then came home. Mary Lynn was doing a good job of filling in for her mother and taking care of the house. And Lance was there and didn't get in the way, to much, but was better at eating than cooking, at least at that time.

Chapter 17:

Quarters for Kisses

It was sometime in the mid 80's that this next started. I had worked, almost all night, on something, don't remember what it was now. I got home in the early hours of the morning, probably 5 to 6, and got up with about 3 hours sleep. I had to be somewhere at 10:00am. I got up and she was already up and doing. Imagine that, with 2 young kids, 8 & 10 or 10 & 12, something like that. I always kissed her the first thing in the morning when I woke up, if she was there. And then when I was leaving for work, or where ever I was leaving for. She went with me or met me at the door and kissed me again. On this day she had gotten her first kiss in the kitchen and when I was ready to leave, and she wasn't at the door, I told her I was leaving. She called back to wait, she needed another kiss before I left. So I went back into the kitchen and embraced her and kissed her. She smiled and said something about leaving without kissing her was just not acceptable. I laughed, and while still holding her, I said "That while the first kiss in the morning was free, the ones after that were 25 cents each". She laughed and said "That's fine with me, do I have to pay cash or is my credit good?" I told her "Your credit is good with me." She said "Alright!!!" She threw both her arms around my neck, pulled me to her and kissed me, quite thoroughly. We were both somewhat breathless when she let me go. She put her hands on my chest and gently pushed me back and said "Now, put that on account". She was smiling and was lucky that I had to be somewhere. Or maybe not. She was quite prepared to happily take responsibility and accept the resulting response for her actions. She knew what my response was going to be. I was able to mumble out something like "You just wait till I get back". She laughed and said she would be here and waiting. And yes she was. This stayed with us the rest of her life and we had lots of fun with it. We might be some where in public and we would kiss each other and one of us would say, "Put that quarter on account." or "That will be another quarter." or "You want that quarter on account?" We did get some funny looks, at times, but that was okay, because I loved her and didn't care what they thought.

Chapter 18:

Rotary Massey Ferguson Combine

In my 32 years of being employed by the Gigot Family I had many experiences that are worth recalling or sharing. This is one them. Over the years the Gigot's had a good working relationship with Massey Ferguson, farm equipment builders. The Massey combines for years were very popular with many farmers and/or custom combine operators. My Dad was one who like Massey. When we went into the Custom Harvesting business, Dad favored Massey combines. While I preferred John Deere. So we wound up buying International Harvesters or just Internationals, who later became Case International Harvester or Case IH. Now over the years Massey would bring ideas or test machines to the Gigot fields for development and testing. I remember one of these was a twin engine combine that was actually cheaper to build than the conventional Model 760 that was in production at the time. People just didn't take to the idea of 2 motors. But by using 2 motors, one was used for the propulsion and the hydraulics of the machine and the other for driving the thrashing part of the machine. Drive lines, gear boxes, and such could be built smaller and lighter because of the less required horsepower by the smaller used engines and so was cheaper to build. The drive engine didn't require as much HP because it didn't have to supply the thrashing part of the machine the required HP for thrashing and propulsion. So this machine never saw the light of production, but I thought it was still a good idea or concept.

Another machine that they decided to develop was a large rotary machine. While other companies already had or were in the process of doing this, Massey was in the process of field testing a proto type machine. This would have been in the early 1980's. During the year in question, they arrived at the farm with the machine and a crew of engineers, mechanics, and machinists to support this machine and make it work. As I remember they had both 8 row and 12 row corn heads with the machine. The Gigot operations were set up with 16 row planters, cultivators, and other support equipment so it worked best to use 8 row corn heads in the harvesting of the grain. But this machine was large enough that it would handle the 12 row head satisfactorily. All the way through the fall harvest they worked at perfecting and getting the bugs out of this machine. For the most part it ran with Terry and Jerry Gigot's combines, on a daily basis. In some cases they had to hand make parts as needed for this new machine. They were confident that they were really building a superior combine. And this one was reportedly at or over the million dollar cost mark at this point in time. At this time Mike Gigot was running 8820 John Deere combines. He had switched to the JD's because of the availability, previously, of new Massey's. I would at times go out and run one of Mike's combines at night, after I left the grain elevator (Southwest Corn) where I ran the elevator and grain dryers. This was a needed break from the daily job and I liked running combines. I did this all the time while Mike was still in the corn farming business. I also would, most years, take off from work using vacation time to make extra money and cut wheat for him in the summer. This let his regular help stay on the corn farming part of the business. I liked to harvest wheat and corn, and so I was pretty good at it and had lots of years of doing it. I started running a combine when I was in the 4th grade. We had moved off the farm by then and were living in town. I would go and stay with my grandparents on the farm and would help, or get in the way of, their neighbor, our old neighbor. He started letting me run his combine while cutting wheat. I started early at this, too. Back to the rotary, after working on this all harvest they were ready for the big test. Every year, that it was possible, Terry would get me out of the elevator and out to the field and into a combine for a day or several days. He knew that I really liked and wanted to run a combine. This year I was out there for a couple of days, with my first job being to help put the straw walkers back in one of the 860 combines. Terry and Jerry had 3 860 Massey's, and one White Rotary machine at the time. I would be running the 860 that we put the straw walkers in. We had 2 circles, PV 5 &6, together that would let us have full mile long rows for the test. The 3 860's were up the road on PV #4 field, shelling corn there. When they were ready to run the test, they pulled me out. I went down and got ready to run the test with this 860 Massey. The test was run using the Massey Rotary, the White Rotary, and the 1 Massey 860. Now I had wanted to run the test with one of Mike's 8820 John Deere's but was told "No". Now why I was picked for this test, I don't know. Maybe they (the engineers) thought that it would show the rotary in a better position, beating the 860 by a wider margin, with a less (their thought) experienced operator on the machine. We had to go and park on a marked spot and they fueled and checked all the settings on the machine, and then I had to wait for the go ahead to start the engine. We also had an engineer ride with us to certify the test. While waiting for the go ahead to start my engine, I asked the engineer about the test and how I was expected to run it. He explained the test and said to run the machine to the best of its ability. As I remember they were going to check ground speed, acres per hour, bushels per hour, fuel consumption, field loss, cracked grain, foreign material in the grain, and maybe some other things that I'm not remembering any more. That was what I wanted to hear, about the running of the machine, because I ran somewhat different than their normal operators. The Gigot brothers are very competitive, at every-thing they do and in running with Mike's crew I would do my best and was reliable. And when he needed someone to run late at night or was short an operator, and I could do it, I was there to run for him. And he had said if they would let me run the test, then I would have, my pick of his John Deere machines. I told the engineer that I was going to run the engine against the tach and would have to slow down when we unloaded the corn, on the go. We unloaded into a grain cart, as I remember we each had our own grain cart. I had to do this to hold my RPM when I unloaded. More horsepower was used on the unloading auger. He said sure, that would be fine and he understood what I was saying and was going to do. We would have 3 miles of corn each, a mile down, a mile back, and then the 3rd mile back down the field to the finish. I was to go first, okay, I'm ready. We finally got the signal to start, and I fired up the engine and moved into the field. Not much to tell about the actual test, the field was flat, for Southwest Kansas, so no problems there, we made our run, I ran the engine against the tach, slowing down when unloading and then back up on speed after I unloaded the grain. We had grain monitors, to show if we were losing any grain, so I was watching for field loss. After I was finished they had me park on a designated spot, they fueled and checked the machine and I was told to go to the shop. I said "No". I would head back to help the other 860's with the last field, for the whole year. We all wanted to be finished for another year. The other 2 test machine operators chose to go to the shop. We didn't take to long to finish and were told to leave the machines in the field, but move the trucks and other equipment home. So I made 2 trips driving in loaded corn trucks, we didn't dump them that night. We were more than ready to go to the after harvest party, that had already started, even though some of us hadn't finished yet, but we got there eventually. The others were already ahead of us, meaning those that had stayed to finish, so that there could be an after harvest party, but that was okay. People were there from all the crews and were having a good time. As far as I remember all the Massey people were there also. The wives were invited and welcome but most, like Kate, chose to stay at home. The first order of business was a cold beer and the second was I wanted to find out about the test. So I looked up one of the head engineers and ask how the test went. He said "....... you" and walked away. Everyone of them that I tried to talked to would just walk away from me, the others didn't say anything. I finally caught up with one who had been coming down for a lot of years and we had been on friendly terms all this time. I asked him what was wrong with everyone. He said "You don't know?" "No, I don't". So he explained that I had smoked the other 2 machines, on every test category except ground speed. "What???" "Yep, you just threw out 2 to 3 years of work for them on this machine. And they wanted to know why I wasn't running that machine, regularly, instead of doing whatever I did, regularly. My question was why I hadn't been allowed to run their test machine, because if I could do that with their "Old obsolete machine" (their words), what could I have done with their 'new' machine, they still didn't want to talk to me. Sometimes in trying to build the odds in your favor you overlook a better solution for the problem. They never considered the operators when they were setting up their test. They should have had each operator run each machine as part of the test, and noted the experience or lack of experience of each operator with the individual machines. This would of made the test more fair and realistic. I guess its nice to be a well kept secret, in some circles anyway. These were some of the many experiences that I had while with the Gigot family.

Chapter 19:

Clarence Gigot

Clarence was the Gigot brothers father, and to those that applauded the Gigot brother's accomplishments, and rightfully so, I would say, if you think they were accomplished you should have known and looked at their father, Clarence. First, he was my friend, and a good friend. He was a kind man, who loved children, his and others. He was always there with a helping hand and a kind word. He was sharp, in farming and in a business sense. He not only was successful, but started all of his kids in the farming business also. To me, anyway, he would tell the stories of his history and of the country's history. Here was a man who had lived it, not bragging, just telling. How I miss those stories of the early life in this country. I can only relay the information that I remember, so I won't claim this to be complete or maybe completely accurate, but only as I remember it. I think he came from Wisconsin as a young child, was born on October 23rd, 1904. They moved to Kinsley, Kansas, when he was about 4 years old. To my recollection his father was a Mill Wright by trade and this meant in those days he could build about anything. His father built or helped build a lot of brick buildings in Kinsley, and a number of them are still standing and in use today. I'm not remembering how many years they lived there before coming to Garden City to live. This would have been around 1920 or 21, when he was about 16. They first lived in the area of where Garden City's Airport is today. They had 2 sections of grass there and ran cattle.

He told me of having 2 horses and he rode those fences every day for 2 years, and he had enough of horse back riding to last him the rest of his life. Now when we were building the race track, which is known as Airport Raceway, he would come and watch. He would come at or about Noon and maybe go to lunch with Mike, Terry, Jeff Gigot and Steve Proehl, but I only remember him doing that once or twice. Usually he would show up just after they left, and I would say "You just missed them, they just left to go eat" and he would answer "NO, I didn't miss anybody", and would stay and talk to me through the lunch hour or until they came back. I would have my lunch with me and would offer to share, sometimes he would take the offer of part of my lunch, to share with me. How I enjoyed these times when we would set and talk of what we were doing or of times gone by. One day we were setting there and talking and looking at some cottonwood trees. These were to the west of us and a little north. He said that they looked familiar. As we set, looked, and talked for a while, he said "I guess they should, thats where we used to live and I planted those trees". We decided that the angle was different from what he would normally have seen them from, in times past. That was when he told me of the 2 sections of land mentioned previously. In, I think, 1923, friends of his father told him not to buy cattle that year, as it was going to be a bad year for cattle and that they would 'break the market' that year. So his Dad didn't buy cattle and they wound up returning or selling the land back to the bank and buying and moving to the location on TV Road that was to become their home for many years. There they or his father, started the farming operation that would continue for the rest of his life.

Sometime in the mid 1920's he and his brother were hired by a man to break out and plant a quarter of ground, just over into Haskell County. This was not to far from the home place. They agreed to do this and purchased a steam driven tractor and a breaking plow for that purpose. I am not remembering now how they got fuel and water to the field, for the tractor, but they got it there someway. The tractor had a large operators platform on it and they secured a folding cot on the platform so that one of them could sleep while the other ran the tractor, thus enabling them to run 24 hours a day, with stops only for fuel, water, or break downs. They got the quarter of ground broke out and planted to wheat, received their pay and Clarence went across the road and put a down payment on the quarter of ground there. I'm not sure now if his brother was a partner on this or not. He broke out the new quarter and got it planted to wheat also. I'm thinking he said that he raised 27 or 28 bushel wheat off this ground the first year. He said he had enough to pay everything off, including the ground, and go to town and buy himself a brand new car. Everything was paid off and he had a new car, and a quarter of ground but was broke. Such was life in the fast lane in those youthful days. I have cut wheat on that quarter a number of times, both of them for that matter, and baled a lot of alfalfa on the first, with feed, straw, and milo stalks being baled on the second one, at different times. Because in later times he acquired the first quarter also, and they were willed to 2 of his granddaughters, with his passing.

The first summer I was in Garden City and in the employ of Southwest Corn, Terry was my boss. I was sent with a 4000 White dump bed farm truck and a pup trailer, to haul 50,000 bushels of corn from Clarence's to W-W feeders. This had a Giesel Engine, this engine had been converted from running on diesel fuel to running on gasoline. With this set up I could hall 1000-1100 bushes of corn each load. Terry said to check with "Dad" on every load, before I loaded, or he would get upset about my not doing so. I checked with Clarence on the first load and he told me and showed me everything. He was there and watch me load the first load. "Okay you've got it, if you need something just let me know." I replied with "Okay thanks". When I came back for the second load I went and found him, where ever he was at, and whatever he was doing. I told him I was back for the second load. "Okay, do you need help?" "No, but Terry said to check with you on every load". "NO, you know how and don't need me, so just do it and tell Terry to mind his own business". "I don't think I will tell him that". Clarence said "Well, I will". So I just hauled and after a few days Terry stopped me on the road and asked how it was going, I told him good and I had so many loads hauled in, and was I checking with Dad on each load? No, he said that I knew how to do it and could do just as well whether he was there or not, so don't waste time and bother him. I am to "Tell Terry to mind his own business, we would handle the corn hauling".

Terry laughed and said that sounded like Dad and to do it however he said to, and I did. And Clarence and I got along just fine. The corn was all haul when it was suppose to be.

Another time he told of the little red haired girl he met and eventually married, what fun times and adventures they had together. It was so enjoyable to listen to him talk of those days when they were starting out. I sure hope she had red hair in those days because that was what he said.

East of Highway 50 on Annie Scheer Road, about 2 to 2 ½ miles on the north side of the road, on the field we called Mike #4. This had been the headquarters of the Bullard Cattle Company. It was reported to have been the largest free roaming cattle ranch in Kansas history. They free roamed or ranged cattle from Ingalls or Cimarron, Kansas to Lamar, Colorado, and from the Arkansas River to the Cimarron River. A fair sized area of land, especially on horse back. Not sure of the date any more but Clarence was still living at home with his parents. His dad took him up to this site. There was 30,000 head of cattle, loose, being herded by cowboys riding around them on horse back. They had been rounded up and brought into the home ranch for sorting, doctoring, and what ever they needed prior to being sold. It seems Mr. Bullard had been diagnosed with cancer and was going to sell out. The cattle were eventually driven to Pierceville, loaded on stock cars and shipped from there. He had 2 children, a boy and a girl, who were socialites and were more interested in partying than running a cattle ranch, they were back east somewhere. So he would sell everything and put the money in a trust that would hopefully take care of them in the years to come. Clarence's Dad said "Boy, you look at this and remember, because you'll never see it again" and he was right. According to Clarence, he never did, he saw 30,000 head of cattle on a quarter of ground, 160 acres, but with fences around them and divided up in to pens with cattle in the different pens. This was quite a sight, seen through his eyes and with his telling of it. Mike has told me at least parts of this also. The headquarters was out towards the center of the quarter with a large water well, in the same place as the irrigation well is now located. They would pump water and it would run into a series of tanks, stair stepped down the hill, to the southeast. As the upper tank got full it would go out an overflow and run into the next tank and so on clear down the hill to the bottom. If the last tank got full it would run over onto the ground and make a pond with the overflow. This location is still able to be picked out after all these years and the ground is definitely different, through the years of build up of sediment and moisture. If you work the ground, you can see the difference. I would like to have seen that sight with him those many years ago.

When I would cut wheat for Mike in the summer, if Clarence wasn't done with his wheat, then Mike would say "Head to Dad's and get him finished". If he didn't say so or I didn't talk to him I would just head that way. If I didn't know where he was at, I would call him, in the evening before or that morning and ask where I needed to be. He never had to ask what I was talking about or doing, he knew. He would tell me where he wanted me and that's where I would be. I would pull in and go to cutting, check behind the machine (s) and keep on going. That's all that was needed between us. One time I finished on Mike's, Mike #10, and we came down and he was on PV #3. East and south of his house. He had told me where he would be or Mike had. So I just pulled in, checked behind the machines, and kept going. This was during the noon hour and if some one didn't come and relieve him he would not go in to eat. So one of the boys or I have been known to do it, would come and relieve him. Terry was on Clarence's combine and caught me when I was unloading onto a truck. Terry told me I was in trouble with his Dad. I said "Okay, what for this time?" Terry said that I had come into his field and not checked with him before I started cutting. You had to always check with Dad before you started cutting on any of his fields. Okay. We went back to cutting. Clarence returned and got back on his combine and when we finished for the day, we were on another field. When we quit for the day and we were talking at the pickups before going home, I told Clarence that "I guessed I'm in trouble with you". He said "For what?" I replied "For pulling in and starting to cut without checking with you." Clarence "Who told you that?" "Terry." Clarence "Oh, that kid!" And he added "No, you did just fine, and that's what you were suppose to do, you know that". "Well, I thought so but that's what he said." Clarence "Tell him to mind his own business and we'll take care of mine." Again I said "No, I don't think I'll tell him that". He said "Well, I will." And he did, when he saw him.

Clarence seemed to always be thinking of me, if he was cutting wheat and I hadn't been down, he would come by the elevator and stop and see me and ask "Have you been cutting wheat?" "No, I haven't made it out yet." He would respond with something like this "Well, I've got something to do today, so if you can, you better come down and run my combine for awhile, so I can get away." "OK, I will be down as soon as I can get there." When I would get there he would put me on his combine and say he would be back, sometime. I'm not sure if he ever had anything to do, at least that couldn't wait. He made sure that I was on a combine for at least an afternoon. And he didn't like to give up his combine. He did it though, so I could run too. I believe he cut wheat for about 70 straight years, he never missed a year. I miss him, and I looked for him to show up in the field, to check on me or see what I was doing for 4 or 5 years, after he was gone. I never quit looking but also knowing he wasn't going to make it.

I time, when I was a Deputy Sheriff, I heard a call on the radio. I was at home in the evening, and had a scanner to listen to radio traffic. The call was an older man had had a heart attack, while running a tractor. South on Highway 83, to TV road and then 5 ½ miles east, on the north side of the road. Clarence's home was 5 ½ east on the south side of the county road. I was off and running, scared to death, fearing the worst and hoping for something better. I got there in a pretty short time, and was flying down TV road, I saw the tractor in the field before I got there, and standing in the field was Clarence. There was another man on the ground. I was able to take another reasonable breath, again. Clarence's brother in law had been running the tractor and had the heart attack, Clarence had tried running along beside the tractor and was going to try and get on the tractor to stop it when it ran into a mud hole between the fields, and the disk went down in the mud and killed the tractor's engine. Clarence removed the body from the tractor, by himself, and laid it on the ground, but it was already to late. Nothing could be done, as I remember it was a massive coronary. We waited together for the ambulance to get there and talked about what had happened. He had come to the field and was setting in his pickup watching. We discussed what could of happened if he had tried get on that tractor while it was moving, if he had slipped or stumbled but he said he had to try and that he was glad when the tractor and disk had gone into the mud, so was I.

I remember of his telling of going to see Johnny Adams, the father of Fern Batchelder, to discuss farming some of Johnny's ground. Johnny was an old time cowboy and ran cattle and as I remember did not even know how to run a tractor or want to. When Fern was still at home she did whatever farming that got done. Johnny lived about 6 miles west of Highway 50 and 1 ½ miles north of the Haskell County line. This house looked to be the old stucco type walled structure, not so, those wall were made with high grade concrete. When I went down with the 645 Allis articulating loader to push it in, I couldn't do anything to the walls. Even with a short run and bump, I just marked the wall, using the corner of the cutting bit I couldn't make a hole in the wall. It was built to last and was very sturdy. They wound up bringing in a large crawler dozer to push it in, I think they used a 41 Allis crawler. This was a big dozer. The blade was 8 foot tall and 20 foot wide, the whole unit weighted about 160,000 pounds. Clarence had gone down on Sunday, after church, for dinner and to discuss the land deal that they were working on. He said that he didn't know Johnny very well and had heard stories about him. Maybe he was different or as some said 'a little strange'. I would suspect that living out there by ones self would make all of us 'a little strange'. Especially if we stayed and prospered, which Johnny did. Upon entering the house Johnny invited him to sit down, but first Johnny pulled the cushions from the couch and chair and checked to make sure nothing else was in or under the cushions. A little strange Clarence thought, but not that big a thing. Johnny was cooking in the kitchen and said it was almost ready. He noticed Clarence glancing into the bedroom, and the bed clothes were thrown off the bed and were on the floor. So Johnny decided to tell him about this, he said you never set down in the couch or easy chair without pulling the cushions to check for rattle-snakes. For they like to come in and crawl up into the gaps around the cushions and just lay there. And you never get into a bed with out checking between each piece of bedding first, because the snakes will crawl up and into the bed and lay between the individual layers. Even I can see where it might be somewhat surprising to slide into bed and find you had unwanted company in the bed. I'm sure. So you threw the covers off the bed and made it when you were getting in to it, no surprises when getting into bed this way. Clarence said that he did watch, EVERYTHING, a lot closer the rest of the day, while he was there. Johnny explained that the house had a partially finished basement and the snakes could enter through the unfinished part. Then they would come up the stairs into the house and, sort of, make themselves to home. I'm sure I couldn't have lived there but then that was one of those different worlds and I guess I'm just not cowboy enough, or tough enough, to live like that. The snakes would even come into that basement and "den up" for the winter. I can't imagine living there with, maybe, hundreds of rattlesnakes in the basement. I don't even care if it was winter and they weren't moving or moving slowly, I would have done something different. Anyway the encounter was successful and they make a deal for Clarence to start farming some of Johnny's land. This lead to the farming of about 31 quarters, eventually. I was there when we did finally push in this house and was prepared for the, suspected, snakes but we found none in the house. I wasn't there when they ripped up the concrete floor in the barn, part of the barn had a concrete floor. The wood from the barn was dismantled and hauled away by someone and so the floor was done at a different time. That's where the snakes were, many, many snakes were under that floor. Snakes and pieces of snakes were all over the tracks on that dozer, and as I remember the operator was very glad that he had tight shutting doors on the cab. That was "spooky", in his words. Anyway this became part of the Batchelder unit and was actually circle #3. I did help some with the breaking out of this unit. I didn't help with this quarter.

I remember getting 'lost' in a blizzard on the south Batchelder, the part over in Haskell county, before it was broke out. I had been down there scouting for deer and the blizzard came rolling in, I was out in the middle of a large area of native grass and sage brush. Almost instantly you could not see anything. There was one prominent hill and I decided I would keep it off to my left and drive north until I hit the road. I was going slow, because of the visibility and seemed like it was taking a long time to get to that road. I came up on some ones vehicle tracks in the snow, and thought what kind of an idiot would be out in this weather driving around. I looked at the tracks a little closer and realized that the idiot in question was setting in my Bronco. I had gone full circle around that hill without even realizing it, until I came up on my own tracks. That's how bad it was. I usually have a very good sense of direction. I decided to take a different approach to my problem. I put the hill behind me and would try to drive straight away from it. If I could hold my line I would eventually get to a fence on the east, a road on the north or another one to the west, or go a long ways to the south and eventually come to another fence. I know, not much of a plan, but it was the only game in town, at the time. You didn't come up with anything better, at the time, as I remember it. Because when I decided to take this approach, I wasn't even sure which side of the hill I was on. I thought the east side but I had lost my sense of direction and other than the silhouette of the hill, for reference, and it was fuzzy in the blowing snow. I could tell absolutely nothing from the landscape, everything was already covered with snow, and everything looked the same. You couldn't even see the hill at 50 yards and with no other background, everything was white, you had a very lost feeling. Well it worked anyway, and I was able to drive a straight line for about 3/8 of a mile. I know how far it was because when I came back later and I checked. I got to the fence and followed it north to the road and back to a more civilized world. A very eerie and lost feeling, I assure you. Can you imagine what this would have been like before roads and fences, really gives meaning to being lost and helpless, and maybe even worse. God does look out for us fools, or idiots would maybe be another good word here.

Another time Terry told of going out for the evening, actually he went to Dodge City, and saw Connie Ray, his future wife. She shared an apartment or house with Barb, I not sure what they did that evening but Terry says that he was tired and slept on the couch for awhile and then got up and went home. He had missed Dad and Mom's curfew but that was okay he would cut his engine before he got there and coast into the yard, slip into the house and into bed. Dad would never even know. Well things went as planned, he was in bed and asleep when Dad came to get him up, about 4 or 4:30 am. He did not get much sleep but Dad never said anything so he had put one over on Dad. He had to go cultivate milo all day on an open tractor, no cab, but it was worth it to put one over on Dad. Now Clarence told a little different story, when he told it to me he didn't know that Terry had already told me the same story. Clarence's version went like this, Terry had gone out that night, to go see Connie, and was to be home by curfew, I think that was 11:00pm, but not for sure. He wasn't home on time. And Clarence was awake when he came coasting into the yard, and "silently" slipped into the house and went to bed. Clarence said he gave him about 15 or 20 minutes to get undressed, get into bed and get to sleep. Then Clarence went in and got him up so he could get an early start on the cultivating. Normally he wouldn't have got him up this early but everything considered he needed an early start. And normally he would have shut down during the middle or hot part of the day but it would be good for him to just keep running. And he was ready for bed that night after a full day on the tractor. Now Bud Byer, Barb's father, told the same story from Barb and Connie's point of view. When they had quizzed Terry about getting home, he said he could stay out late if he wanted to, Dad wouldn't care, especially if he didn't know. He could slip in and get in bed and Dad would never know. Dad slept so sound he would never even hear him when he slipped into the house at 4 in the morning and went to bed. It was pretty funny listening to the 3 accounts of the same story and Terry thinking he had put one over on old Dad, and Dad knowing that he hadn't put anything over on anybody. Just to prove it he got to run the tractor all day long.

In about 1977 in the fall, we had been working everyday for over 2 months and we were shutting everything down for a day, a day off for everyone. Mike stopped by and wanted to know if I was going to sleep all day. I laughed and said I wouldn't remember how to do that. He said he was going down to his Dad's to shell a circle of corn, 135 acres, and wanted to know if I wanted to take one of his Massey's and go along and help his Dad and Max Davis. Max was Clarence's son in law, Jennifer's husband. They were going to shell Jen's #1 circle. It wouldn't take long with 4 machines and we would be done early. I said "Okay, I'll go". I was to meet him on Mike #9, his machines were located there. They would be serviced and ready to go. Meet there about 9:00am. "Okay". We moved down to Clarence's and pulled in and started shelling with the 2 7720 machines of Clarence and Max. I told him that "This was different, daylight and standing corn, I wasn't sure if I knew how to run". Everything I had being seeing was at night and with down corn in the field. Mike laughed and said to tough it out, just raise the head up off the ground and go. We were finished by early afternoon and Mike said to leave the combine there and take the new 1978 4x4 Ford Pickup home. That he was driving, and just keep it the rest of the week. This pickup was for some one at the shop, but Mike wanted to put some miles on it first. So I took it home and drove it for the rest of the week, the guys at the shop were upset or concerned that I had the new pickup but Mike said to keep it, so I did and I guess they eventually got over it.

Chapter 20:

We are a family of shooters

To get started and establish a record, we are a family of shooters, as in guns. Although Kate did not compete or have any desire to, she did learn to shoot and would upon occasion join us in plinking. Mary Lynn, Lance, and I are all somewhat accomplished and to different degrees of ability. Mary Lynn has hunted with me since she was less than a year old, actually she started going with me when she was about 3-4 months old. Sometimes with her mother and sometimes just the two of us. We would go hunt coyotes and I did some calling with her along. She started shooting at a very young age also. Mostly 22 caliber rim fires, air guns, and some with the center fire or larger guns. She started shooting in the National Guard Air Rifle shooting program when Lance was in it. It happened that their practice night was the same as the night that I ran Police Combat shooting for the Gun Club. So Kate would take Lance to practice and since Lynn had to go along, she started shooting with them for something to do while they waited for Lance. Some kids go to Little League, but Lance played soccer. She progressed until she went to the State Championship Matches at least 2 years, as a shooter on the team. The last year that she went, because she got to old, she was on the first team from Garden City. As I remember, which could be faulty, she placed 7th Individual in the state competition, and was on the 1st place State Championship Team. Her team placed 1st, 2nd, 4th, and 7th individually. After the rifle competition was finished, the people running the competition announced that there would be a special air pistol competition for all the competitors, guns and equipment would be furnished. No one knew this was coming so no practicing had taken place, you went in to the competition cold, what you see is what you get. Well when everyone had finished our little girl was 3rd in the State Air Pistol competition. She did upset a lot of boys who thought that they could shoot. She was interviewed, by whom ever was covering the shoot, radio and TV, and was asked where she had learned to shoot like that. She answered that she had been taught by her Dad and been shooting with him for a long time. Which she had, she shot 22 bowling pin competition for a lot of years. While she shot all events, there were 9 individual events, her specialty or best was the 22 rifle. In the club yearly competition she was often 3rd overall for the season, of course she was behind her old Dad, who was also her teacher and a friend of ours whom we shot with for years. As in the state tournament, a number of shooters would want to know how she got third place, and were told she had beat them. She probably never won an individual nightly shoot but she was always close to the top and did not have any bad scores. The 22 Pin Shoots were on steel silhouettes of bowling pins and were timed by electronic timing, the base course was 5 pins on 16 inch centers and shot at 25 feet for handguns, and 25 yards for the rifles. The regular club events were shot 3 times each and all counted, total fastest time wins, then your best scores, for the year, were totaled and averaged to decide your placing, we used 50% of the events available, plus 1 more, for the annual score. So consistency was a must if you were going to win or place. She also competed in the 2 day week end shoots that we held and was very much into the competition. These shoots also had classes for women and children. She does have her own guns and if she doesn't have one she borrows from me. And I don't want her shooting at me, she's pretty good, but then she had a good teacher.

Lance is a very competitive person, and also a competitive shooter. He has been going hunting and shooting with me since his mother would allow him to go, which was before he could walk, he started hunting coyotes with me when he was maybe 4 months old, like his sister. He has set in the pickup and out in the sagebrush and called coyotes with me. He has been shooting since he was about

6 and while he is actually faster than I am, he still can not beat me consistently, yet. Maybe now or before long, I think. He has shot the 22 pin events almost as long as I have, and I started them. Actually I was the main one involved with the invention of this particular sport and it has spread quite a ways in all directions. Lance has shot Police Combat, Steel Silhouettes, International Practical Pistol Shooting, International Revolver, Bullseye, Bowling Pins and whatever else that has come along. He used to go with me to local shoots and then traveled with me to out of town shoots, before he was old enough to be allowed to enter and compete. When he was old enough he started competing in the local shoots and eventually in bigger and out of town shoots. I remember we went to Guymon, Oklahoma to an International Practical Pistol Shoot when he wasn't to old, but was old enough to be allowed to compete by the rules. These shoots were governed by the International rules, so National Classifications were used, if you had one. I was class C and Mike Homm, who went with us, was class D. Lance was unclassified so they put him in D class. They had a local classification system that they used for local shoots, but since we weren't classed locally they used our National Classifications. Most of these shooters, from Guymon, used high capacity 9 mm guns. Mike and I used 45acp 1911Colt type, semi-automatic handguns, with 8 round magazines. Lance chose to use my 45 Auto Rim, Smith and Wesson, model 25-2 revolver, with 6 ½ inch barrel, this was a 45 caliber, which used 45acp ammunition with a full moon clip that held 6 rounds together so that you could load and eject all six at one time. This type of shooting requires speed, accuracy, powerful loads, movement, reloading, utilizing cover, multiple targets, different positions, and problem solving. The courses of fire that day were set up with the extra round capacity guns in mind but they also favored the thinking shooter. It was set up so that you moved to a cover position, for the shooter, and engaged 3 targets with two shots each, then moved to another position and more or less repeated the same thing, after 3 such engagements you would move and shoot a stop plate and stop the clock. If you have not been keeping track, that's 19 rounds required. You are allowed to shoot extra rounds with no penalty except time used. The targets were scored 2 best hits, no penalty for extra holes. The shooters using

18 round magazines, with one in the chamber could shoot the whole course without a reload. If you made all your shots good, it could make for less time used. However if you were skilled at reloading, on the run, then you could reload and be ready when you reached the new position and give up very little in elapsed time. Where someone seemed to have set these courses up to favor the high capacity magazine guns, it also worked very well for shooters who were skilled and well practiced in the art of reloading on the move with 1911 Colts and also full moon clipped 45 revolvers. When everyone was done I had won overall, while not expected was with in reason because of my known abilities. Mike Homm won Class D, which could be expected, and with Lance placing 2nd, which was not expected from some "green" kid. He made believers out of a lot of grown men that day. They were mostly shooting 18 round semi-automatic handguns, he was using an "old fashioned 6 shot revolver" and had beaten them on their home ground. He picked up a lot of admirers that day, and I thing to a man that they conceded that they had been bested and acknowledged that they were glad for him because he had done it. They did tease him about giving them lessons and maybe they had should give up their autos and get revolvers like him, because if they learned their guns, as well as he knew his, they could maybe compete with the "kid". It was quite a day for Lance and me also. Like I said he has shot and competed a lot over the years and is very good when it comes to shooting, and no that's not a proud father talking, that's a veteran handgun instructor talking. I was certified and trained by the FBI, and certified by the NRA, and recognized by the State of Kansas as a Police Firearms Instructor with some where around 20 years of experience, as a Police Firearms Instructor. I have trained several hundred shooters and worked with more. I was a certified instructor on the FATS Simulation Machine, at the Garden City Community College, used in the firearms training of law enforcement officers. I was listed as an instructor at the GCCC for a number of years. So I do not make that observation without basis for doing so. With maybe just a little partiality.

Lance's wife Katy fits right in with the rest of us, she has started shooting with us too. Although not for very long, she is showing promise too. She has plinked with Lance and I, and has participated in several 22 Bowling Pin Shoots with us. She is learning and an avid pupil. Probably our best moment so far, was at one of the shoots we took 1-2-3 in the 22 Single Action event. We did make our presence known, I think we were all happy with the fact that she had done so well, so quickly. I'm beginning to think that maybe new shooters in this family have to be able to shoot single action, maybe a law or something. Back in my heavy competition days I was one of the top single action shooters, on bowling pins, in the country (as in the USA), in both 22 and center fire handgun events.

We all have many stories and memories of our shooting experiences, both good and bad.

In my years with the Finney Co. Sheriff's Posse we had 3 females join, wanting to be Deputies, and had to be trained. The first one was back in 1979 or 1980 and was not welcomed by everyone. She couldn't carry a firearm, because she wasn't qualified, and then she could only work with 2 of our Deputies. This was a ridiculous situation. I did get her qualified and then asked Kate, after explaining the situation, if she cared if I worked with her, and of course Kate said it was okay. Then she had to sign a statement saying it was okay for me to work with Ellen, a female deputy. Give her a gun and a badge and then not trust her to work with a male deputy. Please consider the men too, we were fully sworn Law Enforcement Officers and had to get our wives written permission to work with a female deputy, it really inspired confidence. She didn't last to long anyway, didn't think that law enforcement was all she had expected, imagine that.

The other two were something else, when we held the board on them I was one of two who voted "no" on the first one, she was a self confirmed recovered alcoholic. She had 10 children, and as told by her, 2 were alcoholics like her, 3 were addicted to cocaine, 2 were addicted to heroin, and 2 were suppose to be okay, I don't remember about the other 1. She was accepted for training. Oh, and she was married. She was a self proclaimed firearms expert. The second one was, maybe, okay. I did vote to accept her, single, 20 something, blond, good looking, and seemingly reasonably intelligent, her relatives were okay also. I knew her Dad and of and about her Mother, she was accepted too. The Sheriff was upset and came to the next meeting and told us about it, and blamed me personally and told me so. I told him I only have one vote. It didn't matter I should have convinced the others that they weren't qualified. I suspected that there was more to it than was stated, but didn't say so in open meeting. As punishment I got to train both of them and one of the other 3 'male' recruits. The one with 10 children, wasn't doing to well and got in serious trouble in firearms training, when she pointed a loaded gun at me for the third time. The first time I blocked the gun, the second time I blocked her arm and rocked her somewhat when I deflected the gun, the third time I blocked the gun with one hand and stopped her with the other arm, quite roughly across her chest, I hit her hard. I then had her unload and holster her firearm and leave the range. She would not be allowed back on my range again. I did write this up in a report and submitted it to the Sheriff's Department. The other department range officers would have to give her the rest of her firearms training and qualify her, if she was to continue. She still had to continue the other classes, and pass, to make it to graduation. She did quit soon after this because it would seem to be obvious that she was in trouble with her training and attitude. The other girl, Kathy Enslow, did very well in firearms training and well in all of her training. When she got to the street she did good also. One of the ones I trusted at my back when we went into hostile situations. I knew if I got my butt kicked that there would be two of us getting our butts kicked. I did trust her and she was a good deputy. We worked a number of things in the line of duty. When we went into the bars, whether for a bar check or where there was a problem, she never backed up or backed down. Whatever it was she was right there in the middle of it. Whatever the situation she was right there and was willing to learn. If she was my back, she was there and would be doing whatever she could to cover me or keep someone off me. She was well on her way to making a good cop, and she was always welcome to work with me, and I did not say that about everybody or actually very many. As luck would have it we all got called in to go on a big raid. It was a drug and illegal alien raid/bust. We had 20 some deputies on the posse and 3 of us got to go in on the 3 entry teams. I was always picked for these assignments, some of us are just good, or have people fooled. When we were briefed and given our assignments, Kathy was setting with me and wanted to get on the entry team with me. Since she was suppose to go with me where ever I went, and she did, she was still on probation. I promised to try and see if I could get her on the entry team. When I talked with the Officers running the operation, I was told not likely, given her experience. But I try not to forget my friends. I had a friend on the detectives who said she would try to get her on the Evidence Team, which she did. Kathy was happy, but got a rude awakening to the world of law enforcement. It seems some or all of the bar girls were distributing drugs, cocaine. They had packets of it hidden on their person, after the bar had been secured, and we started processing people, these girls requested to go to the bathroom, independently and one at a time. They were escorted there by female officers, and unknown to their guards, they concealed their bags of cocaine inside their person and were returned to the holding area. The problem was that their bodies started absorbing the drug, and they got high. It was quite evident that there was a problem, so they were taken to, the bathroom I presume, and strip searched to the extreme and the drugs had to be removed and collected as evidence, not the exciting world of law enforcement she had envisioned. Shortly after all of this she did resign and found other things to do, in Oregon. I did miss her as she was a good officer while she was here. I guess this was a contrast in 2 trainees that happened to be women or females and the differ- ence in there attitudes and back grounds. One I didn't trust in any sense of the word, and the other I trusted completely. I knew Kathy's physical limitations but would never have hesitated on any situation, that comes to mind, to have entered or proceeded with it, she would have been there and I knew it. That is what I thought of her and the trust I had in her. There were a lot of others, maybe, more qualified, but that didn't mean a thing when you didn't trust them.

I liked working with kids, others as well as my own, and have worked with quite a few over the years. One that gave me great satis- faction was Casey Kidder. Casey shot with the gun club and with his Dad, Roger Kidder. Among other things he shot on our regular club Bowling Pin shoots. When we shot what we called the "Beer round" after the regular shooting had finished. And no, kids and juveniles did not drink beer at these shoots or gatherings, there was "Soda Water", or known in some areas as pop, colas, soft drinks or whatever you prefer to call it. What this was, is everyone that wanted in, at no additional cost, would draw a number and you were paired up 1-2, 3-4, and so on. Each team had 10 pins, these were set on 8 inch centers, with the middle one, of the 5 pin set, left out, you had to knock the pins off the table. If your team had the fastest time you were awarded 1 point, 2nd 2 points, 3rd 3 points and so on, after each team had shot. Then everyone drew again and it was repeated. This was done as often as everyone desired or we had time for. At the end, each shooter's points were totaled, and shooters ranked least to the most, and the bottom 25% had to bring the liquid refreshment for the next shoot, buyers choice of beverage. We also had a family rule of only one looser/buyer per family, trying to keep undo financial hardship off anyone who had kids participating. Roger wasn't letting Casey shoot in these because he thought that some of the guys might get upset if they lost when drawing Casey for a partner. Roger wasn't worried about Casey loosing and having to buy, but other people's feelings and attitudes. Upon finding this out I told him that Casey was entitled to shoot just like everyone else, but he wasn't going to allow him to shoot. Now one thing about Bowling Pin Shooting, at the Big Shoot at Second Chance (as in body armor) in Central Lake, Michigan and also in my shoots, the rules are "rule number 1-range master makes the rules, and rule number 2-see rule number 1". So I said that he was going to shoot and if anybody had a problem with it, to see me. Better yet I would just take him as a permanent partner and we would take on the field. Casey and Roger appreciated this but thought it would be unfair to me, wrong, I'll take my chances with a kid any day. So that was the way it was. I told Casey to just fire one shot and get one pin, if there were any left then fire one shot and get one pin, don't worry about missing I could do the missing for both of us. While we may not have won a lot of the go rounds, we also never lost any, and did not have to "buy" for 11 shoots running. At the 11th shoot we won every go round and of course was the top team for the night. By the 12th shoot the guys who had complained about having to shoot with a kid, were complaining that it wasn't fair that I always had a "good" partner, so Casey went back into the pool and drew with everyone else, and while he didn't do as good, maybe, as he had when he was shooting with me, he still did okay and had more confidence when shooting with others. He still didn't buy anything for the whole season, nor did I. He and I both still remember that summer and smile (I know I do) when ever thinking about the guys who didn't want to shoot with a kid, they might loose, and the shooter, who was a kid, who just whipped their butts all summer long. I have a lot of memories like this and can honestly say that no one ever complained about drawing one of my kids for a partner, and no they wouldn't let me take either one of them and take on the field, because there was no handicap in shooting with either of them. And that is the proud father talking and maybe the experienced range officer also. We always pushed for letting the kids shoot and in having there own class, and if they wanted to, to jump right into the open class and take on the field, which a number of our kids did, and they said to leave the kids class for the ones who wanted it. We also tried to always have a women's class, because a lot of the ladies were intimidated by shooting with the men.

A couple of more that come to mind are Clint and Mitch Howard, I worked with their Dad, Mike Howard, some, and he helped me a lot with gun club things. These 2 were like Lance and went with us all the time and I am afraid that I was guilty of forgetting their ages, at times, when it came to shooting, and was always getting myself and maybe them in trouble for letting them get in and shoot with everyone else. This never caused any problem as far as safety was concerned, because they were safer than many of the adults and took responsibility for their own actions. We lost Mike to throat cancer when he was 44 and the boys were not quite "grown up", but I would pick them up and take them to the shoots until Clint was old enough to drive and then they came on their own, and still are today, and are two of the top members in the club.

Rollie Leighton's 3 boys, Garand-Bill-Sam, are some more who fit into this same category, I think all 3 of those boys got me into trouble for letting them shoot at some of these shoots, never in trouble with safety or as far as the shoot was concerned, but with mothers, fathers or others, who thought that they were still to young, maybe they were and maybe they weren't, they were always safe and were supervised and coached. And I suppose we had way to much fun for some people. The 3 boys, or men, have or do shoot on a national level in the shooting sports and I like to think that I played a little part in them getting there.

The Big Bowling Pin Shoot that I/we ran in May each year, until 1991, was probably the second largest pin shoot in the country, in terms of the amount of events and shooting that took place. And usually this shoot took place on Mother's Day week end. Not only did we shoot all day Saturday and Sunday but we had a free feed on Saturday night, to read Bar-B-Q. We would feed, I think. up to 400 to 500 people at some of these. Kate was always in the middle of these, getting things done, serving food, preparing food, or whatever needed to be done. I usually didn't get to eat at these because I was still tied up at the range working on the shoot results or what ever needed doing. She would fix me a plate and bring it to me so that I would at least eat something. If she had time she would sit with me while I ate. I always liked to thing it was my good company, but it may have been to make sure that I did eat. These feeds took place at the picnic area, at the range, that I built with my usual crew of help. I hesitate to start naming people because it is so easy to leave some one out on things like this, but will name the main crew who were always there, Mike Howard, Bob Billbe, Gary Billbe, Mike Homm, Jerry Bitter, Jeff Stasch, Les Bishop, and the many others who helped build the things we did at the range. The picnic area was a 40 by 40 covered area with tables and benches. It also had a buried steel encased cooking pit, with a winch for removing the lid and raising and lowering the cooking platform into the pit. You then could swing the cooking platform to a processing table. We had running water and I planted trees around it. I haven't been there for a long time now. Never did get the sinks mounted and plumbed in. Eventually I would get to the picnic area to partake in the free beer that we (the gun club) provided. We had a lot of fun and make a lot of friends at these shoots. We drew shooters from all over the Mid West, mainly, some from the south and the east coast. One year we even had 2 come from Denmark, they had a blast and met a lot of good people who they became friends with.

Chapter 21:

Hunting and shooting

In the winter of 75-76 when I joined the Sand and Sage Rifle and Pistol Club I started something that would continue on until the present. When we started the Life Membership program to raise money to purchase a range of our own, I joined as a life member. I was already a Life member of the National Rifle Association and I am now a Endowment Member. I have been very active as a shooter and a hunter over the years. I could hunt in the winter months when it was slow, at work and I shot at the club events, as I could. This was at least 2 fold, I had something to do and it helped put food on the table. I made some extra money reloading ammunition and casting bullets. I started doing leather work and sold some of my work and this helped with extra money also. Belts and holsters were my main stays of leather work but I did other things, too. I probably made about 150 to 175 holsters and a lot of belts. The belts were every-thing from plain, functional, and finished natural color, to fancy art work and bright acrylic colors. I really like working with cut figure designs and bright colors. Horses and wildlife were my favorites, but did a lot of other stuff too. What ever the customer wanted. I made Yosemite Sam key chains and art work, they seemed to be favored items but really didn't make money on them as they took to much time. Basket weave belts were good sellers also and they were fairly easy to make, design wise, after you have made some you start learning how to do and start gaining speed.

With my active mind I was always coming up with new ideas for shooting events and things that would keep the interest up and the shooters coming out. We were already doing Police Combat shooting, Bull's-Eye target shooting, and Bench Rest. Silhouettes and Bowling Pins were started in 76 and Bowling Pins continues still today. I took over running the Bowling Pin Shoots in mid season, officially, in 76, and continued into the 90's when I finally gave it up because of work, not enough time. I did start the 22 Bowling Pins as a practice for the center fire guns. When I designed the first set of steel pins, Mike Howard and I built them and made them so they could be calibrated to a power factor. With the 22 Rim Fires in mind, but not planned as an option to start with. Then we tried the pins with the 22's and a new sport was born. Combat team shooting was another one, assault courses, Hogans alley's or House Clearings were others that were liked. Also home defense scenarios that we set up and ran for everyone's benefit. My 22 sniper course was a blast and was somewhat hard to do. I reduced down regular military targets till they were tiny, then I made steel silhouettes that were swingers, and the same size at the paper targets. They would move when they were hit and did not have to be reset. These were complete and partial targets. Then my daughter and I collaborated and I got some very small plastic toy soldiers. There were 10 different positions and 2 colors, maximum height was 1 ¾ inch, maximum width was ¾ inch, some were considerably smaller . And then we hand painted the helmets and shirts different colors so there was a very broad selection of targets. I built a rack with wooden shelves that would hold soldiers on 5 different levels and about 13 to each level. And then I really started thinking and with some experimentation, I used small squares of velcro, 3/8 of an inch square, glued on the bases and the wood stands and less than a full diameter hit would not take them off the velcro, but a full diameter hit would take them off, pretty realistic and a definite reality factor. The shooter was allowed 5 shots in 5 minutes, with no repeat engagements, to find and engage each of his targets listed on a piece of paper that was opened when the go signal was given. This was shot at a100 feet, with the shooters 22 Rim Fire Rifle and a scope of no more than 6 Power, if shooter had a variable power scope we would set it on 6X and tape it with clear tape, and the tape had to stay on, from a solid sandbagged rest. The shooter had a spotter on a 20X spotting scope helping. When the 5 targets had been found and engaged with 1 shot each, then the shooter could open his bonus paper. He then had 2 more, bonus targets to find and engage, still within the 5 minute time limit. Sounds easy, but you need to try it before you make up your mind. To complete the whole course, you also engaged 10 small paper targets, at another position, and 10 steel swingers at another shooting position.

In starting the 22 Bowling Pin Shoots, we started with the 22 Handgun, 22 Revolver, and 22 Rifle. We added the 22 Single Action Revolver, then the 22 9 Pin Handgun, 22 8 Pin Revolver, later 22 Manual Action Rifle, 22 8 Pin Handgun, still later 22 9 Pin Single Action Revolver, these were the individual events. We had 2 Man Team, 2 Man Team Revolvers, Mixed Doubles, Jr.-Sr, and we had 3 man team at 25 yards, Rifle, Manual Rifle, Handgun, we had this on the menu but only did it a time or two. This was a lot of fun, especially when I wound up with Sky Leighton on my team, along with Chad Weiss. Now I know there are those that think that the team pairing were rigged, but honest, they just worked out that way, it was done by the standings at the time. And it was pretty tough for anyone to beat us, with Sky on the Rifle, Chad on the Manual Rifle, and me on the Handgun, to read a Revolver, yes a revolver, an 8 3/8 barrel at 25 yards is deadly. I didn't borrow it to anyone that night either, I guess I did offer it though.

When I hunted coyotes it was for the sport, first and secondarily I was able to harvest furs. There was also the livestock and pet predation from the coyotes, to be considered. This also brought income in to our family. If you have never done it, you should try calling coyotes in the dark, on snow, with a preferably full moon. It can get very eerie, interesting, and exciting. For you are now the hunted, and you never know what is coming to check you out. I have actually felt arctic owls, other owls too, when they come over you on silent wings, and yes you can feel them when they glide in on silent wings, from behind you, and that shadow will make the hair stand up on the back of your neck. I do not recommend trying this for the weak of heart. In the night I have called in not only coyotes, but owls, bobcats, foxes, mountain lions, dogs, cats, deer, and all kinds of little critters that are out in the night, on business of their own. Calling in the daytime, in addition to the above, I have also called in cows, horses, sheep, turkeys, elk, black bear, and things that I never saw, but have heard them and seen the bushes and brush moving where they had been. The night calling I'm talking about, was done on snow with the moon light and artificial light was not used. And it does get wild when you use artificial light but that is not legal in most places, now, when you have a weapon in your possession.

Having hunted a lot of different things, including man, I do know something about the hunting sport. Searching for people is also a task that I have participated in, day and night. Having been in on several search missions for downed Aircraft, that is somewhat different but still the same. And the different terrains involved makes for all kinds of different problems.

Chapter 22:

The Second Bear Hunt

Having met Mike Grosse in1984 and hunting with him several times, I have some good stories from that source.

The first bear hunt, in 1984, was covered earlier in the book. The next year, 1985, I came back for another bear hunt. This hunt took place in the Gunnison, Colorado country and was a 5 day hunt that stretched in to 6 days of hunting and I was there for 7 days. For this hunt I didn't do anything but hunt, and go out with the guides in the early morning to check baits, re-bait and or rebuild bait sites. I again carried a 44 Magnum handgun, but this time I carried my Smith and Wesson model 29, with an 8 3/8 inch barrel, this gun was my favorite and I have used it for almost everything that I used a handgun for. Obviously not for 22 rimfire events. Sometimes when I got a new one I would carry the new one, instead of it. Mike put me on a stand that was west and south of Gunnison. It was beautiful country, mountains, trees, lots of green grass, flowers, other vegetation and a tumbling stream. The stream was about 15 feet across or more in some places. We had to stop down the road, because the road was blocked, with a locked chain across it. Because the roads were unreliable, impassable at times,do to winter weather and it was better if people stayed out of this remote country until the weather got better with the coming of spring and summer. I would be required to walk, on the road, for about a mile, as I remember, then I had to go down to the stream and cross it and go into the trees, to the stand. The stand was in a natural small clearing in the trees, it had been used long enough that area around the bait site was white and in there in the shadows, with no direct sunlight you had a natural white back ground for your target. I had brought a bucket of molasses with me, this is second only to honey for attracting bears. I had brought a small container of the molasses to the bait site and when I got there, the first thing I did was put some around on the bait site. I know, I know, but I like sweetening the odds, I know, but I can't help it. The first evening was a beautiful evening, clear skies, nice weather, and a gentle breeze going down the canyon, south to north, I was facing west and had a good view in 3 directions. A good view for about 40 yards to the north. I could see the stream through a lane down through the trees to the northwest. I could only see about 30 yards to the west. To the southwest the view was clear for about 30-35 yards and to the south, maybe, 40-45 yards. To the east, it was to my rear, if I had turned around, I could have seen for 10 to 75 yards, depending on the individual spot. The bait had been being hit almost every night, and the indications were that this was a big boar. From the tracks and evidence, this was what was indicated, and no other bears were coming in, so this too indicated a dominate male bear. There would be little, if any, activity, they told me, until about 7:00pm or after. About 6:00pm I heard the bear come out, back up on the moun-tainside behind me, of whatever he was in. I swear I could hear him stretch and moan, and kind of thrash around a little, maybe scratching, then he started down the mountain. It seemed that he didn't care if he made noise or not, I think he was under the opinion that the area was his and he was all alone. He came slowly and would growl occasionally, and sounded to be wandering around. Just an educated guess, but he must have been over ½ mile away when he started down. This was kind of a spooky feeling, knowing that he was there and coming in to me, and making no secret of his presence or the fact that he thought he owned the territory. He took his time and circled to my right, or to the north. I know that he was not to far away but stayed out of my sight. He circled far enough out that I could never see him. He got to the stream and I don't know if he drank first or not, but he jumped into the water and splashed around playing or cooling off in the water. While I never saw him the sounds were just as good as if I could see him. I could track him, as to direction, at all times because of the sounds, and could guess at the distance, although this was only an educated guess. When he came out of the water I could hear him, and then he shook himself off. I know that he couldn't have been to far away because of my being able to hear him and this was made more difficult by my hearing problem. However when it is still, I can hear sounds but have to interpret them, at times, so with the conditions being what they were, I could probably hear sound further away than I would have been able to normally, as far as distinguishing and interpreting sounds. After he shook himself off he started to the south. When he came to my scent trail, all of his sounds stopped. He had discovered that I was there, somewhere. And now everything was different, there were no more broken sticks or branches, no more tracking him by sound, I knew he was there but not exactly where anymore. It was very quiet, I could hear birds and the leaves rustling in the breeze, the bubbling and splashing of the running stream, but no sound from the bear. To say that I was experiencing a high, would I think be an understatement. I doubt that people who take their stimulating drugs, ever experience anything better or even close to this. It was me and the bear. Now the ball was in his court and I did feel somewhat inadequate in competing with his senses. He had the advantage, in my opinion. I had not done everything I could, to neutralize his superior senses. After a while, he was off to my left front, out of sight, and I couldn't tell how far he was. But he was there, and he would woof at me, pop his teeth, and growl. I have to assume that this was at his displeasure with me, for being inconvenienced and not being able to come on in for his supper. He knew it was there and he knew I was also there. Woof, woof, gggrroowwll, pop and snap. And he wasn't coming in as long as I was there. I waited until it was full dark and then a little more, hoping he would take the chance on the darkness to come on in and eat, but I know he knew how the game was played. The vehicle had come and stopped at the chain across the road and I knew that the guide would be impatient with the waiting for me and might be thinking I was lost or something. This was the same guide that I had when hunting the year before. He had been told not to come in, I would come out when I was ready. With the white circle around the bait I was willing to stretch the time, at least a little. This white circle came from all the bones that had been eaten on the site over the years, small pieces being dropped and pushed into the dirt, this made a wonderful shooting background, for the hunter, but not especially good for the hunted. I finally conceded to the bear and snapped a stick to let the bear know that I was moving and he would move away or at least be aware, that I was moving. I holstered my handgun and climbed down from the tree stand. I then drew my handgun, again, and started trying to move, as quietly as possible, away from the area. I went to my right out of the stand area and circled back to the path I had followed coming in. I did go to the right because, while not being to bright, I did know the last place the bear had been was to the left. I crossed the stream and moved back up on the road and headed down the road to the vehicle, that was my ride back to the cabins. I met the guide part way up the road and we walked back to the vehicle together. When we were in the vehicle and turned around, headed back to the highway and then to Mike's house, north of Gunnison, I told him what had happened. He wanted to know if I thought the bear was still there? My best guess was he was still close and would come on in to the bait after he knew for sure I was gone. It was a long ride home, but I didn't get sleepy, I would guess the dregs of my high were still with me. I had to relate to Mike, and everyone else, about my adventure and he asked "If I was I wanting to go back the next day?" I guess I would rate that as one of those "Dumb questions" and I was going out with the guides in the morning for the usual rounds on the bait sites.

I was up and ready, bright and early, and waiting on the guides. After breakfast we took off on our appointed rounds. We had a series of stands to check and re-bait on further east of and besides the area where I had been the day before. Some had been hit, but one was destroyed. Logs 8 to 10 inches in diameter had been thrown out of the clearing, rocks the size of basketballs or bigger were thrown around like marbles. The tracks and the marks on the trees showed that this was a very large bear. We rebuilt this bait site and moved on. We were back in around noon or a little after and I told Mike I wanted to set on that destroyed bait site. He said no, because a hunter had just taken a very good bear on that stand on Friday , just 4 days ago, and it was likely that this was a roaming or wondering bear.

I returned to the same stand as the previous night and the bear came in again, but it was a little more reserved in coming down off the mountain and in his approach. And I didn't hear him go into the water, on this night. Where I had put out the molasses the night before, it was gone. He had licked it off or eaten it, and where I had put it on the end of a very porous, spongy, decaying log the bear had eaten about 8 inches of the molasses covered wood. This wood was fairly soft and the bear liked the molasses. He again stayed out to my left front and woofed, growled, and popped his teeth at me, the same as the night before. I stayed until 10:00pm but with the same results. He was an older bear and knew how to play the game. I again snapped a stick and walked out, again going to the right away from where the bear was or had been, and the guide had waited in the vehicle.

The next day was a repeat of the previous day, with the same bait site being again destroyed. We rebuilt it again and I, again, told Mike that I wanted to set on that stand, he again said no.

On the third day, Wednesday, the bear did not come in and I heard nothing, but the bait pile had been hit, I had put out more molasses and it was pretty much gone, again. The next morning I again went with the guides, the bait site that had been destroyed had been hit but not destroyed as severely as before.

On the fourth day, Thursday, the bear came in again, but was really a repeat of Tuesday, we weren't fooling this bear. I even tried to mask or hide my scent by putting some kind of cover scent on my boots, but it didn't work. He was there but was not coming in, until I left, and then he would come in, and hit the bait. Friday morning was a repeat, also of Tuesday, the bait pile was destroyed again. Again I requested that stand and was again turned down.

On Friday before we went out, we discussed the situation on the stand I had been hunting on, Mike wanted me to try one more time, so even though I believed that this was not going to work, I went back, one more time. The same results, we were not going to fool this bear with out changing tactics drastically. This bear knew how the game was played, I would guess that this bear had been educated. Meaning that he knew about man, bait sights, tree stands and had probably seen a hunter in, enter and/or leave a tree stand over a bait sight. I thought that, to try and fool this bear, take 2 people in, and one go to the stand, as a decoy, and the actual shooter to take up a position, on the ground, but further up the canyon, it would be necessary to play it by ear, as scouting would tip off the bear, but Mike didn't want to put me on the ground. So we had the same result.

I had told Mike that I would stay and hunt 1 more day and I still wanted to sit on the stand that had been destroyed everyday this week. Mike said he would put me on a different stand and we would decide which one later in the day. I did go out with the guides again on Saturday morning with the same results we had all week. When we got back in, Mike said that he had gone west and north of Gunnison, to an area that had been impassable until a short time before, because of the snow. With the warm weather we were going to try and go into some stands that had not been hunted this year, at all. They had been getting some of them baited by going in on ATVs and some walking, for the past week. We would go as far as we could in a 4 wheel drive pickup and then unload a couple of ATVs and go as far as we could with them and then walk about 3 more miles. I would go the last ½ mile or more to my stand by myself. Mike had forgotten his flashlight, left it in the pickup, so I gave him mine. This worked out pretty well and I found my stand and got into it okay. The only problem was it was a lot darker here, than on any stand I had been on to date. About 6:00 I heard a bear start in, from off the mountain to my left front, southeast, and he worked around to straight in front of me and came down a trail, straight in to the bait.. It got dark a lot quicker and when the bear came in I could not see him or her. I knew where the bear was, first on the trail and then on the bait. The bear was 10 feet from me, on the ground, and I could hear it eating on the bait but couldn't see even an out line of the bear. I wanted to try a shot, but would not, without being able to see. I would have been tempted, if I had my flashlight, to try a shot using the flashlight as per my law enforcement training of shooting in the dark, with a flashlight and a handgun, tempted, but I don't know if I would have or not. I was aware of the light coming up the road, before I heard anything and the bear was still feeding. So I snapped a stick and the bear faded into the forest. Although the bear was quiet, in leaving, I was so close and it was so quiet, I actually heard him move off in the darkness. Mike froze in place when I broke the stick and knew instantly why I had broken the stick. He waited and then came on in. I came down from the tree stand and we walked out for at least a mile before we either one spoke, needless to say we were both disappointed. We walked on to the ATVs and rode to and picked up the other hunter, and then on to the pickup, loaded up and went on to the house. He invited me to stay one more day, no charge, he also didn't charge me for hunting on Saturday. I had to get headed home and would go to work on Monday morning. No bear, again, but lots of hunting and did enjoy the experiences. Kate was glad to see me when I got home and was fully expecting to be putting bear meat in the freezer. And was disappointed, for me, in my not being successful but we were both glad that I was home.

On Tuesday night Mike Grosse called and apologized. The stand that I had wanted to hunt all week was successful on Monday night. A new group of hunters came in on Sunday and several were new bear hunters from Louisiana. He put one of them on this stand, on Monday, because it kept getting hit every night. Along about 5 to 5:15pm a bear came down the trail straight across from the hunter. He didn't know if this was a big bear or not, having never seen one before. The bear got to the edge of the bait site and stopped, and would not come on in, deciding that something was wrong, he would walk away, go out of sight, and come back, he did this several times. When he was there, he would look away and then back trying to catch something moving or to figure out what was wrong. Finally he turned 180 degrees to the hunter and stopped and looked back, one more time, the hunter decided he had better shoot. He came up with his rifle, a 300 Winchester Magnum, and fired at the base of the tail. The bear went down and got up and ran off. The hunter decided he would just stay in the stand and wait, which he did for a fairly long period of time. He came down before dark and looked at where he had shot the bear and there was some blood. He went back and set down with his back to a tree and waited for the guide. The guide came in before dark and they went and looked. The bear had gone only a short way and then bedded down for awhile, the bed was there but the bear was gone. He left a lot of blood in the bed, but was not leaving a blood trail when he left. They went on out and when they got in told Mike. Mike, the guides, and all the hunters went back the next morning. They were expecting to find the bear in a short distance. The bear continued to go along the ridge and would periodically lay down and leave some blood. I don't remember the distance, over a mile, but eventually, the bear was following the ridge, turned 90 degrees and went straight down off the ridge to the stream, for water. Now usually a bear that is seriously wounded will follow a straight line, and stay on high ground, and try to go out of the country, or until it dies. Or if not wounded to bad will wonder around some and find a place to lay up for awhile and then go to water. This one was not doing either, really. After the bear went to the water, he either drank first or went into the water and then drank. They couldn't tell which way he went. They looked on the far bank and found nothing that would indicate that he had crossed and left the water. Mike went down stream with half the hunters and one of the guides went up stream with the rest of the group. Mike went down stream and around a couple of bends in the stream and after going around the second one, lying on a sand bar, was the bear. Mike was carrying a Thompson-Center Contender, scoped, in 30-30 caliber, he was on the bear instantly but the bear was not moving, just laying there with it's head on it's paws, with the eyes open. After waiting a short time he circled the bear and got a limb and poked the bear, and then poked him in the eye, the bear didn't move, he was dead. He checked the bear and it was still body temperature, he had been waiting for them, or waited watching his back trail, was what Mike figured, and had finally died while waiting. The others caught up with them and they decided that they would cut a pole, tie the bears front feet and back feet together, put the pole between his legs, and carry him out. When they tried this with 4 men on the pole, they could not pick him up and get him off the ground. So Mike field dressed him and they tried again. They were able to carry him out this time, and got him to the check station for the Colorado Wildlife and Parks. There he was weighted and checked by the Game Wardens. The bear's estimated live weight was 720 pounds. The biggest black bear ever taken in Colorado, seems like in the continental United States. I don't know about Canada or Alaska. This was a very big bear. Bears are normally scored by the skull size, length plus width. This one didn't have the skull to go with his body. As I remember, the skull scored 21 something, not a world record. He kept telling me "You said that was the place and that you had wanted to hunt that stand, but I hadn't listened". Such is hunting.

Chapter 23:

The Buffalo Hunt

I didn't hunt with Mike for a number of years, money and time away from work, pretty well covers the situation. So here is the story about my buffalo hunt in south Texas in early 1999. I had purchased a share in Mike Grosse's outfitting company, Outdoors Adventures Unlimited back in the early 1980's and had been building up hunting credits for about 15 years. I wanted to go on the Buffalo or American Bison hunt, in south Texas, in February 1998 but it had not worked out because of timing and other things. So in late 1998 I did book the hunt for the first part of February, 1999. The hunt was on a ranch in south Texas that had a population of free roaming buffalo, they had been there since about 1950. Numbers ran from 800 to about 1200 depending on the year and the range conditions. The ranch was 57000 acres and was split by the highway, with about 17000 acres on the east side of the highway and the balance, with the headquarters on the west side. The ranch had been the project of some Hollywood type, I never heard the name, and was built up pretty nice. The main ranch house was big and very nice. It had a number of bedrooms and was quite spacious and comfortable. It had a big, fenced backyard with a pit BBQ, built in BBQ grill, tables and benches, lounge chairs, swimming pool and lounge area for parties or gatherings. They also had cabins and a bunkhouse or two. Besides buffalo there were Barbados sheep, actually a mouflon from north Africa that had been let run wild and had cross bred with, possibly, domestic sheep, so was now not considered a pure breed hence the Barbados name, goats, Aoudad, turkey, Javelinas, were all available to hunt, for a fee. The hunt was $250.00 for 3 days and 4 nights, everything included except your personable gear. And then you paid a trophy fee for what ever animals you harvested. Buffalo was $2475.00, any buffalo, Barbados were $325.00, Aoudad was $325.00, seems like the goats were $250.00, maybe $200.00 on the Javelinas, and turkeys were $100.00, and not sure about anything else..

In planning for the hunt I wanted to take the buffalo with a 44 magnum revolver and cast bullets, that I cast myself. The handgun was the same 8 3/8 barrel, blue revolver, that I had used on the second bear hunt, just mentioned above. Also while being a little bit crazy, I am not stupid and wanted Rollie Leighton to go along to back me up with a big bore rifle. In the remote possibility that somehow I would be less than successful with the handgun and needed my butt saved or something.

I started working on the hunting ammunition right away, this would require a harder than normal bullet, to get better or deeper penetration due to the size and structure of the animal. I worked on the bullets, I cast them of a harder alloy of metals and then to make them even harder, I used a tempering process. This required that the bullets be heated in the oven, Kate was always so tolerant and patient with me, for a specified period of time and then could either be allowed to cool or drenched in cool water for an accelerated cooling which also hardened the outside of the bullet even more. I worked at this and finally got what I thought I wanted and that I thought would work. Then they were loaded into finished ammunition, which I have done for years. I already knew the powder charge I was going to use, and the other settings for reloading. I only had to load them up. Then it was on to the testing. The accuracy of the ammo was very good, which I knew it would be from past experience. This being the same bullet that I had used for years, just a different alloy. Then the testing or actually shooting of the bullet into different substances to check for performance. It would penetrate, but when it encountered major bone it would blow up or break up into to many pieces, not what I wanted at all. I tried it on deer size game and while it was effective on this type or size of animal it would not be on the larger buffalo. Time was short so I contacted Sierra Bullet Company and talked with one of their "bullet smiths". I explained what I wanted to accomplish, what I had done and the results, and now I was needing help in solving my problem. We discussed it and he like my approach and understood my results, so I needed another bullet. They had a 250 grain full metal profile bullet that had been developed for target shooting, on steel targets. This bullet while not designed for game and would not expand, seemed to fill the bill for what I needed. This bullet, he assured me would not deform or breakup, so I decided to try it. It worked very well in the testing and shot with good accuracy also. In testing this load, I walked into the farm shop one day and there on the floor was a used bowling ball. I asked who's it was and why it was there. One of the guys said it was his, he had gotten a new ball and he had the old one in his pick up and just set it on the floor, in the shop. "Why do you want it?" I replied with "Yes I do". "What are you going to do with it?" My response "I'm going to shoot it with a 44 magnum and try to break it". "OK, you can have it". So I took it and went to the Hay Barn and put it in front of a sand bank, backed off about 25 yards and tried to shoot it at an angle where it would not bounce back at me. When you launch a projectile at a heavy hard surface and you don't get penetration, the projectile slingshots back at you at an angle that is approximately the same as it goes into the target. If it goes in at 90 degrees to the surface, it comes back at the same angle. It might not be good to ask me how I know these details. When you add the rounded surface of a bowling ball it can also changes the laws of return flight. It took a chip out of it as I had hit to close to the edge, and no penetration. I dug the bullet out of the sand bank, and it was in near perfect shape. So I went back and tried it again, a center of mass shot. The bowling ball was reduced to a lot of small pieces, dust, fragments, splinters, and a few large pieces about the size of a medium sized potato. I dug the bullet out of the sand bank and it to was in near perfect condition, it could have been reloaded, in a shell case, and fired again. I got a box from my pickup and picked up what was left of the bowling ball. I went back to the shop and showed them what a 'used' bowling ball looked like. The previous owner got a little upset and wanted to know what I had done to his ball. Shot it with a 44 mag like I had said I was going to. He didn't think I had been serious. Weelllll, I was and I did. "Did he want me to glue it back together?" "No!!!" He had been going to keep it for a back up. Not no more. I said "I asked before I did it and you gave your permission". "But I didn't think you would do it." What can I say, it was fun, and the look on his face was priceless. I had had a discussion in town, at a local gun store, with a store employee who assured me that a 44 mag would not break a bowling ball. He stated that "I would need a 50 Action Express if I wanted to do any damage". Trying to make a sale? I just happened to stop by the store when I was in town and asked if he would like to see what a 44 mag would do to a bowling ball. Sure he would. A little more damage than what he had predicted "didn't he think so, too?" He said "Oh, I knew it would". My reply "But that's not what you said". "Well I meant that it wasn't as destructive as the 50 AE." I was willing to bet that the 50 wouldn't do as much damage but he would not actually put up any money.

So now all we had to do was pack, load up, and drive the long distance to Iraan, Texas. The name, Iraan, came from the first settlers, a man and his wife, who prospected, settled, and started the village or town. When a name was needed to establish the town, for the Post Office, the people couldn't agree on a name, so they finally agreed to use the man's first name, Ira, and his wife's first name, Ann, for a name for the new town, hence the name Iraan. We did head for Texas, we picked up Kim, a guide from Eastern Kansas, somewhere, and gave him a lift down to Iraan with us. We got there in the late afternoon, settled in, in the main house and made ready. Then we went with the outfitter, Mike Grosse, the guide, Kim, I forget his last name, to town and had supper. We were the only ones on the ranch except for a man and his wife who worked and lived there, in the foreman's or Segundo's house, year round.

The next morning we got up and went to town for breakfast and came back and went hunting. Buffalo were all over around the ranch headquarters, cows with calves, and yearlings and older buffalo cows, but no mature bulls. This could be explained in one word, water. We started hunting and looking at buffalo, we were in a Chevy Suburban

4 wheel drive vehicle. While we glassed and checked out the brush and thickets we stayed on the trails. These paths were for a 4 wheeled vehicle, it was more Rollie's and my way to go to the ridges and glass the other side and to look at everything we could see, but Mike didn't want to leave the trails. After looking for a couple of hours and covering quite a bit of country, from the trails. We still had not seen a mature bull and to ourselves, Rollie and I were questioning the strategy of staying on the trails, but not openly, yet. We finally got up on top, the country was flat and you could see a long way, like a table top until you got to a canyon. We wound around on trails, up on top. There were a number of thickets and the trails wound around them. We were coming up to where 3 fences came together dividing the land up into 3 different pastures, however, the gates were left open and the buffalo could go where they wanted to. Standing in the gate, where the 3 pastures fences joined, was a large bull buffalo. This was a big animal, and he was by himself, probably a good sign. We got close enough to get a good look and even to me, who didn't have much to judge him against in the way of past sightings. He looked very big and after looking at his horns in the spotting scope we all agreed he was good. I said he was definitely good enough and lets go for him. Mike and Kim decided that this was the "Diablo Bull", a known trouble maker. Known for tearing up fences and getting out onto others peoples property. There had been an effort to kill him for at least 3 years. He was anti-social and would not let even other buffalo stay around him. And they said he was no longer breeding, a real loner. Later he was aged at about 17 to 18 years of age, this is an old buffalo. While we were looking at him, he was looking at us. We decided to back up and ease away from him and try to make a plan to get where I would have a chance for a shot with the handgun. When we started backing away he followed, just walking. I don't think he was wanting directions or conversation. We kept going and he stopped. We decided to back on around a thicket, staying on the trail. When we got out of sight I would step out and they would keep going, he was coming again. Sounded like a good plan but was to simple, I guess, to actually work. He stopped and would not come on around the thicket where I could see him. I couldn't tell but he turned around and went back to the gates and took up his former position.

Rollie came and got me and we went back to the vehicle. We decided that I would head to the canyon lip about 1/4 to 3/8 mile away and move into a thicket. They would go back to the bull and start him down along the fence on the game trail and he was suppose to follow it to the canyon and down the trail into the canyon. Sounded like another good plan and was somewhat simple and should work. I guess I'm usually optimistic and that's one reason why I hunt. I was a ways from the bull and would walk a circular route, to the thicket, on the canyon rim and take up a position inside the thicket, find a spot where I had a window to shoot through when the bull came by the thicket. They allowed me time to get in position and then they moved in on the bull. They drove up fairly close and the bull just stood looking at them. Mike got out and moved toward the bull thinking he would move away. Wrong, I really believe he thought that HE owned the territory. He started pawing the ground and throwing up dirt. Mike tried to move him but he wasn't moving, he owned the place. Mike decided he might be better off in another location, given the bull's attitude. And started moving back toward the Suburban, the bull had went to his knees and was hooking his horns into the ground and tearing pieces of sod out of the ground. He made a false charge and Mike got around to the right side, of the suburban, and got in. Kim had to move over and drive. He put the vehicle in gear and accelerated out of there. Rollie said that the bull charged and came up behind the vehicle close enough that he couldn't see his head in the back window. He had to be within inches of the back of the suburban. Now I couldn't see any of this but when the bull charged I could feel this through the ground. When he was chasing the suburban I could feel him and tell he was going away from me. When he gave up on the suburban and started arcing away from it I could tell this through the vibrations in the ground. I set there and could feel him turn almost a 180 degrees and was coming back at me, some of this was possibly hearing. Great, running right at my back. I turned my head and looked over my shoulder and he broke over the roll of the ground towards the thicket and the canyon, oh and little old me. When he came to my scent trail he turned and followed it towards the thicket. I don't know if he was following my scent or just following the natural path. I was thinking that it was going to get awfully small inside that thicket with both of us in there. At this time I wasn't sure I could break him down, to stop him. That was a very reassuring thought. When he got to the thicket he turned to his right and followed the edge of it around to the trail and towards the canyon. At last, he was following the script. We didn't get to find out how small the inside of the thicket was. Of course he was coming on a dead run and was about 25 yards away. I started swinging my revolver on him as he came around the thicket, being able to follow him in the gaps in the vegetation. When he came to the gap, that was my window, I was pretty close to point of aim on him, with a small sight change, on his side, I swung and fired on him as he was going through the window. I had the flash sight picture that I was 2 inches low, of the point of aim, when the gun went off. You not only have to be in the right spot, for shot placement, but have to time it for the leg to be in a forward position when the bullet gets there. If the leg is back it covers the heart. If you hit him when the leg is back, then you have to go through the leg to get to the heart, a risky shot at best. Because even a large powerful bullet will not stay on a perfectly straight line when going through bone. The buffalo had started to jump when he was getting to the lip on the trail leading down into the canyon, so he was going up when the gun went off, making the bullet hit low. I knew that I had blown the shot, because of the flash sight picture. I was upset with myself for not making the first shot a good one. I moved and watched the bull go down the canyon to a grove of scrub cedar trees. He went into the trees and turned facing me at about 125 yards. I sighted on him but did not want to try a shot at that distance and face on, not a good choice for shot placement. Mike came up while I was looking at the buffalo. The buffalo turned and went into the trees, and was headed down canyon. Mike wanted to know what had happened and I explained it to him. That I had hit him about 2 inches low. He said "No, You missed". I said that "No, I did not missed, that I was about 2 inches low". He said that "I saw the bullet hit on the other side of the bull and that it was a miss". "No, the bullet went clear through him and he had a hole through both lungs." We went about a half of a mile down the canyon, the suburban was setting on the rim of the canyon. Kim and Rollie were there watching the bull with spotting scope and binoculars. We got there and Rollie said that he was bleeding out of his nose. To clean out the nostril indent, the bull was licking his nose, like a cow does, but buffalo do not usually do this, so it was a lung shot. Kim said he thought so too. Mike said "No he missed", again. I answered that "No I had not missed. but I did hit him about 2-3 inches below the heart". The buffalo would stand and pick up his left fore leg and hold it up, like it was hurting, then would put it back down, gingerly and kind of feel the ground and shift it around, as if looking for the right spot, and then finally put it down and put his weight on it. Mike said that "Maybe you hit him in the leg?" "No, first I knew where I had hit and 2nd there was no evidence of a wound on the leg". You could see, through the spotting scope, the indication of an entry wound on the side of the buffalo. I said that "We have a wounded buffalo and he's not getting out of the canyon". I then reached over and took my Ruger No. 1 rifle, in 375 H & H caliber, out of the hard case scabbard and loaded it with a round from my pocket. When hunting with this rifle along, I always carry 5 rounds on my person just in case. Mike wanted to know "What are you going to do?" My reply "I'm going to kill that buffalo". He said, "Now wait a minute, we would, but with the handgun like I wanted to". We settled down to talking about how to get in and finish the job, that I had started. Mike wanted me to go up canyon and down the side into the canyon and move in on the bull from the side. I wanted to go down canyon, to where I could get down, and then move up wind. Go up the canyon and come in on him into the wind. "Your hunt, your way." Mike said "Okay, if that's the way you want to do it, we would do it that way".

Mike wanted Rollie and Kim to stay on top with the vehicle. "No, Rollie came along to cover my back". Or butt if you must know, and he was going with me, with a rifle. My choice was the Ruger 375 H&H, his was the 45-70 lever action. With him, hopefully, not doing any shooting, but if he has to shoot, he should shoot what he wants, and the 375 was a single shot, I'm thinking that 1 is enough. However the 45-70 was a repeater, so bring the 45-70. Down we went into the canyon, and then up the canyon towards the buffalo. At about 80 yards from the bull, there was a raised ,flat topped, outcropping of rock. Rollie and Mike got on top of this so they would be out of the way, have a good view, and also, for Rollie, a good field of fire, on the chance that I would need his help. I moved on up canyon, behind the cover of a large thicket, this thicket would take me to with about 30-40 yards of the bull. When I ran out of cover I started crawling to get closer and to try and get an angle for the shot. Every time I got in to a position where I could shoot, the bull would move and put another tree covering his vital area. Talk about knowing what you are doing, he did, and frustrating it was, for me. I could look back and see Rollie and Mike, and with a form of sign language, we could communicate. After several attempts to get on the bull, I looked back and asked what to do, they indicated they didn't know either. So on toes and elbows I started working back to get behind the thicket, and try and decide how to get to the bull. When I got out of the bull's sight, I looked at Rollie and he indicated that the bull was coming to me, just walking. As I moved around the thicket, the bull would hear me, I assume, and change his direction to the new spot, he did this several times and then came to the thicket. When he got to the thicket he started going to his right which would bring us face to face if I kept going in the same direction that I was going. I was kept informed by looking to Rollie for information. When I was coming across the down canyon side of the thicket the bull was coming down canyon to meet me at the corner of the thicket. At what I thought was 15 yards, but was actually about 25 yards, I lay down on my stomach and with gun drawn waited for him to come around the corner of the thicket. He got to the corner and when his eye cleared the cover he stopped. I could see his face from back of the eye forward and the bottom of his legs for about 5 inches, of hoof and leg. We stayed like this for at least 15 minutes, you want to talk about tension, and getting tired of not moving. I would lower my head to relieve the tension on the back of my neck, for long periods of time, it seemed, actual times were maybe 2 or 3 seconds, then I would have to raise my head back up. I know how quick a buffalo can move. The buffalo laid down right there and I couldn't see any more of him than I could before. I looked to Rollie and Mike, and asked, through sign language, what should I do. They didn't have any ideas either. Back up on toes and elbows, keeping the gun in front of me and at the ready position, backing up and trying to get out of sight, and expecting a charge at any time, none came. I got back far enough to go sideways and got out of sight. Up on my feet and around the thicket I go. I worked around until I could finally see the buffalo, straight down his back line, not where I wanted to shoot. To get some angle I started side stepping, to my right. I finally was out in the open and the bull finally noticed me and did a double take. I froze in place, at the ready position, and waited, expecting a charge or something. Nothing happened, he would stare at me and then slowly look away, then snap back around with his head to look at me again. This went on for a couple of minutes, he finally got to his feet and started to walk away, the angle was bad but I tried to lead him and imagine where the heart was, through the length of that 'big' body. I tried the shot and went in at about the last rib, trying to get the angle right to reach the heart. I had my only failure of a bullet at this time. I broke the first rib and then when the bullet hit the second rib, right at the edge of the rib, at just the right place on the bullet, where the copper jacket and the very small spot of lead came together on the nose of the bullet. It actually started splitting the bullet jacket and it broke up somewhat, about 75 to 80 percent of the bullet went left through the lungs and into the offside shoulder. The rest was a small piece of the jacket and pieces of lead core and they followed the ribs up along the side into the near side shoulder and they stayed there under the skin. All of these pieces were recovered later. This kicked the bull into high gear, still running at the same angle away from me. I tried another shot guessing at the lead and fired, the bullet went by his shoulder, just missing, and under his chin cutting hair from under his jaw but not actually touching him. But it did cause him to swing to his left. They told me later I was always in motion going toward the bull. Common sense intelligence would maybe say that this might not have been the best choice of direction to be going. As I was moving and he was swinging left the angle got better and I tried again to get a bullet into his heart. While the shooting, accuracy wise, might not have been the best and the conditions were not the best I have ever had, I was still hitting him. This shot took him right below the shoulder joint and took out the left fore leg. The leg went almost 90 degrees straight forward and then swung back and hung limp and would bear no weight. While it slowed him down, for he was now running on 3 legs. He did not even stumble or anything when the hit took out his leg. He swung back to his right and I was running behind him and I reloaded on the run with an HKS speed loader. I was cutting across to again get the angle for another shot. I didn't get a shot on the right and we went back left. When the angle looked good again I fired 2 shots, very rapidly, and these both also missed the heart but were again close and close together, less than an inch apart, but lungs hits don't get the job done. He again swung to the right and I was running to the right and closing the distance. Again I got the right angle and fired, one more time. This shot was an inch above the heart, but I got the main artery coming out of the heart. The stream of blood coming out of this wound was about 1 inch in diameter and came back at me for about 25 feet before starting to break up in to smaller amounts and spray, confirmed by Rollie and Mike. I don't know how far away I was at this point but did not get any of the blood on me. I knew now that the bull was dead or going to be. But did he know it? He turned quartering to face my direction and I was going to hit him again. Mike was yelling "DON'T shoot again". I was ready and undecided, but with 3 rounds left in the gun, I was going to do another reload, using another HKS speed loader that I carried. I reached for my speed loader and did not immediately find it on my belt. Rollie yelled, and I turned and looked at him, he tossed me a speed loader and I caught it out of the air and made the reload in a seemingly single motion reload, just like in the movies. You could reload 6 rounds of ammo very quickly with practice. I didn't open the revolver until I had the speed loader in hand. The bull turned and went into a small tangle of brush. Mike came running up and wanted to get him out of there before he went down. Mike was in front of the bull trying to get him to charge, I didn't know whether I would have to shoot one or the other if the bull actually charged. Luckily the bull didn't charge but after about 15 minutes went down in the back, like a dog setting down. Then after awhile lay down with his legs under him. It was about another 15 minutes before he finally expired. This whole thing took considerably less time to happen than it did to write it. I would guess that from the first shot to the last all happened in less than 1 minute. Everything seemed to be in slow motion and I did not remember advancing on the bull while I was shooting But I was. I didn't consciously do it, I just did it. I was standing at the ready this whole time in case he did get back up. When it was finally over, amid the congratulations and hand shakes from Rollie and Mike, the nervous reaction hit and I was shaking some what. While I had seemed to be cool and calm while this was all going on I wasn't any more. Wow the adrenalin had been flowing and I was really feeling it now. Kim made it down and we took pictures and were starting to field dress him. I wanted to help but they wouldn't let me, while they said I was the hunter and didn't need to help, I might have been a danger with a knife at that time. So I was sent back to the ranch to get a jeep and trailer that we could get down into the canyon with. We would winch him onto the trailer for transport back, to be hung at the ranch, for cooling and skinning.

Buffalo-February 1999-Iraan, Texas

We figured we had our work cut out for us, in getting him loaded on the trailer. He would have weighed over 2500 pounds live weight. A lot of game animals get smaller when you actually get them on the ground, not him, he was still huge. We backed the trailer up close and put a piece of plywood down and started it under him the best we could. We put a chain around his neck and 2 hand winches hooked to the front corners of the trailer. We started pulling, do to the way he was laying he started pivoting his shoulders first and as they came on to the plywood he actually got easier to move. The trailer was a tilt bed and we had it up and the plywood on the back edge, so with several re-hooks we slid him right onto the trailer and proceeded back to the ranch headquarters. When we tried to hang him in the barn, the bottom of the rafters are only 12 feet off the ground and with his hind legs pulled up past the rafters we still couldn't get his head off the ground. We would skinned him down and then raise him some more until we got him as far as we could off the ground. We skinned him clear down and then removed the head and cape, for a mount, he was still big. We were finished and cleaned up and it still wasn't noon. Mike asked if we wanted to go to town and eat or eat our sack lunches and continue hunting something else. Lets go hunting, we can eat after dark. The weather was suppose to be cool, but it was 75 and so the next morning I took the carcass to a packing plant to cool and for processing, I did not want to loose that meat. The packing house was over 100 miles away in Midland, Texas. We did keep some steaks and some roasts and the rest was made into hamburger. The hump roast is really a treat, very good eating. You usually get 2 hump roasts from a bull, a big bull will produce 4 roasts from the hump, this bull produced 6 hump roasts and you could cut them with your fork. The actual weight of this buffalo is unknown but was estimated by the dressed weight and the hanging weight at the processing plant. Their guess-estimation was 2700 to 2800 pounds live weight, based on the carcass weight. I did have a shoulder mount done and the back hide or what is left after you take the cape for the mount will still cover our queen sized bed. I had this hide tanned hair on, for a super nice buffalo robe. Kate would never let me use it on our bed, and I asked several times, but no she wouldn't change her mind. I have no idea why she didn't want to use it, but usually when she said no then it was no.

He was scored for the Safari record book and he would have gone into the record book at number 14 largest ever taken with a handgun. And according to known records or anything we found, he was the largest ever taken with an open sighted revolver. He would have gone into the firearms book at 68 to70 in a tie. This would be for all time. I had the score sheet and the application all filled out but decided to not send it in. Not sure why but that's how I felt at the time. We ate buffalo meat for about a year and it was all good, no cholesterol either.

I am not sure but would guess that we did donate some of this meat to the Emmaus House for their use, Kate was very good about sharing with others and I did share with some of my hunter friends.

Chapter 24:

Buffalo Hunt Part 2

After we had finished hanging, skinning, and skinning out the cape of the buffalo we were ready to go hunting again. And the target this time was Barbados sheep, this is a Mouflon sheep from North Africa that had been brought to Texas and released to roam wild in this new land. They have roamed wild every since, but have possibly cross bred with other sheep and are not pure bred any longer, so they are called Barbados. They are a small sheep and it doesn't take a lot to put them down, so I chose my Ruger No. 1 in 375 H&H Magnum to hunt with, a little bit of overkill maybe, but it works for me. We crossed the highway and hunted for sheep on the 17,000 acres that was on the east side of the highway. We hadn't gone to far when Mike and Kim, who were in the front seats, spotted a couple of Rams. They were able to look them over and so did Rollie. I couldn't see them and didn't want to move around and rock the vehicle for them, in getting into a position to be able to see them. They decided that one was really good and the second one was not to bad either. They watched them and I finally got to see their rumps as they went into the brush. We got out and started down the trail, Mike said to follow him and he would step aside and tell me to shoot and I was to shoot. Mike went first, them me, then Kim, and Rollie brought up the rear. We were moving down the trail, in this single file order, and I turned around to Kim and quietly asked "Which one of the two was I to shoot?" He said "The big one". "Which one is the big one, I never got to see either one of them". He got a blank look and said, after hesitating "The one on the left or in the lead". "Okay, thanks." We moved further down the trail and Mike stepped sideways and said "shoot". The rifle came up, I got on the left or lead animal and squeezed off my shot, the shot felt good and under recoil, through my scope, saw the one I shot, jump and swap ends and disappear. I saw the other one turn about 120-150 degrees and ran off into the brush. Mike said come on and we moved or ran to the right front, towards the canyon. This canyon paralleled the trail that we had been driving on. We got to the canyon rim, having seen nothing of the sheep. Rollie and Mike went up canyon and Kim and I went down canyon, looking for any sign of the sheep. Nothing was seen by anyone. I told Kim "I want to go back to where they were when I fired". He said that "Mike doesn't want you to because you had missed the shot". "No, I don't think so, and that's where we should start looking". We headed back and Rollie and Mike were waiting for us and I again said "I want to go back to the spot where they had been when I fired". Mike said "No, it was a waste of time as you missed". Again I said "No, I don't think so". Rollie said "No, he didn't miss". Rollie had seen the bullet hit, hair and dirt had blown off the sheep where and when the bullet hit. After a bit of discussion, which I did not participate in, we were lead back to the suburban and moved out of the area. Now I would like to say here that this is not the way Rollie and I hunt. You make every effort to find and follow up downed animals and make sure that all efforts are exhausted to end any suffering that they might be having. That this bothered me, and Rollie too, would be an understatement. I did not speak again for some time, it should have been a give away, to anyone that knew me, and it was to Rollie. We continued to look for more sheep and found some across one of the canyons and had to drive quite a ways to get to them. We had looked over this group and Mike decided that there was at least one that was a shooter. The sheep have different color combinations so they are fairly easy to tell apart. When we got around the canyon and into the area where we thought the sheep should be, we stopped and started looking, I had still not spoken and was more than a little upset about what had happened. When we found the sheep and I located the one that they had considered the best one. I came up with my rifle and said "cover your ears". I made sure of my point of aim and fired as soon as I was on the sheep. I watched in my scope as the sheep was knocked off his feet and fell, instantly dead. I knew where I had hit the sheep, just like the other one, and knew immediately that he was dead. So I said, sarcastically, "I suppose that one ran off too". This one never got out of my sight and was very visible on the ground. We moved up and field dressed the sheep and took pictures. We loaded up and went back to the ranch headquarters. We went to town and ate supper and then came back and went to bed. While not being able to sleep, Rollie and I discussed the day's activities, I was still upset about the first sheep. I knew that my shot had been good. He said that the second sheep was good but the first one had been a lot better. I had never seen the first one's horns, so I didn't know about that. And we were still not happy about the whole situation.

The next morning I was still worrying about the temperature, in relation to my buffalo meat. So I decided to load the hanging carcass into my pickup, cover it up, and take him to the processing plant, in Midland, Texas, which we hadn't been going to. I wanted to get him in the cooler and then have them go ahead and process the meat and make the hamburger. No use hauling the bones home and we were going to be in need of space. Then they would quick freeze all of it for the trip home. In doing this I was gone for Rollie's sheep hunt and it was over with by the time I got back. While the horns were different in shape they actually scored almost identical with mine. When measured and scored both would made the Safari record book. His had a more tight curl where mine unwound to the side, more like a spring, where his stayed closer together and closer to the head in width. We decided, that while we looked some more, we were probably done shooting. For while we are always hunting, we didn't find anything else that we wanted to shoot. We did do some exploring, looking around, and target shooting while we were still there. One of the things that we did was shoot at a hill or bluff at about 400 yards. In shooting the different guns we had along, both Mike and Kim participated in this with us. We had been commenting on the accuracy range of the handguns we used and we took some good natured kidding about being able to shoot long distance with our 44 magnums. Now one thing that we are both good at, was shooting handguns at longer distances, than most people think reasonable. There was a 18 to 20 inch hole in the bluff or hill and we were asked if we could hit it, I said maybe and tried, my first shot was a little low, Rollie's was right on the edge of the hole, as I remember, and then he fired again and we could see nothing in the way of a hit. Amid the laughs we were told that he must have missed the whole side of the hill. Not likely, I fired again, with the same result and we were still taking the same kind of ribbing when Rollie fired again, with the same result. At first laughter, but about that time hundreds of bats that had been roosting in the hole started pouring out of the hole and flying off in search of a quieter roosting place. Maybe we hadn't missed the whole hill side, the bats didn't seem to think so either.

Later Rollie said, that I had left his speed loader on the ground in the canyon where I had shot the buffalo. No, I didn't. I stuck it in my pocket and forgot about it. That's the only excuse I can come up with for forgetting this bit of information. I will claim to have been somewhat busy at the time and for some reason not paying much attention to anything else while being involved in the bottom of that canyon, with that buffalo. Maybe I could plead temporary insanity or something. There are those who would readily agree to that, especially, considering the circumstances. I still haven't returned his speed loader, but maybe I will get around to it one of these days.

We were sitting in front of the headquarters in a jeep, looking around. We were using binoculars, and spotted a chain gang, down on the interstate highway to the south, picking up trash This was a different view, in the middle of a ranch, on a hunting trip. We did do some speculating about this but I guess that is another of those things that's better left unsaid, and maybe left to the imagination of the reader. We might have pulled out early and headed for home but we had to wait for my buffalo to be finished, it was in quick freeze and I couldn't pick it up early. When the time got there, we were waiting at the packing plant and picked him up, and packed out a lot of packages of buffalo meat and got them in coolers and covered and started for home.

We drove straight through so as to get that meat in a freezer, there were a lot of packages to carry in when we got home. I was also ready to see Kate, while I had called her it was better to see her in person. I was ready, maybe to tell her of my bravery or possibly my lack of good common sense. But she would have thought that I was just brave and maybe a little of the other. And as always, she was glad to see me, almost as much as I was to see her, and she was glad of my success and safe return.

Chapter 25:

Another buffalo Hunt

About 2 weeks after we returned from the Texas Buffalo Hunt, I received a phone call from Rollie. Did I want to go on after another bull buffalo? Yes, where and when? He said we would be going north and east of Hays, Kansas to a farm or ranch, whichever name you prefer, to take a herd bull. The people there were going to get rid of all their buffalo and while they were selling most of the cows and younger animals, they wanted to keep and eat their herd bull. They preferred that we not shoot him with a rifle, and ideally we would use a bow and arrow, as this would not upset the other animals. If I remember right, a handgun would be preferred to a rifle, but they still preferred the quiet method of a bow and arrow. I know we set this up to do on a week day, I think it was a Thursday. In this case I would be the back up, with my long barreled Smith and Wesson Revolver, model 29 in 44 Magnum caliber. The same gun I had killed the buffalo in Texas with. I was flattered that Rollie thought that I was reliable enough with this gun to be trusted for his back up. Or maybe he was just sure I wouldn't be needed. Or he just liked my company. Better yet he liked all three, my nerves of steel and superb accuracy, my good humor and company, and he wasn't going to need me anyway, and I work cheap.

These people were afraid if we shot the bull it would upset the rest of the herd. Someone decided that we would make our attempt in the security corral, built out of telephone poles, railroad ties, heavy wood planks, and steel cable.

On the chosen day I got up early and drove to Rollie's, got there and loaded up his equipment and put Garand and Bill, in the back seat of my pickup. We were headed for Hays pretty early. From Hays we went on east on Interstate 70 and then left I-70 and went north as directed. We got there and met the people who owned the buffalo. Introductions were made all around and we went out and looked at the buffalo. He was pretty good sized, about 12 years old, and had good horns. Live weight was estimated at 2000 pounds plus. Not as large as the Texas bull but still a big buffalo. With the fence it made it very hard for Rollie to get in position for a good shot, especially with the bow and arrow, for proper placement of the arrow would be critical. When he was unsuccessful in getting a good position, he said he would just go over the fence and be on the ground inside with the buffalo. I said "No, to dangerous". He said "It'll be okay". Again I said "No". I'm not going to face Karen and try to explain what you were doing on the ground inside that pen, it's not happening. Also I would have to go inside to be in position to back him up. One of us had to be able to drive home. So he took up a position on the fence and we moved up and down the fence, on the ground, in trying to get the bull to turn the right way. Eventually it worked and he got his shot. The shot was perfect, clean heart shot, no reaction from the buffalo, he just stood and looked around and eventually move to the center of the pen and just stood there. As soon as he took the shot, I looked at my watch, for the time. It was 20 minutes before the bull went down and then 17-18 minutes more before he died. The blood was coming up the arrow shaft and arcing off the end and onto the ground. With the arrow shaft in the hole, it restricted the blood flow out of the wound. When all was over and the pictures taken and looking was finished, we brought in a big loader and picked him up and took him out and proceeded to skin and cape him. We didn't get any of the meat on this one but Rollie did get the head, for a trophy, and the hide. George Sumner had gotten there and video taped some of this, I'm not sure how much he did get of the whole thing. But there was not much in the way of action involved, in this one. Made for some interesting conversations though. For me personally I have no desire to take a buffalo with a bow and arrow and have even greater respect for the people who do. And the ones that took buffalo with a bow and arrow from horse back. They had to be not only skilled hunters, archers and horseman,but they needed to be fearless also. This also took special horses, that trusted their riders. As long as a buffalo can go after a lethal wound has been inflicted is truly amazing and awe inspiring. Not to mention dangerous for the hunter and the horse, if you're doing it from horse back. But on the other side when you are personally involved and on the ground, so to speak, things have a completely different perspective. At least it did for me when I was on the ground with the buffalo in Texas, no thought of fear or endangerment crossed my mind, but was still aware of the danger and what was going on, when this was taking place. Under the scoring guides for Safari Club this buffalo scored almost as good as the Texas buffalo. The scoring is done by measuring the outside curve of the horn for length, then measuring the circumference at the base of the horn and then the circumference at the mid point of the length, and then adding all three figures together. Boone and Crockett. does this, but also measures circumference at the 1/4 length and 3/4 length points also. These horns tapered down more as they moved to the ends of the horns than the Texas bull did, not as much mass in relation to the length, another sign of the older age of the Texas bull. A really fine trophy and another adventure for us. In our book of life and in living out our hunting experiences. And as people always do, there were those that scoffed and tried to talk down this accomplishment. I would say to those that did and those that will, "What have you done?" Lets see and hear about your accomplishments. We did and you have heard about some of ours, lets see and hear about yours. Some people just irritate me with their negative talk. Enough said.

Chapter 26:

Lance and Katy

Lance had been living away from home for sometime and we would see him at least every week. I remember him coming out and introducing a girl to me. I was working with the horses behind Mike and Jerry Gigot's homes, where I kept them on pasture. Her name was Katy Gfeller, and she was from Nebraska, originally. He said that she liked horses and she had 1 at her father's house in Nebraska. I was polite and a little interested, but I had heard the "I like horses story" before. They often want to ride but are not to interested in taking care of or learning about the horses or the work involved with having horses. Seems like now, I saw her several times, and she was also into riding 4 wheelers or ATVs, sand buggies, and they had been out shooting some, also. I rode 4 wheelers with them a couple of times on the Arkansas River south of Garden City. Well now this was getting better, horses, 4 wheelers, guns, but nothing about hunting. No ones perfect, I guess. It wasn't to long before he was telling me that they were talking about getting married. In no time at all, or so it seems, a date was set and August 9th, 2003, rolled around quite quickly. They lived here and then moved to Greeley, Colorado area, then to Nemaha, Nebraska, back down to Garden City, and then back to Nemaha. Katy's Dad. Bill, had cancer and they went back to Nebraska to take care of him and with Bill's passing, they are still in Nebraska. Logan came along on August 31st, 2007. The doctor induced labor around 8:00 in the morning and Katy was still in labor that evening. The Doctor decided, after talking with them, that a C-section was necessary because of the size of the baby and it was performed about 8:00pm that evening. Someone had to stay here because of the horses, so Kate and Mary Lynn were headed to Nebraska. Grandma was some excited about the new baby and about being a grandmother. She had said that she would stay and I could go but that really wasn't what she wanted, and I wanted her to go. I wanted to go too but I would be there later and they came down shortly, under threat, and I got to see him too. He is still a joy in my life and I get to see him ever so often. I don't get blamed for spoiling him, because there are to many others closer, that get to do that. But that's okay, as long as someone gets it done. I do get to talk to him on the phone some now.

Ralph & Kate Morton August 2003

Chapter 27:

KU Med Center-Kansas City

We arrived in Kansas City at the Airport and an ambulance took us to the KU Med Center Hospital, we were checked in and they started running tests. I was told that they had a guest house close by where I could stay or I could stay right in the room with Kate. There was a couch that could be converted to a bed or I could sleep on it, as is. They brought me sheets, blankets, and pillows. I still had Kate's quilt and it was better. Kate was retaining fluids very badly, and they wanted to draw off fluids from her body cavity but had to identify the specific cancer before they would do anything. All kinds of test were run and we were waiting for results. On Monday son Lance, his wife Katy, and our Grandson Logan came down from Nemeha, Nebraska to visit. They brought a pizza along and we all had some pizza. Dr. Fleming came in, checked the pizza box and said that he was glad we were into health food. On Tuesday they came again and brought 2 pizzas, different kinds, and when Dr. Fleming came in he checked the boxes and decided we were having a party and he had not been invited. So I did invite him but he said he would have to decline because of his very regulated diet. But thanked us and encouraged Kate to eat. On Wednesday morning we went and they did a ultrasound of her body cavity, to determine the best place to draw the fluid from.

In the afternoon while we were waiting, I was setting by the bed and she said "I need another kiss". "Okay I can take care of that" I got up and leaned over her and kissed her. When I started to straighten back up she said "I guess that's another quarter?" I said that "No, since she was in the hospital no charges were being made and all of them were free". She said "Alright" grabbed me around the neck with both arms and pulled me down to her and proceeded to kiss me 25 or 30 times. She let me up about 4 inches, and we were both smiling and I said "Are you through yet?". "No, with the special on I want some more" "Okay , that's what .I'm here for." With that she pulled me back down an kissed me 8 or 10 more times. When I say 'she kissed me', we were kissing each other, as we always did. She let me back up about 4 inches, we were both getting a little breathless, and I asked "Are you getting tired yet?" "Yes a little, but I want some more later." "Okay, whenever you're ready I'll be here." "OK, but don't go to far, I 'll be wanting some more in a little while". Now Michele, our nurse for the last 3 days, was there and had seen part or all of this exchange. She stepped on up to the bed and said "You 2 are newlyweds, aren't you?" I agreed that we were. She said "I just knew it, I could tell by the way you talked, acted, touched, and kissed". She was real proud of herself for figuring this out. She went on for awhile and said that, "Alright you're not going to tell me, so how long have you been married?" I looked at Kate and we smiled at each other and I said "Over 38 years". She said "I don't believe it, yes I do". She was happy that she was wrong and happy that we were that way, after all these years. We were pleased and happy that it showed after all those years, because I did love her as much as I ever did and I can only say that she said she loved me as much as ever also.

After we had our talk with Michele, our nurse, about the quarters for kisses and that we were newlyweds, for just 38 years. Michele left, on other duties. I had noticed a lady waiting outside our door, she was with the cleaning service that cleaned the rooms. I had noticed her outside for a little while when we were talking to Michele. I told her "Come on in". She said "I had not wanted to intrude while you were busy". I told her "We were just visiting with Michele and you should have come on in". She said "I didn't mean to be eavesdropping but I couldn't help but overhear what you had been saying". I told her "It was okay, we didn't mind". She said "What you had talked about was so beautiful and I am so glad for you". She said that she had been married for a total of 21 years. She was now single again. That they had been mostly bad and unhappy years. Her first husband had been an alcoholic. The second one had been a drug addict. And they had been more interested in their addictions than in her. We both told her how sorry we were for her past experiences. She asked if there were any more like me at home, and I had to laugh. I said that "No, Mom always said that one of me was more than enough for the world to have to put up with, sorry". She said "I was just checking and I don't think there are any good ones left around". I thanked her, and said that yes there were some good ones still left out there, she should just keep looking, maybe she just hadn't looked in the right place yet. Kate said that she would pray for her and maybe she could find a "good one" with a little more looking. She should just keep praying and believing, and asking for God's help, and she would find someone. We talked with her for a little while longer and she said she had to better get busy, she finished with our room and again thanked us for our consideration and words of encouragement. They meant a lot to her, that someone still cared and would take the time to talk and tell her so, especially when we had our own problems. We both thanked her and said that we wished we could be of more help. Again Kate told her, she needed to talk to God and ask for his help and that he would help and provide. She left then to finish her work for the day. We didn't see or talk to her again.

One other incident sticks in my mind from this time frame. Another lady on the housekeeping staff had come in on Tuesday, I believe it was. We visited with her also. I was trying to get Kate to eat something, anything, and this lady wanted to know why she wasn't eating. Kate said that nothing sounded or tasted good. I told them that maybe I should have brought some of the goulash from home. Kate said that it sounded good and if we had some she would try and eat some of it. I had made goulash at home while we were still in Garden City and had taken some to Kate at the hospital. She had eaten some of it and thought that it tasted so good. The lady said that it sounded good to her too. But she didn't know how to make it. Kate told her that I was the one who made it and I could tell her how. So I did tell her how I made it. If I could, she could do it, it wasn't to hard and you had a lot of room for variation. She said that maybe she could do that and would try and remember the receipt. We talked for a while and she left to get her rooms finished for the day. On Friday she was back and we talked some more and we both asked her if she had made the goulash. She said "No, when I got home, I couldn't remember the receipt". Kate said that I would write it out for her, and the lady said that she would stop back by a little later and pick it up. So I did write it out and had it ready for her when she came back. When she came back I went over it with her and explained everything and asked if she had any questions, she didn't think so, she should be able to do it with the written instructions. But wished that I would just come over Saturday morning and make it for her and her husband, who was sick. We had told her that we were going home Saturday morning. So that wouldn't be possible. Kate said, in all seriousness, that maybe we could wait one more day and I could go over on Saturday and fix them the goulash. I had to say "No, that wouldn't be possible". We were going home the next morning. And Kate said she knew that but was just wishing. Typical Kate, wanting to do something for someone else. The lady said that she appreciated it and that she would be able to fix it herself and wished us good luck and a safe journey home. We thanked her and she left.

About 4:00pm, on Wednesday, they came and took Kate, this was about the only time that they didn't let me go along, but said I needed to stay in the room. They took her down and drew 4 liters of fluid off her body cavity, this is over 30 pounds of fluid. She was a lot more comfortable when she came back. This took the pressure off her body. She had went into the hospital at 151 pounds and weighted 184 when we got to KU Med Center, she was up to 197. We also realized that if they were drawing fluid then they had made a diagnoses, and that we would be hearing shortly. Dr. Strum had been in that morning and talked with us about a possible transplant. We would all know more a little later.

On Thursday morning, not to long before noon, the liver cancer specialist came by and talked with us. She said maybe the easiest way would be for us to tell her what we knew. So I told her what I knew and understood and Kate agreed that she could add nothing to what I had said. Then the doctor told us the rest. What we had known was pretty accurate but that a transplant wasn't possible do to the progression of the cancer and that no treatment was going to make any difference, it would just cause her a lot of pain. And in her opinion would not extent her life, any, either. And that Dr. Watkins had been very good on his original diagnoses but that instead of 6 to 11 months we should be thinking of 3 to 6 weeks. This was very bad news and for the first time I was unable to take it. I broke down and was silently crying, Kate reached and pulled me to her and put my head on her shoulder/chest and she was comforting me. I was suppose to be there to comfort her but as her norm she was strong and secure, do to her faith in God, and was comforting me. The doctor said she was sorry that she did not have better news, but that was what she had and was her best opinion. I regained my composure and thanked her and that I appreciated her forthright honesty and it was, in my opinion, better to have and deal with the truth than to try and do otherwise. The doctor left then and we just set and held hands and I lay my head on her and tried to grasp, the all, of what we had been told.

Dr. Fleming came in, with the whole team of cancer doctors, not to long after this and per his habit checked her lunch, which she hadn't eaten any of, and wanted to know why she had not eaten any of her lunch. She said she just wasn't hungry. He said that he was really disappointed because he had went down to the kitchen and fixed her cheeseburger himself and she had not eaten any of it. She smiled and said she would try and eat some when he left, and she did eat several bites after he left. He then proceeded to tell us the same things that the liver cancer specialist had but he used different words. He told us that the hardest thing, outside of hearing this news, was to have to tell it and that this one was especially hard. We had gotten to know Dr. Fleming and a number of his team and they all are exceptional people and I can't say enough good things about them. Dr. Fleming ask Kate what she wanted to do and she said "I want to go home". He said "I will see that it happens". He put people in motion instantly to accomplish this. He ordered portable oxygen tanks for us to take home with us and that everything would be done and taken care of right now, if not sooner. When he had given all of them their instructions and saw that people were carrying them out, he then set and visited with us for awhile. But there was nothing for him to say that would make things better today. On Friday when Dr. Fleming came by on his rounds, with the team, he asked the different team members and the nurse how things were progressing for our departure, he was assured that everything was ready, he noticed that there were no portable oxygen bottles there and he had ordered them the day before. He was told that they would be there when we needed them. He said "I ordered them to be here and I want them here, now". People were moving, and when he walked out of the room they wheeled in 3 portable tanks on wheels and parked them in the room. When I asked "why now", I was told Dr. Fleming said now, and around here that means "now".

I called Rollie and told him we were going to be ready to come home Saturday morning. He had told me previously that he would take care of arranging our transportation home, and he said that he would take care of it, not to worry about it. I also gave him the diagnoses. He would call me on Friday with the details and the 'who' was coming information.

As had been my habit, I called Margie that night and updated her. I also told her that if she wanted to see Kate she needed to come right away, not next week or sometime, now. She would start making plans right away. I called Mom and Dad and as I remember Margie took care of telling the rest of Kate's family about the latest news.

Chapter 28:

Kate Goes Home

T hen Saturday morning came and we were ready, and our ride was coming. Bill and Steph had come down on Friday night. Bill called from Steph's sister's home, she lived in the Kansas City area, and said they were leaving for the KU Med Center and would be there before 9am. Bill was Bill Leighton, middle son of Rollie and Karen Leighton, who has been mentioned else where. Steph is Bill's girlfriend, Stephanie Leiker, from Wakeeney, Kansas. Steph is going to school to be a nurse and already works on an Ambulance as a technician. The nurse, we had a new one this day, was in the room when I talked to Bill on the phone and said "No, we wouldn't be able to leave for maybe 4 hours". I said "No, we're leaving". She said we would just have to wait. I was leaving the room, going to get a hold of the doctor that had just left, Dr. Strum. The nurse said she would do it. Doctor Strum came back, with others from the cancer team and said they would take care of things and we would be able to go shortly, if not sooner. We got out of there just shortly after Bill and Steph arrived. We had to get Kate and our stuff down to the van, go by the pharmacy and pick up her prescription. Then the big thing was getting her in the van, she was so sore we could not pick her up, we tried several ways and none of them were working. I suggested a back board, stand it up and get her against it and lay her down and slide her in on it, then she would roll herself over and off the board and we would pull the board out, it worked. We were headed home and she made the trip without to much discomfort.. When we finally got home Kate wanted to go out and see Dolly and just be outside for awhile, which we did. We went out back and she got to see and pet Dolly. They were both glad to see each other. We stayed outside until she got tired and was ready to go in. We finally went into the house and she got into her bed in the living room and we tried to settle in. When we were in Kansas City she kept wanting to get up and walk to try and get some of her strength back. She kept telling me that she wanted to be able to be my "Mate" again. Am still not sure why the switch from wife to mate. But it must have had some special meaning for her, and she didn't tell me anything more about it, when I asked. I still haven't figured it out yet, maybe someday I will.

She had a bad day on Tuesday and I thought she was over medicated, so I cut back on her pain medication. She finally came out of it on Wednesday morning, around 3:00am. She was struggling a little and I ask her "What's the matter?" She said "My night gown is hurting me and I want it off". "Okay, I'll take it off for you". I got it off and laid it back over her. She picked it up and threw it off the foot of the bed, "I said I wanted it off". I picked it up and laid it on the foot of the bed and told her that "Not very long ago it would not have been a problem, as I would have been tearing it off for her". She smiled at this. I kissed her. And ask if she wanted a rub down. She said yes. I gave her a rub down with lotion and she said she felt better. She was resting easy and I spread her gown back over her. I was constantly giving her the 'free' kisses she wanted and desired. She always responded until between 4 and 5 on Friday morning. When she didn't respond and her breathing was changing, I called Katy, my other daughter, from the bed room to help me. I called the nurse, who called the doctor, and said she would call me back. I called Charlotte, Kate's good friend and told her what was happening, and she asked if I wanted her to call Pastor Lenoir and I told her yes. Lenoir called me in a couple of minutes and said she and husband, Joe, would be on their way shortly. When she and Joe got there we talked a little and prayed and talked to Kate. Lenoir told her that we were all okay and taken care of and she needed to worry about Kate now. After a short time Kate opened her eyes and looked at us and then closed them and in a couple minutes she quit breathing. We kept asking her to breath but she never took another breath. Her heart kept beating for awhile and then she was gone.

Chapter 29:

The Aftermath and Life without Kate

Mom, Dad, and Susan got here on Thursday afternoon and had gone to town and gotten a motel room. Margie and Paul where leaving San Francisco early on Friday morning and would be in at noon. Someone called Lisa and Julie and told them and they flew to Albuquerque, New Mexico and drove on up with Aunt Mar and Uncle Geo Hon, on Friday. The Memorial Service was held on Sunday, September 21, 2008, Kate's birthday. This was done to accommodate her family. Very short notice for other friends or no notice at all, but I felt it was necessary because of Kate's side of our family.

Life is suppose to go on and I was going through the motions, but I really didn't care if I lived or not. There were days and then there were bad days and then worse days. I had made the commitment to go to church, because of Kate, with Pastor Lenoir''s urging and because I needed it. Before, I didn't feel that I needed to go to church, she was my spiritual leader. I don't claim this to be right or the way it should be, but I think this is the way I felt, maybe she was a substitute for church, as far as worshiping went. I don't really claim to know. And my experiences with other people and other churches, I wasn't much on going to church. It wasn't that I didn't believe in God, it was I had seen to much of people who claimed to be church people, but were not what I would call good, practicing Christians. I have to admit that as a group the people at the Word of Life Church, Garden City, Kansas are very hard to beat or find fault with. They have been there individually and as a group. I will start here with some of my writings from the time after her Memorial Service.

Oct. 6, 2008

Pastor Lenoir, Joe, and all at the Word of Life Church

I have been wanting to find a way to express my sincere thanks or thank you to all at the church for your love and support during the difficult times with Kate's hospitalization and passing. A thank you card just didn't seem to be enough. To all of you who helped in the many ways that were needed, you are appreciated. Words alone cannot express my feelings. Kate was such a good, kind , and loving lady. Everyone felt they needed to say these things to me, and it was much appreciated, however sometimes I would get amused and/ or even a little annoyed at people, although trying my best not to show it, for trying to tell me about the woman I had been with and loved for over 38 years. I say this in complete honesty and candor and mean no ill will or hard feelings. Pastor and Joe were there and did so much for Kate and I, and all of the family and friends, again words are not enough to express thanks, in this most difficult of times.

I was in church Sunday (and really Kate I was) and in listening to Pastor Lenoir speak, of the people who thought of this wonderful church, what is the people, being less than what they deemed it should be, I was moved to speak, but with me, hard to do in front of you all, the word that comes to mind is ignorance, because no one with first hand knowledge could possible speak or think that way about this church or group. I thank God for all of you and what you did or wanted to do for us, I really know the meaning of the frustration of wanting to help someone and not being able to, and trying to do anything that you can but it is not enough. Sometimes just being there is the best you can do.

I would like to share something with you that is somewhat personal and then again is not. When Kate went to the
hospital in Garden City, I had wanted to take her somewhere
else for a second opinion but she said no, for whatever reasons
of her own, and I kept asking her but I couldn't/wouldn't
argue with her, although I wanted to. On the second Friday
that she was there Pastor came and visited and told her that
she should go and get a second opinion, among other things,
I wasn't their at the time but came in after Pastor Lenoir had
left. When I got there she told me that Pastor had been there
and thought we should get a second opinion. My reaction
was a quite "good idea", inside I was "amen, finally" and
then my thoughts were "I could kiss that woman". Please
bear in mind that I had not kissed another woman, to include
even our mothers, its just not my way, since Kate and I first
met. We have been putting together a memorial to Kate for
her family's newspaper and in writing for that I included
that incident in just that way except for when I said "I could
kiss that woman, although I haven't , I may still". And the
editor, edited it out, along with several other things, because
this language was inappropriate and improper, after she had
agreed that my words about my wife would not be edited,
without my permission, or I would not contribute. Now this
edition of the paper is still in progress, so don't give up hope
yet. When I came to church Sunday morning my protest had
not been answered, and I was getting a little more upset.
When Pastor Lenoir and Joe were on their way to the fellow-
ship hall she stopped , hugged me and asked how I was doing,
I think I said okay but that maybe she shouldn't (in jest) be
hugging me as she had already go me in trouble this week.
When she inquired as to how , I relayed this information to
her and said that I did not understand, I didn't feel I had said
or done anything wrong or inappropriate. She agreed and
said certainly not , that she was "ready and willing, anywhere
and anytime", another load gone, to which I said better not
here, in church, and she stated, here in the church was fine
with her, with Joe agreeing whole heartedly. I may still kiss

this wonderful lady who has become such a good friend, and is a credit to the church, community, and all mankind. I almost asked her if she thought that they would have thought it would have been alright if I had said I was going to kiss Joe instead, but I restrained myself. I did pass this exchange on to the editor and although she hasn't responded directly on this, she did send me a couple of notes saying that my corrections were received and would be taken care of, and that when the special edition was completed it would be forwarded to me for proof reading and approval. So hope this has been taken care.

I do hope that this "confession" does not offend or bother anyone here, it was to simply relay my feeling and demonstrate the kind of person you have for a Pastor. There I go, trying to tell you about someone you already know, love, and appreciate so well

Thanks again so much for a job well done.

Sincerely ,

Ralph Morton

October 7, 2008

Hi Mom and Dad and others,

Was having a bad morning this morning and was determined to change my mind set and did so by thinking about 'good memories of Kate', will put some of them down here to share with you.

Kate made me some slippers, they were crocheted using heavy yarn and were very warm, they were dark red, maybe cranberry red, red being my favorite color and goes with my eyes. I would come home and put them on to warm up my feet, after being out in the cold all day. Kate had a habit of slipping them on and wearing them around the house during the day, and then when I got home I would have trouble finding them. She would have to tell me where she had left them or take them off, and I would tease her about wearing them and she would give it right back to me and tell me she just did it so she would be nearer to me by wearing my slippers and was keeping them warm for when I got home and then she would laugh at me and/or we would laugh together. I would sometimes tell her that I wished they were big enough so we could wear them at the same time, and she would ask me if I thought that our feet should be going the same way or opposite directions. Now don't go jumping to conclusions, that can get you into trouble, and I should know. If the feet were going in opposite directions it was a whole lot easier to kiss her, of course this could have other advantages too. But if they were going the same way it was easier to walk together. We got a lot of mileage out of these slippers. Amazing how much fun you could get out of a pair of red slippers.

S he also made me a number of jackets over the years, a white leather jacket, a green denim one, a camouflage and red reversible, a light weight camouflage one, probably some others also.

The camouflage and red reversible one was for hunting, and was suppose to be orange instead of red but she would tell be that red goes with my eyes better so I would just have to live with the red. This jacket was a little oversize, for wearing hunting clothes under it, but I would tell her if she stood real close that it would go around both of us, so she would stand real close and I would wrap my arms around her and close the jacket behind her and she did fit inside, and boy was that a warm jacket. And this was a really good jacket and the number of things you could do while wearing it was truly astounding, and I think I tried most of them, one time or another. And I still have it.

The white leather one she made for me so that I could go to functions, dressed up, on the motorcycle and still be protected by leather. It was pretty neat having a white leather jacket to wear, still have it too. Darn, she didn't fit inside this one with me.

The green denim jacket has a embroidered picture on the back of Wiley Coyote and the Road Runner. It is a treasured possession and I do still wear it, most recently to church on Sundays. Some very special memories were sewn into these items.

I'm sure most of you don't know that she did hunt with me some, not as much as I wanted but maybe more than she really wanted. It was quality time spent together that maybe wasn't really her thing. But she did it for me and to be with me doing something I enjoyed. Now the most undesirable part of hunting is the killing, and I do understand that, for both of us. But one year she put in for a deer license, part of this was so we would have venison for Lance's diet, and we hunted deer together. I was able to get her in reasonable distance for a shot which she did make and hit the moving deer, she had stopped her swing when she squeezed the trigger and hit him to far back, I was backing her up and though the deer went down I quickly put in the finishing shot. She was both happy and sad at this, happy that we had together been successful but sad that it ended in death. Although she still has gone with me after this she never again shot anything. And I never ask her to participate again, as to the shooting part. We still harvested game and processed the meat together, and she did willingly process and prepare the meat for our and others to use. We did donate wild game to others, for their use of it in feeding themselves and others. We did so enjoy the mornings when we would be out and watch the sun rise and the awakening of a new day. And although we were limited, somewhat, with the raising of the kids, and the limitations, placed on the hunting by them, we still did participate in this when we could. The sharing of God's beauty in nature was one of our many pleasures that we so enjoyed sharing. As stated else where, I never could get enough of her, doing most anything. I am working on the writing of my buffalo hunt, but I get distracted from it, easier than other subjects, and am not sure why this is. Maybe its because it is about me only. For someone who was always wanting to be doing, I could set and watch things just happen for the sake of learning, whether it was wildlife, horses, or people. And she understood and when we could share it, it was so much better, except maybe the girl watching, but we did actually do that together and in a constructive manner, at times. I know that one is hard to believe but it did happen, we have set in open air cafes, and other places, and discussed different things about the passerby people, men and women, clothing or lack there of, jewelry, attitudes, hairdos, or the way the were actually put or fitted together, long or short legs, long or short waisted, necks, heads or whatever, part of this was the seamstress in her and the artist in me, it was just about being together.

Well its time to get up and get ready for work, so I will finish this later, I have a couple of other things to include in this, so I will be back.

I used to watch the deer and learned so much about there habits and there nature by just watching. Kate didn't understand, at first, what I was actually doing, when I was doing this. And then I got her to go with me, to one of my favorite spots, and watch and I could tell her where the deer would be, what they were doing and going to do, and if spooked depending on where the threat came from, which way they would go. The exceptions to this were the big or older deer who had survived, they would at times do the unexpected or the abnormal in trying to escape and/or survive. This was something that you can not teach, you have to want to learn and have the patience and time to spend in learning these things. Everyone can't or won't do these things. And while Kate appreciated them, she didn't think she would ever try to do it, it just wasn't her thing or her way. And that was OK because one person in the family, who was a little strange, was enough.

I deleted out a section of this about the kids allergies that was covered elsewhere.

Speaking of hunting, I got invited to go hunting in south Texas, down at the Light Ranch, headquarters in Cotula, Texas. This invite was extended through Dave Lowe who was the Manger at Gigot Feeders, Feed yard. Do to corn harvest not being finished I was unable to go when the rest of the group were scheduled to go, so George Light said that I was welcome to come later, whenever I could and to bring 3 friends with me. This was really nice of him and his family, not only to let me come later but to get to bring 3 friends with me. I had invited Chris Hammer, Merle Bishop, and Lloyd Crouch to go with me. We were to go about the first of December, Lloyd managed to fall down, hunting, in a corn field and ran a corn stock, or a piece of one, into his eye and couldn't go, so Merle didn't go either. Chris and I went by ourselves. We had a good time hunting deer, javelina, wild boar (hogs), and quail. While we didn't get to shoot any wild boar, we did take deer, javelina, and quail. Phil Lyne, George's son in law, invited me back after deer seasons to hunt hogs on horse back and with dogs. Wanted to so bad but just couldn't afford another trip at that time. These people hunt deer, it is almost a religion with them, also big business, they sold guaranteed hunts for deer, so big a rack, and that cost $5000.00, so high in the Texas record book another $5000.00, Boone and Crockett record book another $5000.00, and if he went over a certain score for the record book then it was another $5000.00. For those of you not keeping score, that's $20,000.00 for one deer. I told Phil that I would just shoot does while we were there, he laughed and said shoot anything you see, those prices are for others, you are our guest and there are no fees for you. WOW thanks. I still shot does while I was there, I wasn't going to shoot a deer that was worth 5 to 20,000 dollars, even if it was free, for me, if some else shot it, it was worth that much money to the family. While hunting, (another little girl story), Phil said he was going to bring his daughter along if it was OK, sure it was okay, her name was Sam, short for Samantha, and she was 4 years old. Now they have rules in this family, you have to be 5 before you get to shoot your first deer. And Sam's sister was 5 and got to shoot her first deer and javelina just before we came down to hunt. The main thing we were doing was game cropping, removing unwanted animals from the herd. Chris got a shot and wounded a deer and he and Phil were going to go after it. A doe crossed in front of us and Phil said he wanted me to go and intercept that doe and shoot her, indicated where she was headed and told me how to get where I could get a shot before she got away. Sam wanted to go with me and Phil said it was OK with him if it was okay with me, I said it was. I told her stay behind me and when I said to "cover your ears", she would cover her ears, she said she would, so off we went into the brush, it worked perfectly and we got the doe. I field dressed it and drug it back to the pick up. Phil said that I need not have gutted it, he had people paid to do that, OK, next time. They had got their deer also, so we were ready to go, we got in the pickup and started driving, that was when Sam spoke up, Dad, what Sam, can I shoot the next deer?. No Sam you know you have to be 5 before you can shoot a deer, oooohhhh kay, (pause) Dad, what Sam, can I gut the next deer, Phil was very busy looking out the window, hhhmmmm, no Sam, you know your mother won't let you have a sharp knife, oooohhhhhhh kay, (pause) Dad, WHAT Sam, on the next deer you do the cuttin and I'll do the guttin, okay? Now Phil was very very busy looking out the window on his side of the pickup and of course I was very busy looking out the window on my side of the pickup, "We'll see Sam". Sam never did get to shoot or cut or gut a deer while we were there but I'll bet she has by now. This was a wonderful family, George and his wife, their daughter Sarah, her husband Phil Lyne, and their 2 daughters. George had 2 or 3 boys and I only remember meeting one of them, briefly, and they all were deer hunters and cowboys. Phil Lyne was the PRCA all around cowboy in 1971 and 1972, a real cowboy and a good friend.

Well these were memories I concentrated on to get my mind off other things, and it seemed to work. Well will go on to bed for another night. Good night to all.

Love

Ralph

Hi Mom and Dad,   October 23, 2008

With so much time on my hands this morning and being so busy, thought I would send a couple of more pictures from your visit on May 14 & 15, 2008, think I may have already sent them, not sure, so will send them anyway.

The first one is of the mare (Ruby) and colt (Star) that was born the morning of the 14th of May
the second one is maybe self explanatory
the third is Kate (trying to hide behind her Dad), Dad, Mom, Mar, and Geo
the fourth is an ice cream cake for Mom and Mar- for Mothers Day
the fifth is a flock of wild turkeys that I took up at Rollie's they actually come right into Rollie's Dads house and will feed on whatever they find and he puts out food for them so he and his wife (Helen) can watch them out of the window

Rollie thinks that Star is the best horse that Kate and I have bred, we had bred and raised both of the parents so were especially proud of this one, think we were on the right track in developing a better horse. We thought that this one was a little extra special since he was born on the day of your visit. He was so standoffish after the first day when I did handle him (called imprint training) and it was fun for both of us to get his trust, so we could have him willingly let us handle and pet him, took me longer to develop this in him than usual, compared to the other colts we have raised, and Kate won him over soon after I did. A lot of them were this way from day one. As I have said, I get along with kids, dogs, and horses, its everyone and everything else that I have problems with. And Margie has taken to telling me when I say this, "and women", and I started out saying "well one anyway", to which I have amended to "maybe two", and now to "okay several". Its rare when I can't make up with a child, or a dog, or a horse very quickly. I believe that partly this is because they look at or in you and see. They see you for what you are and there is a certain amount of trust there almost immediately, and when it is not there, there is a challenge that I really respond to and do work at getting that trust. One of those 'rare' things that Kate never spoke about, I'm sure, was our neighbor south of Garden City, Larry Johnston, he had a number of horses and did raise some, he had a 9 month old colt that had never been touched, by human hands, and was wild (translates to scared to death) with humans. They had go nowhere with her, and asked if I would try to do something with her, and I agreed to try. I named her Cherry and it took me several weeks to get her to let me touch her, willingly. I also cheated, because I also fed her, and most people understand what you can do with a feed bucket or a dinner table, it helps, so when I finally got her trust, enough to start working with her it would go very quickly for awhile and then, maybe, slow down but we were making progress. I was working with 4 colts at the time and started catching them, at night, and tying them up to feed them. Getting them educated in as many different things as possible. Cherry would also test me at times, and one thing that she would do, is walk up behind me and put her lips on my right ear. If you think that was fun, the first time, you probably haven't had your ear bitten recently, but I just gritted my teeth, and stood there. She would continue to do this until she was over 2 years old, when she went to Oklahoma for further training as a roping horse. After a time or two, it didn't bother or worry me anymore, but I did a lot of other people. I remember the first time Kate saw this happen. I knew Cherry was behind me and was probably going to do it, so I was watching Kate for her reaction, and I got it. She got an 'huh oh' look on her face and started to tell me to watch out but never got out much more that "watc" and then a look of amazement, and asked what Cherry was doing. I said "she's kissing me on the ear, why are you jealous?", and she said "no". Then I explained that she had started doing this to test me and to see if I trusted her, and since she never got a reaction one way or the other, just continued to do it. I think I took her to 5 horse shows and did quite well, 3 firsts in class, 1 second in class, a Reserve Grand Champion quarter horse mare, and a Grand Champion and Best of Show. We were always entered into the quarter horse mare class. As I remember Kate went with me to 4 of those shows and the one that I went by myself was the one that I didn't do any good in. It was truly amazing to have seen Cherry when I started with her and then when I was finished. I think I actually loved that horse like I did 3 year old Julie, but I didn't get to spend a year and a half with Julie. My hurt feelings, again, no 3 hear old Julie to go with us to Ethiopia.

Well will send this and do something else, constructive. Steve called a few minutes ago and sometime today, at my convenience, I have to haul a "level dumping bucket" for a big loader down to High Plains Feed Yard at Montezuma, Ks. And that will probably be all that I do today as it's raining, trying to sleet and turn to snow.

Thanks for listening

Love
Ralph

Hi Mom and Dad ,   October 25, 2008

I slept late this morning, 3:30 am, actually I was awake
and didn't look at the clock until 3:15am. stalled 15 minutes
and then got up. Don't really have to work today, but have to
go in for a safety meeting and will change a headlight on my
truck and put grease on the 5th wheel, the part the trailer sets
on and turns on, pivot point. Think I will go north to Rollie's
this weekend. Don't know if you remember or not but we
had a colt born the morning of Kate's passing, they found
her about the same time as she was leaving us. This is the
first time that I have been able to objectively think about this
occurrence. She so loved the new babies. She would sometimes make a little fuss about having another horse around to
take care of, but try and keep her away from that new one, or
better put might be to say 'not to get in her way ' when going
to see or check on them. It reminded me of someone who was
prone to complain about an extra, perceived, burden maybe,
but actually liked and was happy about it. That was Kate. She
loved and enjoyed so much those new babies. And was so
delighted when they would come to her and want her attention. She really enjoyed it when this would happen and got
so much pleasure from it, but not quite admitting it. Although
would admit to me later when we would be enjoying a 'quiet
time' how much she enjoyed and appreciated those times and
opportunities and that she was so happy, to be here and experiencing these things with me and would not change it for
anything. I would squeeze her hand , hug her tighter, or whatever worked (whatever I had a hold of or could reach), and
would kiss her, at least once, and charged no quarters. Needless
to say that I miss her and will miss those situations. Anyway
have not got to see the new baby, we stopped there on the
way back from Utah, but it was getting dark and momma was
not letting me see or get near her. At times have had a strong
yearning to see this new little girl. Have been asked several
times, by different people, if I was going to name her Kate,
and I try to tell them as nicely as possible, that no, and am not

interested in sharing that name with anything or anybody, at least not yet. We have a string of descendants that we have been naming, all of them beginning with the letter 'S', this wasn't planned but started working out that way and started continuing to do this. Will have to give some thought to this one. The last one was Susan, Star, Smokey, Sky. and Stormy. The 5 paints were Reno, Rusty, Rebel, and Rio. And then the last one was Joshua, bet you can't guess who named that one, and then the one sorrel was Daniel. Joshua was always Kate's favorite although she wouldn't come out and admit it, without a little prodding. I remember that morning so well, I went out to check and then called Kate, on my phone, that she needed to come out, of course she knew what I wanted, he was somehow different, Rollie and I had both liked his mother, and he bought her before I had a chance, Joshua was just people friendly from the start, I climbed over the fence and looked him and momma (Inky) over and he came right to me and I started rubbing on him and a little scratching, when Kate got there he turned to looked at her and started working his way closer, a little at a time until he got close enough that she could touch him and started petting him, that gave her such satisfaction and joy. This one belonged to Rollie and when I told him about Kate's feelings for the little guy, he said he would trade for Rio (who wasn't named yet because the vet said he would never live, but he sure did and does eat a lot for a dead horse, he belongs to a friends granddaughter now) and I/we said no, later he kept telling her she could have him but she would never accept him. Rollie said that the offer stands and still does today. It is with great satisfaction that I view these horses today and see how willing and well mannered they are and are so good with people and espe- cially with kids and babies, knowing that we accomplished this together. she was such a joy to be with and around and the feelings of accomplishments are so good and strong, and I expect will always be so.

Well, guess I had better start thinking about a shower and heading to the office, won't be much to it, just watch a film and a few words of talk. We have to attend at least 3 of these per year for insurance purposes.

Do hope you enjoy this and get some sense of the feeling(s) we shared in this.

Have a good day and hope to talk to you soon.

Love
Ralph

Hi all,   Oct. 25, 2008

It is with very mixed emotions that I send these pics to you all this morning. these are of the filly (girl) colt that was born the morning of Kate's passing. They found her, up at Rollie's, at about the same time that Kate left me/us. I m not sure how I feel about this colt at this time. We normally viewed the addition of new life, especially in our horses, with a lot of joy and happiness. Although this was there, did not seem to be to the extent that would have been there under other circumstances. I guess that this has changed like everything else seems to have. I didn't get my hands on her, as momma is very protective, and being out in the pasture only got with in about 30 feet of her. Did see and get my hands on Star, the colt that was born when Mom and Dad were here on May 14th, He remembered me quite well and wanted attention, since we had raised his mother and she has always been very friendly, we figured he would be too, but was not after the first day, we slowly won him over. I will send pictures of him in another email. For some reason didn't want to include them in this one, like I said very mixed emotions on this one.

At least I spared you of my ramblings this morning. Hope you can enjoy these pics and will try to send the others later.

love to all
Ralph

October 28, 2008

Hi Margie,

Thank you again for the email, it was beautiful and so are you. I printed it out so I can take a copy with me. It is so true and fits not only my current situation but all situations. You have really made my day, again. I have to be leaving here before 3 am, headed to Kearney, Neb. to check out hay to buy and bring a load back. I was torn between forwarding it to everyone and keeping it for myself. Will send it tomorrow but it will be mine for today. I know that you understand. I will send one picture with this, its of Spec, sometimes others just know when we need a hug or a little special attention, she came up to me the other day in the pasture and just stood, touching me, not demanding, not anything but there, somehow she knew and was just being there for me, her hug was a little different but was there just the same and I did hug her back. Don t know how long she would have stood there but we did for awhile and then some of the other horses, who had been holding back decided that they wanted their turn with me and had waited long enough, started pushing forward and although she stood her ground I turned her loose and moved to some of the others, she just stood and watched me and then after awhile moved away. A little later I went back to her and did hug her again and gave her some attention that I had not done before, I had just stood there with her, and know that in my own mind, she was there and understood. Just like you. Its nice to have at least 2 friends. and although I have more, you 2 are both so very special.

thanks and love ya
Ralph

Hi Mom and Dad and others,   Nov. 2008

Have been thinking the last couple of days as I have done a lot of driving this week. A lot of things have been on my mind. So will write about some random things that have been occurring to me.

I went to the VA Hospital in Wichita on Thursday and after they got through with me in x-ray, I went on to Ortho, to get the steroid shots in my knees, when Tiffany, the nurse , was giving me my preliminary check, before she checked my blood pressure I told her not to bother as it was high, she asked how I knew this? I know. She started asking questions while going ahead and taking my blood pressure, I told her about losing Kate. We had something of a conversation and she notified the mental health team and asked if I would as least talk to them, I agreed to, but not to hold her breath. She also got to Susan the Dr. that gives me my shots. I have been seeing Susan for about a year and a half and we get along quite well. The first time I saw her she told me I had 2 bad knees, wow, you are really sharp how many years of advanced schooling have you had to be able to tell that, we both laughed and have been friends ever since. If you had told me before I talked with her that someone would be sticking needles in my knees that day I would have told you, that you are crazy. But she talked me into it or rather convinced me she could do it painlessly. If I trusted her and relaxed my legs and didn't move I wouldn't feel anything, Almost true, but I didn't have any pain and it helped by the time I got up and walked to the door. They hadn't told me anything when I went down for the appointment so I didn't wear swimming trunks or shorts. When she asked if I had worn swim trunks or shorts, I said"Nno. are we going swimming?" She laughed and said "No, but I was going to have to take my pants off". We could get a gown or something, whatever I wanted to do. I said "Okay". She said "It didn't matter to her if it didn't matter to me". I took my pants off. Its been a standing joke between us when I walk in she tells me I have to take my pants off. She really knows how to start a meeting off right. I might add that she was pregnant at our first meeting, I didn't know but suspected it. Then when I went back for my second round of shots, I got Rebecca to give me my shots. I wasn't overly enthusiastic about the change, but found out Susan was not there. They didn't say but she was out for the birth of her baby. Rebecca was okay but she wasn't Susan. I asked if she was as good as Susan in giving the shots and she said she didn't know but I could give her a chance and judge for myself. She's not as good at giving the shots, and I do feel, maybe, it's the trust factor. Don't know if it made any difference but after I told Susan the next time, I've always seen Susan since. She was ready for me Thursday. I walked in and she didn't tell me to take off my pants, but said she thought I could pull them up high enough for the shots today. She then asked how I was doing and I knew she had been told. Everyday is new and different and I'm still here. I had some pictures for her of Susan, the colt, that Kate and I had named for her, and she said "Really, and was I serious". "Yes I am, anyone that I let, and look forward to, sticking needles in my knees can sure have a colt named after them". I showed her the pictures of Susan and the colt that was born on the 19th of September, on my viewer. She surprised me with pictures of her year old baby boy, she really helped make my day. Kate had went down with me but would never go in with me, as she couldn't stand to see the needles in my knees. Susan asked about Kate and I showed her a copy of the Sandoval Sun and her pictures on the viewer. In looking at the pictures she said that "She was so beautiful and so young, for this to have happened and you have to be and have every right to be so proud of her." And of course the doctor is always right, this one any way. She started reading the Sun and said that she wanted to finish but was not going to have enough time, so I left the copy with her and she said that she really appreciated it and that it was most kind for me to do that. I told her "Thank you, but you have already spent an extra 15 or 20 minutes with me today and put yourself behind". She said that this was time well spent and would do it anytime. When I was finally leaving she grabbed me and hugged me and held me for a little while and said to take care of myself and come back to see her. She could make you want to go see a doctor, if they were all only like her. Tiffany was waiting for me, and escorted me over to see the people at mental health, so I wouldn't get lost, she may know me, cause I thought about not going.

The person there, wanted to know why I wanted to see him, and I said I didn't, that the people at Ortho thought I should, so we talked and he wanted to know if I had a support team, and I told him I did, he wanted to know who they were and I told him, who they were and what they did for me. After talking it over he said I was probably right I didn't need to see him but if I did, he gave me his card. And he wanted me to see the nurse, Collene, before I left. She wanted to do something for my sleeping and I said that I doubted that she could help my sleeping. Everything she wanted to give me would require that I not drive for at least 8 hours, I don't always have 8 hours between coming home and going back to work. And some of them could be come addictive and I didn't want any of them either. So she decided that what I was doing would be okay. I had already told them, they might think I'm stubborn, and I can't imagine why they would think that. She did talk to me over an hour and a half and wanted to be sure I was okay, no, but maybe someday. Had to wait over the lunch hour to check on my hearing aids and they were not done, they are hoping for, before thanksgiving, going to have to hurry.

I don't know if I told you or not, have told some but not others. On Sept. 18th 2008, about 6 in the morning I was up and Kate was awake, so I kissed her, as is my custom to do every morning, when I did this she said "oh , not so hard, that hurts", talk about pain, I said I'll take it easier, and I kissed her again, just barely brushing her lips, and she "that's better". I don't know how to explain the hurt and pain that I felt, that something we had done and enjoyed for so long was now a source of pain to her. But I was so very careful the rest of the day when I kissed her. This might indicate to you the pain she must of been in at times even when she insisted that she wasn't in pain, at least some of the time.

I will relate some of the things about the people where I work. When we went to the hospital, I was told that whatever I needed to do to do it, time off, whatever I needed take it, whether I had it coming or not. If we needed anything, anything, call. Tim Dewey, the father and head man, called every few days asking for updates and checking to see if I/ we needed anything. On the off days Steve Dewey, son, and the one I work directly under, would call and ask the same things. Again, don't worry, your job is here when you come back, whenever that is, it will be here. I was using my vacation time to keep the paychecks coming, and was told if I needed money or a paycheck to call, with an amount or they would just continue to send my paycheck, when I came back to work we would work out a payback plan based on whatever amount I could repay, however long it took. At least this was one worry we didn't have. When Kate passed on Tim called and expressed his condolences for him and Pat, his wife, for the family and the company and all the employees. Steve called also, same things. Come back to work whenever I was ready, no hurry, we need you when you get here. At the Memorial Service Tim and Pat came up and expressed their condolences, again, and Tim said "My God what a woman, we had no idea, and only wished we had only got to know her better, and you haven't been with us long but you are family and don't forget it, if you need anything call me". When I did go back to work, I stopped in to see him, and we went into his office with Steve and daughter Janell, she's Office Manager, and talked about anything and everything. Tim wanted to know when I wanted to come back to work, I said tomorrow, ok if you want to, but take longer if I wanted to. What job do you want? You can have any job we have. I'll just do what I have been, if that's okay? Yes that's fine. Pretty good place to work, I would say. They continue to check on me and ask if I'm okay and need anything. The answer is always the same, I'm still here and what I need is unavailable, someday that answer may change.

In talking with my sister, Pat, today we were talking about some of the things I have done over the years and I promised I would try and put some of them down for her and others who have never heard of these things because I never told anyone, except Kate, who knew just about every-thing with very few exceptions, and these things maybe should be passed along to our kids and any of you who would like to hear. While they are just stories of things, as sisters Pat and Margie keep telling me they are unique in that they haven't been heard before and others haven't done these things and they are worth telling and listening to. And besides the doctor(s) say it's good for me, I'm glad that something is.

One other thing that has been on my mind, I was always wanting to be with my Dad. When I was little if Mom took her eyes off me for a minute, I would be gone, if Dad was around close on the farm, she knew where I would be, generally in the road of whatever he was doing, but don't remember him complaining to much, but of course my memory could be bad. If it was at all possible to help him I was there, whether needed or not. Was always jealous of Tom, he was older and could go with Dad and help, and be with him. Have you ever heard the line "it's not fair, I don't care if he is older, I can do just as much as he can. " God its hard to be little, small, and young" when Dad works around home, as in on the farm. It's a wonder I ever survived but I guess I have had a co-pilot for a long time and he has had a busy time looking out for me, it seems, where ever and whatever I was doing. And maybe it's as Pat says and I quote from a Dec. 30, 1967 letter "I'd say you have a guardian angel riding on your shoulder, I have a feeling you were hurt worse that you told Mom and Dad". Actually it was not an untruth it was just not the complete truth. I rest my case.

Well next time it may be to the jungles of Panama, for trout fishing and other things not encouraged by the US Army.

Thanks for listening and love to you all
Ralph

Chapter 30:

More Memories of Kate

After Kate's Memorial Service, I have talked to a lot of people and the stories of the things she had done for people keep coming in. Some were things that I knew something about and some were of things that I did not know about. She was always doing things for others and not wanting any recognition.

There was the time when she found a girl crying because she wanted to go to church but didn't have shoes to wear, to church. Kate told her to not to cry, that the Lord would provide, and she would join her and they would go to church together on Sunday. She came home and was telling me about this and wanted to know what I thought she should do. I told her to go to town and buy the shoes. She smiled and kissed me, and said "Thanks, I was going to anyway but am glad that you agree". I don't really know if she had already bought the shoes or went in and got them after our talk. But she met the girl, somewhere, and she put on her shoes and they went to church, together. The girl's younger sister was telling Mary Lynn, at school, of this after attending Kate's Service, and how much her family thought of "Miss Kate", as she was know to most, at the church.

Another occurrence happened recently, with our friend Gina. I have always thought of her as Gina Aguilar, from when we first moved to Garden City and lived next door to her Mom and Dad, when she was little. When Gina was 9 her parents divorced. Kate kept in contact with Gina and her mother Virginia over the years. I knew this but I didn't realize to the what extent. She would tell me she had stopped by and saw them but that was about all she ever said. Over the years they were good friends and Gina called Kate "Mama Kate or Mother Kate" and referred to me as "Papa Ralph". I knew that she called me this but really never understood why, but who am I to ask, I can always use another daughter, and not complain or ask questions. Kate might not of told me anyway, if I had asked. Sometimes its easier to look thoughtful, interested and occupied than ask questions you won't get answers to anyway. It also saves wear and tear. Over the years she and Mary Lynn stayed close friends with Gina and her family and I would see her occasionally. Her husband Ralph Guerrero and the kids, Gabby, Audrey, Xavier, Mariah, Octavio, Tiffany, Destiny and grandson Eleazar (Gabby's son), on rare occasions. When visiting with Gina, several times recently, I am always made welcome, really welcome, in their home and they are welcome, always, in mine. She was telling me of some of the things that Kate did for her family over the years, always remembering them at Christmas and at other times as well. One year when things had been a little tight, financially, Kate had come by with an artificial Christmas Tree, it was gold in color and I believe it had decorations with it or they made decorations for it, to supplement what they already had, and they set it up and decorated it, together. She told me that this has become a tradition, they always have a artificial tree and I believe they still have a gold one, color wise, every year.

I am very honored by this girl/woman who considers me a part of her family, of course Kate did the work, and hope that she accepts my feeling that she is indeed a part of my family. There is just such a feeling that she is indeed another daughter, and I just feel glad to see and talk to her, because she is a part of Kate, and that can not be changed or taken away. Thank you Gina for being there.

I have come to learn that I have such a family. Some are related by blood, some by spirit, and some by a desire, to be family. I will take this opportunity to name some who have really come to the front since Kate's going home. Some one has to be first, Mary Lynn would be there, Lance and Katy with Logan, Rollie and Karen Leighton with Garand, Bill, and Sam, Pat Smith my sister, Margie Cassero another sister, Ken my brother, Stephanie Leiker another daughter, Gina Guerrero another daughter, extended but still considered, Joe and Lenoir Randle, Bob and Leyla Daley with Katy (3) and Jake, a lot of people at the Word of Life Church (maybe some more that others but still as a whole group), a group of people that I call friends that are there and to numerous to list. And special unto herself, Hannah Yost, to include her Mother Diana, sisters Rebeca and Noemi, please read below and I hope my words do the story justice.

Chapter 31:

Hannah

This was written on January 15, 2009, in an hour and half. I had an appointment with Dr. Carrie Crownover, at Ft. Dodge, east of Dodge City, Kansas on this day and told her of this happening. She had read some of my writings and ask if I had written it down, and I said "No, I haven't". She said "Write this down, it needs to be done, and it will help you.)

In November of 2008, in trying to cope with the loss of Kate, on Sept. 19, 2008, and before Blue Cross-Blue Shield started taking back the medical bill payments that they had made, I was still having trouble sleeping . In my praying and asking for God's help, in understanding, I was awake in the middle of the night and thinking, and trying not to, God spoke to me and told me that "the way to healing would be through a child or children". I knew I needed to find the way to pursue this. I put in a lot of thought and ran through the known, possible, children, they were all older so would have to look else where. I had seen the notice about the Angel Tree, at church, and had already had this in mind, so I called the church and spoke with Diana Yost about participating in the Angel Tree Program. She said she would check and call me back. She did and there was one child, a 2 year old boy, left on the tree, I would take that one. Was there anything else and she told me that was it. Okay, this will be done. Mary Lynn, my daughter, did the shopping, wrapping and the delivering to the church. On the day after Thanksgiving I got the notice that BC-BS had taken back the payments already made. I was really down and somewhat depressed. The next week they notified me that they had paid KU Med Center Hospital bill. I explored a couple of other possibilities but nothing else came to light. The church was to have the party for the children on December 7th, with Christmas Caroling to follow and then a desert auction, to help raise money, for the children going to camp. Pastor Lenoir and Joe Randle made sure I was aware and I promised to come to these festivities, and I did. Do to a communication problem the party did not materialize and I did not get to meet the young man. We went caroling to the nursing homes and a nice time was had by all. Now I did not do much singing, figured that the residents would enjoy it better that way, and did not really feel like singing much anyway. We returned to the church to a soup supper and started viewing the auction desert items that were up for bids. Now we were there to raise money for the kids going to camp, and not gain to many pounds in the process. Now it seemed like everyone was having a good time, some more than others. Pastor Jeff should have gained at least 10 to 15 pounds and a half. A couple of others were right behind him, I'm pretty sure. Hannah Yost seemed to be an avid bidder also, and could bring smiles to a lot of faces, mine included. Now I had watched her in church from Sept. 28 on, and she was always bringing a smile to me, if not on my face, for sure in my heart. When all the deserts were gone, the goal of $3000.00 was surpassed and everyone could go home with the knowledge of a job well done. I still hadn't been able to make any progress, as far as I knew, on my quest for a start on my inside healing process. I kept thinking and looking for something to latch onto, for I was convinced that this would be accomplished or at least started by a child or children. It came to me while driving that the answer had been right in front of me for weeks and now I needed to find a way to accomplish it. I decided that I needed to get Christmas Gifts for Diana's 3 daughters. I have trouble shopping for myself, never less children, Kate and Mary Lynn liked to do this shopping and always took care of it, I haven't really shopped for about 40 years. Oh man this wasn't going to be easy, but why not take them to Wal Mart and let them pick out their own things. Yes, now I was getting somewhere, but that meant I had to go face and ask Diana, being naturally shy and not wanting to intrude, offend, or worse, to anyone, I had a new problem. How to do this, common sense told me I could go and talk to Diana and she being the person she was/is, it would be fine. Now all I had to do was to convince myself that this would be okay. I had a Doctor's appointment, on December 22nd , I also received notice that they took back the KU Med payment on this day, so I would just go by and see her at the church, no sweat. I got to the church and drove right on by, I can't do this, went on down to Mary St. and started going west, I've got to do this, so I turned around and went back to the church and drove into the parking lot, slowed down to park and drove right on through, I can't do this, went back down to Mary St. and went almost to the by pass and I've got to do this, turned around and went back, drove into the parking lot and parked, this time, I can't do this, I've got to do this, so I went in and talked with Diana, she was most gracious and listened and heard me out and agreed to let me do this with her daughters. She talked with me and prayed with me and made me feel better about my situation. She is a very understanding and caring lady. I told her that we could do this whenever it would work for her, after Christmas would be fine, and she would let me know when she could do it.

She called and asked if Sunday (28th of Dec.) after church would be okay, fine with me. We met after church, at the church, and she invited me to lunch, at Ward's. before we went shopping. Sounds like a plan. We get to Ward's and she says lunch is on her, no way, this is my party and lunch will be on me, since I'm still bigger than she is, she decided to agree and let me have my way. We had a very nice lunch and while she was away from the table I explained to the girls about the ice cream law. And that is, if you go to church, on Sunday, and then go eat lunch, you have to eat ice cream before you can go home, it's the law, I thought I had heard or read this some-where, Hannah, 4 years old, asked "really", I'm pretty sure it is, and she asked how did that go again, and I said that if you go to church on Sunday and then go to lunch you have to have ice cream before you can go home, and the age limit is 15 and mandatory, but sometimes it has a sliding scale and can run up to 65, and over 65 the law doesn't apply anyway. This is only if you go out to other than your own home to eat. She was thinking about this and said she would try to remember this law. Diana said that they could have ice cream, I didn't have invoke the law, this time. I thought she had heard this and was just ignoring me, and was being nice and tolerant to me, actually she hadn't been paying attention and hadn't heard any of this. And I was just trying to keep her out of trouble with the police. I'm not sure what price will have to be paid for this, yet, but pretty sure that this will come back home, eventually.

We did go shopping and had a good time, yes I had a good time shopping with these girls and I know there are a lot of people who won't believe that, but, oh well.

Now to finish off a good story, Hannah is a true blessing to me, she makes me smile, inside and out, and I just feel better when she's around. When I saw her after church on Sunday, the 4th of Jan., she came over and was glad to see me, but I don't think as much as I was to see her, and she gave me a hug, and I felt better than I have for quite awhile. I thank God for the blessing of this little girl who has done, I think, more than any adult has to help me with the healing process, and yes it is finally starting to get better. Thank you Hannah. And you are in line with Lenoir, but I'm thinking you are way ahead, in getting that kiss I've promised Lenoir.

Having been thinking about this, I have decided to add this to this story, had held back at first because of my own feelings on it but think it needs to be said so all can know. When Hannah came up to me in church and gave me this hug, it was around my left leg and knee. This knee has hurt for most of the time for 41 years, thanks to Viet Nam, it bothers me when I stand unmoving for even short periods of time. It had been hurting, a little more, from standing in church without any motion. I didn't realize until afterward that when she did this it quit hurting and only one other person, that I know of, had that ability or effect on me, and that of course was Kate. Yes this was temporary and the pain or soreness came back later but any relief is appreciated. Another thing happened at the same time, (and this is not to easy to write) a lot of the time since Kate's passing I have a knot or tightness in my chest, not sure how to explain this, but it seems to come when church is over or about over and we are going to leave, and at other times also. Don't yet understand this but maybe will figure it out in time. I did have it this day and with Hannah's hug this went away and has not come back, this is the 11th day. Now this is hard to explain and to write, but is the fact. And I could only explain it by saying that this is God working through a 4 year old girl, with her and his love. I am humbled and grateful for this. She has been and will continue to be thanked in my nightly conversations.

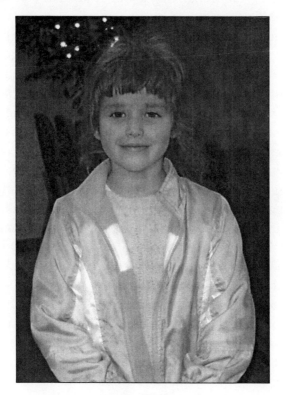

Hannah Yost

This letter was actually started before I wrote the above, but was finished afterward and felt it needed to be included. Ralph

January 12, 2009 (and finished on January 16th and 17th)

Dear Paster Lenoir and Joe,

Just so you know, I do listen and try to learn from you whether its on Sunday or any other day. When you speak of God's plan for us. That it is his plan that includes all of us. I have been listening, and with all of the things I have done and been through, including this last one, I guess he has need of me here. And in thinking about it, thought I would offer these thoughts to you.

He had need of me here in December 2008 to explain the Ice Cream Law to young girls after Church, and to a wise Pastor who did not know of the Ice Cream Law and needed it explained to her. She might have gotten into trouble not knowing this. Or to be there and listen to a smiling mother when she said "You know you can say no to her, you do know how, don't you" and answering "Maybe", and thinking 'sure I do, I just don't want to'. Or in helping a Pastor practice her hugging, with lots of practice she will eventually get it down, but still needs lots of practice. And I will be there to help with practice, whenever I can. And someone had to be there to help a young lady with her picture taking lessons, everyone needs to know how to use a camera. And I guess I needed to be there when this young lady leaned over the table and said "Mr. Ralph, I love you", someone else might have been confused with the use of this name or unprepared for the use of this term. And of course I did know to respond appropriately, with the truth, to her, so that she just beamed with that response. Someone needed to be there with quarters when the young girls had to have a couple of small balls to play with, despite Mom's protest that they didn't need them. I mean, someone has to be there at times like these, its possible that not just anybody could handle these situations. It's a good thing that mothers are also understanding and tolerant of children, big and small, old and young.

On the hugging, you were the first one ever, besides Kate, that I felt completely comfortable with, being hugged, had never been my way, but it did help that weekend of Kate's Memorial Service, I was a lot more comfortable with it, after helping you with your practicing. And like I said before I was hugged more in those 3 days than the rest of my entire previous life, when excluding Kate. So you may be more accomplished than I allowed before, but keep practicing. I think that this possibly goes back to when I was 5 and was trying to recover from my injuries, and would not accept any help, I wanted to do it myself. And if someone hugged me or tried to hug me, I perceived this as trying to help me and I would not allow it, to include my mother. And she respected this in me and did her best to help and that included not hugging me. And it carried over and we never did hug. I think back now and what I must have put her through and then no outward displays of affection, other than an I love you, once in a while. It would be nice if you could go back and do over some of these things, but that is not to be. So I guess I will just to have to let you use me for practice and its okay to fill in for Mom now and again. And that not asking for or accepting help has carried over also, it is very hard to ask anyone for help and have gotten better about accepting it but not to much. But how right it seems to accept help from a small girl, who in her youth, is just being herself. God does work in some not so mysterious ways, at least to some they are not mysterious.

I was also listening when you spoke of seeing a need and doing something about it. And was therefore prepared to accept when a child offered love and trust to someone who was in need of it, and was able to return in kind. I believe the need was there on both sides and maybe was seen by both, for sure by one. I do hope that this relationship can continue and grow because I believe that it will be beneficial to both and maybe to others, on the fringes. I guess you could call it funny, how things sometimes go and evolve, but I see nothing funny in the way I feel about and for this little girl who changed and turned me around. And do so want to help or do anything I can do for her and her sisters, and it might be considered amazing how attached you can get to someone you have never met, but I do feel that way. Maybe its what I have read about, called transference, I don't know if I believe it or not, where you transfer your feelings for one to one or more others. But if this is so, than I have ample love for all three and some more to boot.

In having not gotten this finished this week and having another early morning of not sleeping I have a couple of more things for thought.

I was thinking about if Kate were here and had we brought Hannah, Noemi, and Rebeca out for a weekend, to give Diana a little, of unasked for, time off(?). And Diana thinks I spoil the girls!!! Where I give them ice cream, Kate would have supplied the cookies and cake to go with it. And would have been suppling them with games, puzzles, and other things, in her words, to keep them occupied, but would not be spoiling them in the sense that my giving them ice cream would have been. She would of even let me help. They would of had a weekend of attention and love that would of been hard to beat. We did make an interesting team.

In talking with my sister, Pat, I was telling her of my brothers telling of Kate spoiling me and doing everything for me and I was not really appreciative of her and how awful I was in treating her like this and accepting this from her. And she said she leaned that way herself, until she came and stayed with us for an extended visit. And what an eye opener she got, her words, when she was there and witnessed first hand life in our real world. This was always a two way street with us, and Kate soon set her straight about who did what for whom. She said there was enough love in this house for two or more families. And yes she did spoil me, but she was quick to point out that I returned it. When I took on more work so she didn't have to do anything but what she wanted to, I sometimes worked 20 hours a day and was always working 12 to 16 hours a day and sometimes 7 days a week.

This let her be able to go to church and do the many things that she chose to do, with or without the kids. And while there wasn't an abundance of money, there was enough to do what she wanted and this was because she did such a good job of managing things. Maybe making do with what she had. What a 2 way blessing. I still love her and miss her.

You, meaning the whole Word of Life group, are even changing my vocabulary, and for the better, and while sometimes the words are different I think the meanings are usually the same. When talking about the good things, especially. And when I was disrupting one of your Sunday School classes last week and we were talking about school and/or the learning of things, learn everything you can, it never hurts you and you never know when something is going to come into play and be useful to you or someone else. And we had examples where this had happened in the everyday world of life. And you are saying, you disrupted my what? It really wasn't my fault, okay, maybe it was, but we had a good time, anyway. And my thanks to Chris and the kids, maybe I should say young adults, in the class for a very pleasant morning in Sunday School, for the first time in about 55 years.

Thanks for listening and being there and as always you both are good friends and more.

Ralph

Chapter 32:

Remembering Kids.

Over the course of my life I have been blessed with a number of children that were not mine, by blood, but were still claimed by me. There were of course my own, Mary Lynn and Lance and his wife Katy, and my grandson Logan. These are some of the others that were very important and made a difference in my life.

The first that I remember was Miguel, or Miguelito, who was 4 and 5 when I knew him. He was the son of Teodosia Cruz, in Panama. Amazing how we could converse, with him speaking no English and me limited in my Spanish. We would do little or of no consequence things that occupied us and we wanted to do, and made little sense to others. But that was okay, it made sense to us and he needed attention and a friend. A long time ago but still remembered.

The next one that I remembered and was quite fond of was 3 year old Julie Arthur, Kate's little sister, when we were first married. We made up almost instantly and I had wanted to kidnap her and take her with us to Ethiopia, in 1970, but Kate didn't think Mom would like that. She said I or we had better not do it, Kate did think that she was included in the plan. She never said anything about Dad, so I thought, as an after thought, that maybe it would have been okay with Dad. I'm almost kidding, even now I acknowledge that I would have done it if I had thought Mom and Dad would even had considered allowing it. Still almost kidding. I had taken one of their daughters, maybe I should have tried for two. Kate and

I talked about this for about the first year we were married, and I never changed my position on wanting to, but never intending to. After about the first year she quit bringing it up, because I think she still was concerned that I was still serious about doing it. I never saw another picture of Julie, except for when she was 3, until she was 21 and it was when she had been 18. I think Kate wanted me to still have the memory of the 3 year old red headed little girl that I had remembered for so long. I remember my disappointment when I actually had to acknowledge that she had indeed grown up. I knew she had but did not ever actually admit it, until I saw that picture. The beautiful little girl had become a beautiful woman. And did not ever see her again, until Kate passed away on September 19, 2008. And she had no memory of ever meeting me before, but I still had the memory of her.

There were several children in Ethiopia that made impressions but none that I wanted to kidnap or even borrow for more that a day at a time. When I was building the 7 race tracks, that I built while I was there, the local kids would come and watch and on the rare occasions that I had an interpreter I would talk with them and answer their questions. At times there would be a couple hundred or more and they always got a kick out of the fact that I took time to talk to them and acknowledge their presence. At times when I knew I was going to be there and could get to a store, I would bring them candy or treats of some kind. Kate wasn't keen on the idea of my giving them candy, but I still did. I know this qualifies as bribery. All over the country I was known as "Number 7". They might not know my name but they still knew me, by my racing number. When I or we went down town to local stores I would always draw a crowd of children. Because some one of them would recognize me as "No. 7" and they would crowd around and try to talk to me or try to shake my hand. I always liked to think that it was because I was a nice guy, or maybe my expertise as a motorcycle racer but was probably just the treats. I could always make up with children and went out of my way to do so, especially when I saw or suspected they had a need. When we came home from Ethiopia, I didn't have any more until my own daughter and son came along and was completely infatuated with them, but like all children they grew up. They are still okay, I guess. Think I liked them better when they were little.

While hunting, (another little girl story), at the Light Ranch, Cotula, Texas, I think it was 1984, with Phil Lyne, George Light's son in law, Phil said he was going to bring his daughter along, if it was okay, sure it was okay, her name was Sam, short for Samantha, and she was 4 years old. Now they have rules in this family, you have to be 5 before you get to shoot your first deer. And Sam's sister was 5 and got to shoot her first deer and javelina just before we came down to hunt. The main thing we were doing was game cropping, removing unwanted animals from the herd. Chris Hammer, who came along with me from Kansas, got a shot and wounded a deer and he and Phil were going to go after it. A doe crossed in front of us and Phil said he wanted me to go and intercept that doe and shoot her, indicated where she was headed and told me how to get where I could get a shot before she got away, this was in heavy brush. Sam wanted to go with me and Phil said it was ok with him if it was okay with me, I said it was. I told her to stay behind me and when I said to "cover your ears" she would cover her ears, she said she would, so off we went into the brush, it worked perfectly and we got the doe. I field dressed it and drug it back to the pick up. Phil said that I need not have gutted it, he had people paid to do that, okay next time. They had got their deer also, so we were ready to go, we got in the pickup and started driving, when Sam spoke up "Dad?" "What Sam?" "Can I shoot the next deer??" "No Sam, you know you have to be 5 before you can shoot a deer." "Ooooohhhh kay." pause "Dad?" "What Sam?" "Can I gut the next deer?" Phil was very busy looking out the window "hhhmmmm no Sam, you know your mother won't let you have a sharp knife". "Ooooohhhhhhh kay." pause "Dad?" "WHAT Sam?" "On the next deer you do the cuttin and I'll do the guttin okay?" Now Phil was very very busy looking out the window on his side of the pickup and of course I was very busy looking out the window on my side of the pickup. pause "We'll see Sam." Sam never did get to shoot or cut or gut a deer while we were there but I'll bet she has by now. I had a really good time with Sam in the couple of days that I knew her and have thought of her often over the years. What a true joy children are.

This was a wonderful family, George and his wife, their daughter Sarah with husband Phil Lyne and their 2 daughters. George had 2 or 3 boys, anyway, and they all were deer hunters and cowboys. Phil Lyne was the PRCA all around cowboy in 1971 and 1972, and was a real cowboy and a good friend.

Over the years since mine were little there have been a number that have drawn my attention, some were more permanent than others.

Sky and Scott Leighton would have to be in here, somewhere, of course they were a little older starting out but still qualify in with these others. We did a lot of shooting, hunting, card playing, working, working cattle, fence building, 4 wheeling on ATV's, some socializing, and just having a little fun. Of course they already knew about having a little fun, but at times we might have taken it farther and had a whole lot of fun. It was hilarious to watch them trying to out run a "bad" cow, and when they did finally make it intact. This was especially true when it was slick and slippery. Shooting pigeons out of the air with handguns, skipping rocks and hitting and/or breaking them with handguns, after the first skip off the water. But those are another story altogether. I did hate to see Sky show up at the 22 Pin Shoots with his rifle, he's the only one I ever really conceded to, at least mentally, but only in the 22 Rifle, other events he had to do it if he was going to win, the rifle too, but mentally I gave the 22 Rifle to him. And Scott, when he won the 22 Handgun, best single table, at one of the shoots, when everyone else thought Mike Homm had it won. The Single Best Time, was with unlimited attempts, while the 3 table total was a one time entry. Scott and I knew who was leading but the others were to busy to notice, one of them Leighton kids shooting, and just quietly put in the winning run, he looked at me and I just nodded and he walker over and looked at the written down time and went and put his gun up, I was busy and he didn't say a word to anyone, so later when I called, last call and closed the entries, then the others finally looked at the score sheets and noticed he had a number 1 behind his name, and wanted to know why, well he had the best time and that means he gets first place. Whine, whine, to bad, the winner is ..... I really was glad that he won this event, the 22 Handgun single best time was the most contested part of the shoots and he like me, was really not considered a contender for fastest time, but we all have our day and this was his. They are pretty good kids, ok ok men, now, just don't tell them to loud, we'll have to put up with them, and ask their Mother (Joyce),they can be annoying at times, maybe their Dad (Randy), too, watch those phone wires, Dad.

The Howard boys, Clint and Mitch, they were always around with their Dad, Mike, so were like family. We did a lot of things together and when we lost Mike, I tried to do what I could without be pushy or intruding, it's a fine line to walk. They were treated like adults at these shooting related events and responded accordingly. They are both good men and a credit to their Mother (Nancy) and Father (Mike). We did a lot of shooting together and worked at building things for the Gun Club. They like Lance, were always there with us, helping and doing, whatever came along. They helped with setting up and running a lot of Club events. I am proud of them and proud to call them friends.

Rollie and Karen Leighton's 3 boys, Garand, Bill, and Sam are also family. Watching these 3 grow up and being a small part of it or of them, was a very rewarding experience. We have done so much together that it is a separate story, to even start to cover it. Hunting, shooting, farming, working cattle, riding and working with horses, traveling, sports, playing cards, just listening to them, building fence, riding ATVs setting up shooting events, it goes on and on, and just sharing life. And they are pretty good kids, okay, now they are men but will always be something of kids to me. They do grow up, somewhat, in 20 years. But like me they do still have some of that kid still in them. But they are the kind that when our country needs men, they will be there and sometimes it seems that, that list of men gets shorter as time goes on. They have been treated, at times anyway, like adults for so long that they had to let their body age catch up, in growing, to their experiences. Because in work and play they have acted and behaved like adults for a long time and functioned quite well in that capacity. Sometimes we forgot that they were not full grown, even though they fulfilled the positions very well and satisfactorily. I was always treating them with the respect and responsibility, of older people, when we were at shooting events. They never let me down and performed in a safe and responsible manner, even if their Mother said they weren't old enough to be put in that position. Although she shouldn't of had to, she forgot to let me in on that minor detail and I was always getting them and me, in trouble because of it. And she still hasn't done me great bodily harm, yet, for doing these things. And it still wasn't my fault at Sam's second birthday party.

This group now includes Steph, Stephanie Leiker, of Wakeeney, Kansas, Bill's girlfriend and bride to be. She is another of these special girls/women who has a special place in my heart. I had heard a lot about her, all good except I hadn't met her yet, when she and Bill came to Kansas City to pick Kate and I up and bring us home from the KU Med Center, in September of 2008. She is one who just makes things better by showing up or calling. She may not be perfect but is getting close, likes horses, shooting, guns, hunting and puts up with the likes of me. And I did give her my blue horse, Smokey, or Smoke as she calls him. She is now another unofficial daughter, part of my still growing family.

Matraca Mann was another of the little girls that won my heart right off the bat. Her Dad, Kalo Mann, has been a friend of mine for a long time and I knew him before Rollie and before he married Tammy. It seems after he got married, for some reason, 2 little girls showed up at their house. About a year apart, if I remember right, and I guess there is just something about some little girls that draws out the best (?) in me. When she was 3, Kalo was coming down from Dighton to shoot bowling pins with us on Thursday nights. When he would bring Tammy and the girls along, I just had to give attention to them and especially the smaller one, Matraca. I guess she just tripped my trigger. Anyway we were instant best friends, when we weren't shooting, she was setting with me or on my lap, which was just outstanding with me. I think we probably amused some of the people there but we didn't care, we were in our own world. On one of these occasions she was misbehaving or at least doing something not to her mother's approval. Tammy told her if she didn't behave, what she was going to do was "I'm going to send you home with Ralph". This was fine with her, so while we were shooting and finishing up for the night, and no one was watching, she moved all of her belongings, toys, clothes and whatever she had with her, from their car to my pickup. No one noticed and she was quite proud of herself. We finished shooting and picked up and were done and stopped to socialize and have a beer or soft drink, as so desired. As soon as I set down she was beside me and was pressed, very closely, to my leg, this was okay with me. After the required amount of socializing had transpired, Tammy told her to come and get in their car, they needed to be getting home. She just set there and never said a word. Tammy told her again, and still no response. Then Kalo told her "Come on, we need to be getting home". She says "No". " WHAT DO YOU MEAN, NO, we're going home, get in the car". "No, I'm going home with Ralph, Mom said so." "No Mom was just kidding, lets go." "No, I'm going home with Ralph." So Tammy tried to explain that she hadn't meant it and was just kidding. "No, I going home with Ralph, you said I could." She was starting to cry and I told them that it was okay she could go home with me and I would get her back on the weekend or something. Maybe I was having flash-backs and was planning to keep her, remember Julie. Tammy said "Oh, no , what would your wife say if you brought a 3 year old girl home with you?". My reply was "Thanks", really she would, and she would have. "No she wouldn't, she doesn't want a 3 year old coming to stay." "Oh, yes she does". Tammy said, "What happens when she wakes up in the middle of the night and wants to come home?". "I'll bring her home, but she won't want to". I was pretty sure. "You may have trouble getting her to want to come back". I was just teasing to ease the situation, but was also serious. But no, it wasn't to be, she was crying hard by this time and wrapped her legs and arms around me and wasn't going to let go. They had to drag her off my leg and I couldn't do anything, they were the parents. She was crying, kicking, screaming, and fighting all the way to the car. I felt terrible, another lesson learned, the hard way, and I already knew this, you don't tell anyone, especially little kids, you're going to do something and then don't follow up. Later I told them, privately, if they ever did that to me again I would at least knot their heads. They were just lucky I had put my gun away or I might have broken their wrists when they were dragging her off me. I still have scars, about 3/4 to an inch deep in my leg from her fingers, she wasn't going to let go. They didn't bring her back for awhile and so I didn't see her for sometime. Once in a while on a weekend shoot and I think they always made sure I was busy, before they let her come in, I think I'm kidding. Kate, when she heard this, as soon as I got home, said "You should have brought her home with you". Right, take her away from her parents. "You had a gun didn't you?" I'm pretty sure she was kidding or teasing me, but thought it better that I didn't ask. She was a little bit upset that we put the girl though that. "What about me?" I asked. "Oh, you too." Oh sure, I was playing second fiddle again. In all seriousness that part was not fun and I don't want to do it again. I will leave my gun on, if it happens again, that long heavy barrel will break wrists. I hadn't seen her for about 8 years, and she didn't remember any of this, but she still smiles when she sees me, and as is her habit gives me a hug, and just like Julie, doesn't remember a thing, but I still do. When she was about 13, I offered to bring her home again, to stay for awhile, we had a lot of horses here, and she does like horses (bribery again), and Kate was still ready, willing and happy for her to come, but Mom and Dad didn't think so. I'm pretty sure they were still worried about her coming back. They had just cause for that worry, I would still keep her, but not against her will. She is another good kid, okay, young woman, and makes things better by just being around and you have to admit, there's always something going on in her head, good or bad or otherwise. And she does make me smile, inside and out, others also.

In 1999 Trevor Meier was born, he was the son of Jason and Shelly Meier. The Grandson of Larry and Esther Johnston, long time friends and neighbors, I also put up their alfalfa hay for years. Great Grandson of Ray and Lois Johnston, also long time friends and neighbors, I also put up their alfalfa hay for years. Shelly and Jason were rodeo-ing at the time, well, Shelly took a little time off to deliver Trevor. She was for sure back in 2000, and I tried to make as many practice sessions as I could. And if all else failed I was a pretty good baby sitter, at least I thought so. Trev and I were good friends, and if necessary we could load, push and release calves for Shelly, when her good help wasn't there. Actually Trev and I did pretty good. I carried him at least part of the time and at other times he would stand and hang on to the pipes of the chute and push calves up or help push them up. I did get him a stick so he could poke them and not be sticking his hand through the rails. When September came around and the finals were ready to go in Garden City, Shelly was a Director, for Kansas Professional Rodeo Association, in Breakaway Roping that year. The whole family was in at the Rodeo Arena at the Finney County Fairgrounds. Where they were looking at and broke the new stock, for the finals, out of the chute, for educational purposes. I got there a little late and went up to the Suburban. Esther was there with Betty Dew (Larry's Sister) and some others, all women, Esther was holding Trevor and when I went up to the window, I think he maybe felt in a minority and was ready to leave, he literally dove out the window to me and it's a good thing I caught him. He might even have been glad to see me. I talked with Esther and the others for a little bit, and then I carried him over to the gates for the arena, I knelt down and put him on the ground and he was walking up and down, holding on to the pipes of the gate. Shelly was working Matty or Matlock, one of her horses, in the arena. Trev came down the gate and let go and walked about 4 steps to me, right into my hands. Lots of excitement took place all at once, the Suburban emptied, Larry walked up about that time, and Shelly had been watching and came up on Matty and made a flying dismount, she was very good at this from her High School and College days, goat tying, she was a National Champion. She grabbed him up, excited about him walking, all of the others also. I kept trying to tell them, this wasn't the first time, he had done it several times at home when we were in the home arena. Maybe that didn't count as they had not seen it, but I had. We continued on over the years and then he was performing in the arena himself, and what a cowboy he was turning into. I believe it was when he was 8, he qualified for the Little Britches National Finals in 4 events, and I think that was the year he won his first saddle. And he had this big Silver Belt Buckle, he might of found that somewhere, or he won it for the All Around Cowboy in his age group, that might have been it. He was really proud of that buckle and saddle, and rightfully so. I'm not to sure but think that Mom and Dad were too, not to mention Grandpa and Grandma, and Great Grandpa and Great Grandma. Oh, just another saddle and belt buckle, he can't reach me right now, so he can't smack me, either. I was proud of you to Trev. I listened to a Liberal radio station who had a live sports show, every week day morning, and they were having a contest for area athletes, male, female, and team, for the year. So when they were doing this show I called in and nominated him for Male Athlete of the Year. 8 years old, qualified in 4 events for the National Finals Rodeo, in his age group. We didn't win, but he was third, not to bad considering he was from Garden City and it was a Liberal station. Oh well, I tried, and did get him some air time and it did draw some attention on the air, an 8 year old Rodeo Star, was the way he was announced, or at least one in the making. Give him time, maybe when he's 10 or 12, you know what they say about experience. Go get'em Trev and Good Luck.

The last one, so far, was Hannah Yost. She is so very special. She is another 4 year old girl, and is another friend. Having been going to church from September 28, 2008 till the present, I have watched her in church, most every Sunday and she would just make me smile, sometimes inside and sometimes outside, most times both. She was just being a 4 year old, and that's enough. In looking for something or someone to grab a hold of and to hang on to, figuratively, I spoke with her mother in December about taking her and her sisters Christmas shopping. We agreed to do this at Diana (their mother) and the girl's convenience. Which turned out to be December 28th, 2008, after church. We went to lunch after church and had a nice time. I explained the Ice Cream Law to the girls, after they had asked their mother about having ice cream after lunch. Diana had not answered and had gotten up to get a little more soup, from the soup and salad bar, and so I told them about the law. When Diana came back she told the girls they could have ice cream, once they had eaten all of their lunch. I thought she had been listening and was maybe humoring me about the ice cream, but she hadn't been listening, and had just waited to answer them until she returned to the table. Hannah said something about, 'its good because it's the law' and I had to explain the Ice Cream Law to Mom. The law goes like this, if you go to church on Sunday, and then go to lunch, before you can go home, you have to have ice cream. Mandatory for 15 and younger, with a sliding scale over 15 through 65, and over 65, the law doesn't apply anyway. Now the law only applies when you go to lunch in other than your own home. Diana listened and didn't really comment, so I figured that I might have to pay a price for this in the future. But I can take it, I hope. We went shopping after lunch, Noemi got a hamster, house and needed accessories. Hannah got a toy or toys she picked out and some clothes. Noemi declined to pick out any clothes, because she said the hamster and accessories were enough and wouldn't pick out anything else. Rebeca got a Wal Mart Card so she could pick out what she wanted later and at her convenience. This was a good day and I was content that it had gone well. And it was a start on the healing process.

The next Sunday was the 4th of January, 2009, and I went to church and looked for Hannah upon entering the church but didn't find her or her Mother. When Church was over I saw Diana at the Information Table, taking care of it, and stopped by and gave her a Thank You Card for sharing her daughters with me. I was only able to spend a minute with her as she was busy. When I was leaving Pastor Jeff (Crist) stopped me and we were talking of something. Hannah came around the corner, near her Mother and saw me and called my name and ran over and hugged me around my left knee. I had a tightness or squeezing of the heart feeling that has come and gone, ever since Kate's passing and it was there this day. When she did this, the feeling broke up and fell away. This feeling, of breaking up and falling away, is hard to explain but very easy to experience. What a relief and a comfortable, peaceful feeling this was, after several months of having it. I wanted to scoop her up and hold her, but my conscious thought was "Diana doesn't have 2 hours to try and pry my fingers from around her", so I was content with stroking her hair. When I walked away I was also aware that the pain in my left knee, which is there most of the time, since December 15, 1967, in varying degrees, was also gone. The pain in the left knee came back after awhile but the pain around my heart has not. This whole experience is very hard to explain, and when someone does understand and expresses their feelings, I can only say if you think it is "awesome, great, fantastic or whatever they say", you should try living it. I do know that this is God working through a 4 year old child, but it is hard for me to separate her from the experience, and so she is held in deep affection and respect by me. She is my 4 year old girl friend.

Hannah Yost
June 7, 2009 Word of Life Church

The next Sunday I took them to lunch again, after church, and we did have ice cream and a good time. When we were finished and the girls had gone and looked at the pets, we were at Ward's Flower and Pet Shop with a soup and salad bar, Hannah came back and told me "Mr. Ralph, I love you" to which I replied "I love you, too", she just beamed, like turning on a light bulb. She continues to be a true blessing, and her presence or sight of her is enough to make me feel better and make it a better day. And I continue to thank God for her every night, and like another good friend, Margie Cassero, they continue to help me make it another day in my quest for peace in my mind, for another day.

In trying to understand the feelings for Hannah I will try to write it down like this: When I asked for his help, God responded, in his wisdom he knew that whomever he sent, for them to get through to me would have to be able to make the connection and "get through to me". He knew that it was unlikely for this to be a woman, and less likely for a man. So this left a child. He than crossed Hannah and my paths and what better way than a beautiful child to convey the message of "His Love" than a child. I know that she was a 4 year old child and had no conscious awareness of this, but that she was the messenger for God and carried the knowledge of his Love and Hope, and that he had not forgotten me in my time of need. And who better than a child to carry the message of "God's Love" and children are the "Hope" of mankind. For those that scoff or do not understand I feel sorry for you, and ask that when your turn comes, you do not forget to ask God for his help and for understanding, he hasn't forgotten you, even if you have forgotten him. Maybe he won't sent a beautiful child but he will know and send the right messenger, some would call them Angels, to help you in your time of need. It may not be an instant cure but it will be a start in the right direction. (Paster Marty spoke the other night of help, from the Spirit of the Holy Ghost, but you have to also help yourself.) Also I am aware that it was not just Hannah, but there was a team or group that helped, and while I don't claim to completely understand, I am getting closer, and maybe she is just the point man for the team. And while I am unable to or will not separate her from the truth of this and continue to give her credit and thanks, I am aware of the others who have contributed , and ask that they share the thanks with Hannah, while it may not be openly displayed, it is meant for all of you, and besides she's a lot prettier and more fun to be with.

And if there was ever anyone who would understand and support this it would be Kate, and I still love and miss her.

About the Author

R alph Morton is a Kansas native that has lived in Kansas most of his life. With a few months in Colorado as a child and then a few months in Washington, prior to going in the U. S. Army. While spending 9 years in the Army he was stationed at Ft. Ord, Seaside, California; Ft. Devens, Ayer, Massachusetts; Ft. Clayton, Canal Zone, Panama; Ft. Carson, Colorado Springs, Colorado; Saigon & Pleiku, Viet Nam; Two Rock Ranch Station, Petaluma, California; Kagnew Station, Asmara, Ethiopia. With temporary assignments at Vint Hill Farms, Warrenton, Virginia; Walter Reed Army Hospital, Washington D. C.; Ft. Dix, New Jersey. Born at home, on the farm, in Phillips County, near Phillipsburg, Kansas, into the middle of 5 children, he spent his childhood being a trial to his parents, Orlaff and Sarah Morton. Starting out working on the farm, he has worked in a Bowling Alley, Gas Service Stations, a Truck shop fixing truck tires, motorcycle shops, carpenter work, construction, dirt construction, Custom Harvesting, Grain Elevator, Farming Operation, Alfalfa Hay and Baling Operation, Truck Driver, worked with livestock, and many part time money making jobs. He was awarded the Purple Heart while on duty in Viet Nam. He is a Father and Grandfather, loves children, a hunter, Life member of Sand and Sage Rifle and Pistol Club, an Endowment member of the NRA, life long horseman, a Life member of AQHA, a mentor and teacher of children, he and Kate helped with the Special Olympics for a number of years. He spent 17 years with the Finney County Kansas Sheriff's Posse as a fully sworn officer. Law Enforcement Firearms

Instructor, Hunter Education Instructor, Instructor at GCCC for FATS Law Enforcement Simulator, and is a member of the Word Of Life Church in Garden City, Kansas.

Thank You

I would like to especially thank my daughter Mary Lynn for her love, help, input, understanding, support, and encouragement in everything, not just the writing of this book. She is a true credit to her mother. Also my sisters; Pat Smith for her love, encouragement, understanding, and never ending support, and Margie Cassero the same. Ken Morton for all the help, technical support, and consultations involving this book. The Tim Dewey family for the support and encouragement during this time period. Joe Randle who was always there with support, help, pushing, advice or inspiration. And all the others who were there and contributed in the many ways that they did. And again, especially, Hannah Yost who was just there, being a 4 and then 5 year old friend.

Ralph

LaVergne, TN USA
20 October 2009

161364LV00001B/2/P